World Book

Discovery Science Encyclopedia

Human Beings

M-Z

WORLD BOOK

a Scott Fetzer company

Chicago

www.worldbook.com

For information about other World Book publications, please visit our website at www.worldbook.com or call
1-800-WORLDBK (967-5325).

For information about sales to schools and libraries, please call
1-800-975-3250 (United States); **1-800-837-5365** (Canada).

World Book, Inc.
233 N. Michigan Ave.
Chicago, IL 60601
U.S.A.

The Library of Congress has cataloged an earlier edition of this title as follows:

Library of Congress Cataloging-in-Publication Data

Encyclopedia of human beings.
2 volumes ; cm. -- (World book discovery science encyclopedia)
Summary: "An introduction to human beings, including human anatomy, human diseases and conditions, and human genetics. Features include drawings, diagrams, photographs, and activities"-- Provided by publisher.
Includes index.
ISBN 978-0-7166-7520-4
1. Human biology--Juvenile literature. 2. Human beings--Constitution--Juvenile literature. 3. Human body--Juvenile literature. I. World Book, Inc.
QP37.E488 2013
612--dc23

2013003064

This revised edition:
ISBN: 978-0-7166-7529-7

Printed in China by Shenzhen Donnelley Printing Co., Ltd., Guangdong Province
1st printing March 2015

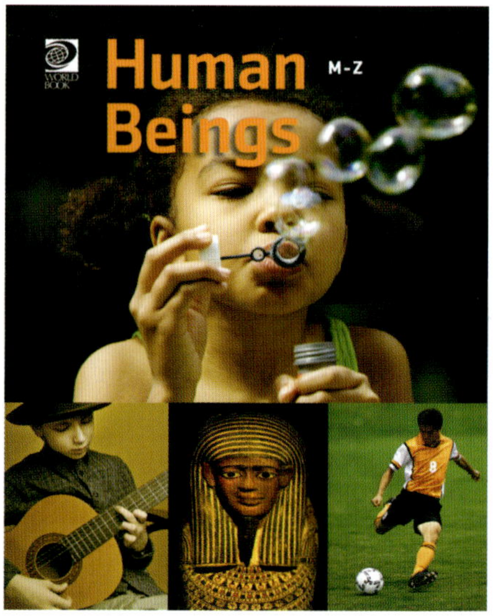

Front Cover:
© Dmitriy Shironosov, Alamy Images
© Shutterstock; © Peter Horree, Alamy Images
© Aflo Sport/Masterfile

Back Cover:
© Tips Images/SuperStock
© Shutterstock
© Blend Images/SuperStock

Staff

Executive Committee

President
Jim O'Rourke

Vice President, Finance
Donald D. Keller

Vice President and Editor in Chief
Paul A. Kobasa

Vice President, School and Library Sales
Sean Lockwood

Director, Marketing
Nicholas A. Fryer

Director, International Sales
Kristin Norell

Director, Human Resources
Bev Ecker

Editorial

Associate Director, Annuals and Topical Reference
Scott Thomas

Managing Editor, Annuals and Topical Reference
Barbara A. Mayes

Manager, Sciences, World Book Encyclopedia
Jeff De La Rosa

Senior Editor, Annuals and Topical Reference
Christine Sullivan

Staff Editors
Michael DuRoss
Daniel Kenis
Nick Kilzer

Manager, Contracts & Compliance (Rights & Permissions)
Loranne K. Shields

Manager, Indexing Services
David Pofelski

Administrative Assistant
Ethel Matthews

Editorial Administration

Senior Manager, Publishing Operations
Timothy Falk

Graphics and Design

Art Director
Tom Evans

Coordinator, Design Development and Production
Brenda B. Tropinski

Senior Designers
Matt Carrington
Don Di Sante
Isaiah Sheppard

Contributing Designer
Lucy Lesiak

Media Researcher
Jeff Heimsath

Contributing Photographs Editor
Carol Parden

Manager, Cartography
Wayne K. Pichler

Senior Cartographer
John M. Rejba

Production

Director, Manufacturing and Pre-Press
Carma Fazio

Manufacturing Manager
Sandra Johnson

Production/Technology Manager
Anne Fritzinger

Senior Production Manager
Jan Rossing

Production Specialist
Curley Hunter

Proofreader
Nathalie Strassheim

How to use World Book Discovery Science Encyclopedia

- Hundreds of illustrations
- Guide words
- Phonetic spellings
- Related article lists
- Experiments and activities
- QR codes

World Book Discovery Science Encyclopedia is filled with information about basic science concepts, tools, and discoveries as well as the world around us. Entries on people who have made important contributions to science are included, too. All entries are written in a way that makes them easy to understand.

Finding entries is easy, too. They are arranged in alphabetical order. There is also an index in each volume. The index lists all the entries, as well as topics that are covered in the volume but that are not themselves entries.

Science experiments and activities are also included in this volume. These and the many other features of *World Book Discovery Science Encyclopedia* make it an encyclopedia that you can use for research as well as reading just for fun.

Easy alphabetical access
Each letter of the alphabet is highlighted to help you locate entries alphabetically.

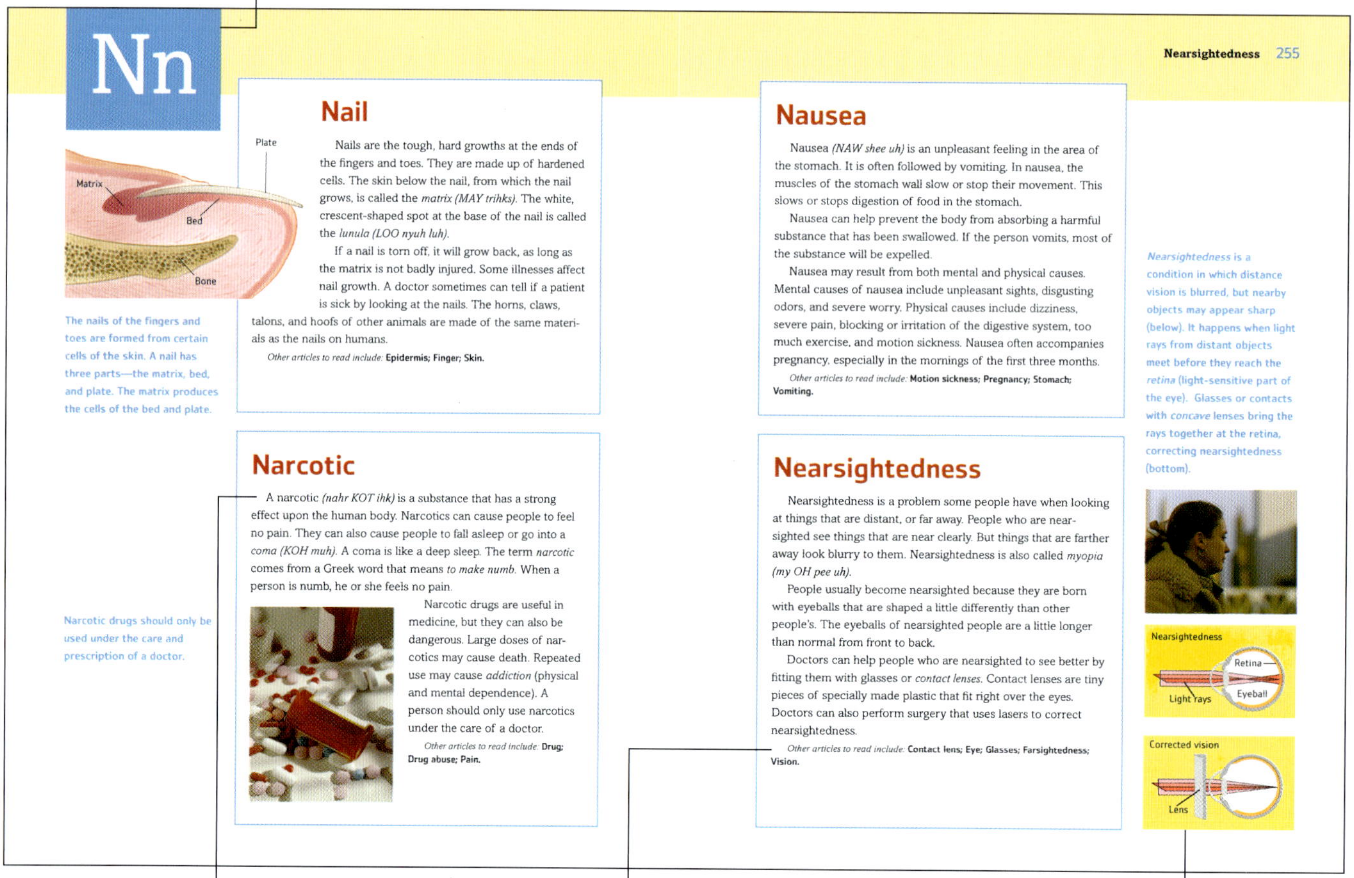

Nearsightedness 255

Nn

Nail

Nails are the tough, hard growths at the ends of the fingers and toes. They are made up of hardened cells. The skin below the nail, from which the nail grows, is called the *matrix (MAY trihks)*. The white, crescent-shaped spot at the base of the nail is called the *lunula (LOO nyuh luh)*.

If a nail is torn off, it will grow back, as long as the matrix is not badly injured. Some illnesses affect nail growth. A doctor sometimes can tell if a patient is sick by looking at the nails. The horns, claws, talons, and hoofs of other animals are made of the same materials as the nails on humans.

Other articles to read include: **Epidermis; Finger; Skin.**

Plate
Matrix
Bed
Bone

The nails of the fingers and toes are formed from certain cells of the skin. A nail has three parts—the matrix, bed, and plate. The matrix produces the cells of the bed and plate.

Narcotic

A narcotic *(nahr KOT ihk)* is a substance that has a strong effect upon the human body. Narcotics can cause people to feel no pain. They can also cause people to fall asleep or go into a *coma (KOH muh)*. A coma is like a deep sleep. The term *narcotic* comes from a Greek word that means *to make numb*. When a person is numb, he or she feels no pain.

Narcotic drugs are useful in medicine, but they can also be dangerous. Large doses of narcotics may cause death. Repeated use may cause *addiction* (physical and mental dependence). A person should only use narcotics under the care of a doctor.

Other articles to read include: **Drug; Drug abuse; Pain.**

Narcotic drugs should only be used under the care and prescription of a doctor.

Nausea

Nausea *(NAW shee uh)* is an unpleasant feeling in the area of the stomach. It is often followed by vomiting. In nausea, the muscles of the stomach wall slow or stop their movement. This slows or stops digestion of food in the stomach.

Nausea can help prevent the body from absorbing a harmful substance that has been swallowed. If the person vomits, most of the substance will be expelled.

Nausea may result from both mental and physical causes. Mental causes of nausea include unpleasant sights, disgusting odors, and severe worry. Physical causes include dizziness, severe pain, blocking or irritation of the digestive system, too much exercise, and motion sickness. Nausea often accompanies pregnancy, especially in the mornings of the first three months.

Other articles to read include: **Motion sickness; Pregnancy; Stomach; Vomiting.**

Nearsightedness

Nearsightedness is a problem some people have when looking at things that are distant, or far away. People who are nearsighted see things that are near clearly. But things that are farther away look blurry to them. Nearsightedness is also called *myopia (my OH pee uh)*.

People usually become nearsighted because they are born with eyeballs that are shaped a little differently than other people's. The eyeballs of nearsighted people are a little longer than normal from front to back.

Doctors can help people who are nearsighted to see better by fitting them with glasses or *contact lenses*. Contact lenses are tiny pieces of specially made plastic that fit right over the eyes. Doctors can also perform surgery that uses lasers to correct nearsightedness.

Other articles to read include: **Contact lens; Eye; Glasses; Farsightedness; Vision.**

Nearsightedness is a condition in which distance vision is blurred, but nearby objects may appear sharp (below). It happens when light rays from distant objects meet before they reach the *retina* (light-sensitive part of the eye). Glasses or contacts with *concave* lenses bring the rays together at the retina, correcting nearsightedness (bottom).

Nearsightedness
Retina
Light rays
Eyeball
Corrected vision
Lens

Pronunciations
The phonetic spelling for unusual or unfamiliar words is given. A key to the pronunciation is in the front of each volume.

Related references
The references listed at the bottom of many articles tell you which other articles to read to find out more or related information.

Illustrations
Each volume of *Discovery Science Encyclopedia* contains hundreds of photographs, drawings, maps, and other illustrations. Each illustration is labeled or explained in a caption.

Guide words
Guide words at the top of a page help you quickly find the entry you are seeking.

Activities
Many activities are found in *Discovery Science Encyclopedia.* These simple activities, which can be done at home or in the classroom, extend or enrich the subject of the article they accompany.

Experiments
Many experiments are found in *Discovery Science Encyclopedia.* These experiments extend or enrich the subject of the article they accompany and are suitable for use at home or in the classroom.

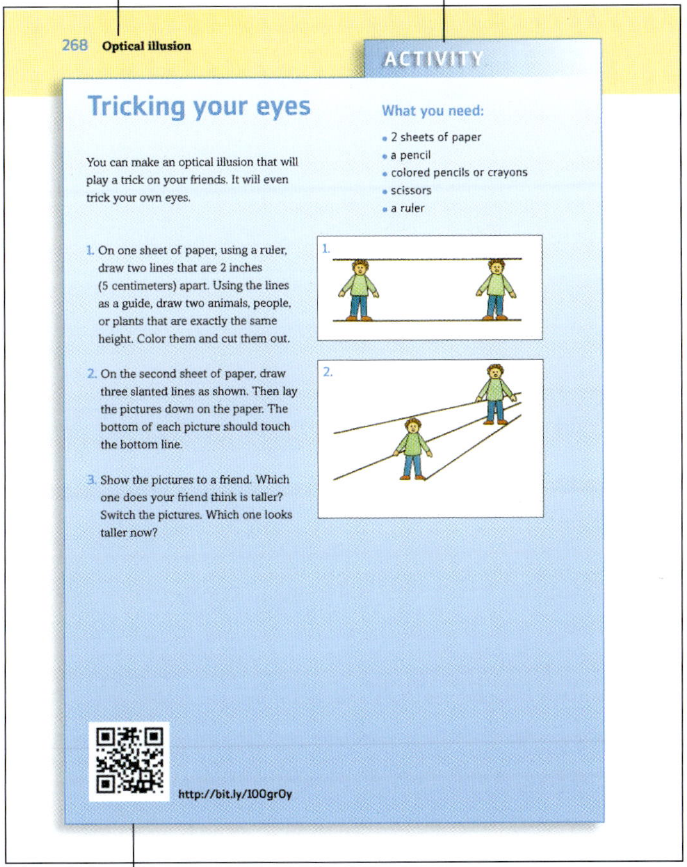
268 **Optical illusion**

ACTIVITY

Tricking your eyes

You can make an optical illusion that will play a trick on your friends. It will even trick your own eyes.

What you need:

- 2 sheets of paper
- a pencil
- colored pencils or crayons
- scissors
- a ruler

1. On one sheet of paper, using a ruler, draw two lines that are 2 inches (5 centimeters) apart. Using the lines as a guide, draw two animals, people, or plants that are exactly the same height. Color them and cut them out.
2. On the second sheet of paper, draw three slanted lines as shown. Then lay the pictures down on the paper. The bottom of each picture should touch the bottom line.
3. Show the pictures to a friend. Which one does your friend think is taller? Switch the pictures. Which one looks taller now?

http://bit.ly/100grOy

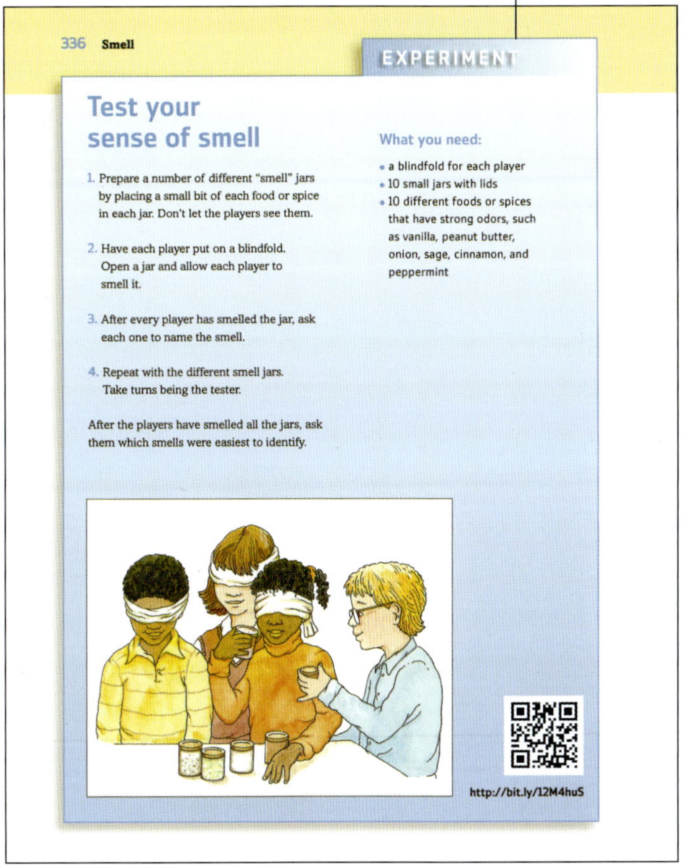
336 **Smell**

EXPERIMENT

Test your sense of smell

What you need:

- a blindfold for each player
- 10 small jars with lids
- 10 different foods or spices that have strong odors, such as vanilla, peanut butter, onion, sage, cinnamon, and peppermint

1. Prepare a number of different "smell" jars by placing a small bit of each food or spice in each jar. Don't let the players see them.
2. Have each player put on a blindfold. Open a jar and allow each player to smell it.
3. After every player has smelled the jar, ask each one to name the smell.
4. Repeat with the different smell jars. Take turns being the tester.

After the players have smelled all the jars, ask them which smells were easiest to identify.

http://bit.ly/12M4huS

QR codes
This symbol is a QR code. You can find QR codes on all the pages with experiments and activities in the *World Book Discovery Science Encyclopedia.* Simply scan a code with your smartphone or tablet to see a video about the experiment or activity or related information about the subject of the project. (You will need to download a QR code reader to your device if you have not already done so.) If you do not have a mobile device, you can still access the videos linked to experiments and activities by keying in the URL beneath each QR code into a browser on your computer.

Key to pronunciation

World Book Discovery Science Encyclopedia provides the pronunciations for many unusual or unfamiliar words. In the pronunciation, the words are divided into syllables and respelled according to the way each syllable sounds. The syllables appear in *italic letters.* For example, here are an article title and the respelled pronunciation for it:

Absorption *(ab SAWRP shuhn)*

The syllable or syllables that get the greatest emphasis when the word is spoken are in capital letters *(SAWRP).*

Mad cow disease

Mad cow disease is an illness that affects the central nervous system of cows. It causes odd behavior, difficulty walking, and death. The scientific name of mad cow disease is *bovine spongiform encephalopathy (BOH vyn SPUHN jih FAWRM ehn SEHF uh LOP uh thee).* Mad cow disease damages an animal's brain so that the tissue looks like a sponge when viewed under a microscope. Scientists believe that eating infected beef can cause a similar disease in human beings.

Mad cow disease was first identified in the United Kingdom, in 1986. British sheep sometimes suffer from a disease called *scrapie,* which is similar to mad cow disease. Scientists think the disease passed from sheep to cattle when the cattle were fed the brains and spinal columns of sheep that had scrapie.

Other articles to read include: **Brain; Disease; Farm and farming.**

A meat inspector checks a cow carcass. Scientists believe that eating infected beef can cause a form of mad cow disease in humans.

Magnetic resonance imaging

Magnetic resonance imaging (MRI) is a method doctors use to inspect tissues in the body. Doctors can use MRI images to see injuries, disorders, and diseases without the need for surgery.

Some other imaging methods use *X rays,* a form of energy that can be harmful to body tissues. MRI uses magnets instead of X rays and is therefore a safer imaging method. MRI uses powerful magnets and cannot be used on people who have metal devices in their bodies. Such devices include *pacemakers* (devices that regulate the heartbeat) and artificial joints.

An MRI unit contains a large magnet, radio devices, and a computer. The magnet creates a magnetic field around the patient. The computer creates an image from the signals produced by the radio devices.

Other articles to read include: **Medicine; Radiology.**

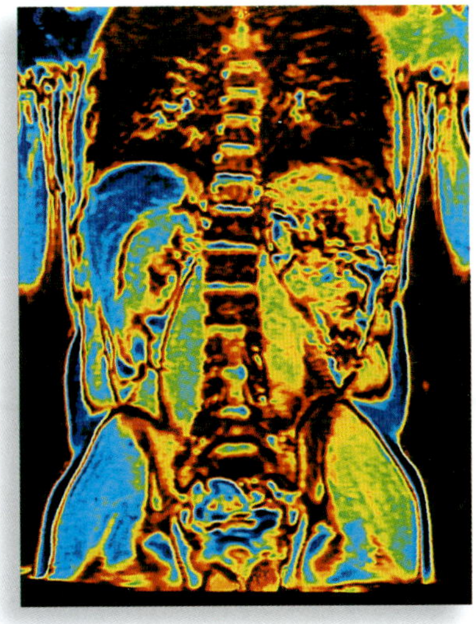

Magnetic resonance imaging (MRI) enables doctors to see through bones and organs.

Mosquito bites can spread malaria to human beings. Public health officials try to reduce mosquito populations by spraying pesticides in regions where malaria is common.

Malaria

Malaria *(muh LAYR ee uh)* is a widespread human disease. It is caused by single-celled *parasites (PAR uh syts).* Parasites are living things that live on or inside other living things.

The parasites that cause malaria are tiny. They can only be seen with a microscope. They enter the body from the bite of a certain kind of mosquito. Such mosquitoes live in tropical places, where the weather is always hot and wet.

People with malaria get chills and fever every few days. They may also have headaches, muscle pain, and upset stomach. Doctors can protect people from malaria with medicine. They often give the medicine ahead of time to prevent malaria in people traveling to places where the disease is common.

Other articles to read include: **Disease; Fever.**

People in many parts of Africa suffer from malnutrition. These children are refugees from war in Rwanda, a small country in east-central Africa. They are waiting in line for food at a relief camp.

Malnutrition

Malnutrition *(MAL noo TRIHSH uhn)* is an unhealthy condition in which the body is not getting the right amount of food or the right kind of food. People can be malnourished even when they eat too much food. They can become malnourished if they do not get enough vitamins or minerals or if the body is unable to use food properly.

But malnutrition usually occurs when people do not eat enough food, which is called *starvation.* People can become malnourished if they are poor and cannot buy or grow enough healthy food. People caught in such disasters as flooding and war also may have a hard time getting healthy food. People who are malnourished can have cramps, diarrhea, weakness, and various kinds of diseases.

Other articles to read include: **Eating disorder; Diet; Famine; Food; Nutrition.**

Mandible

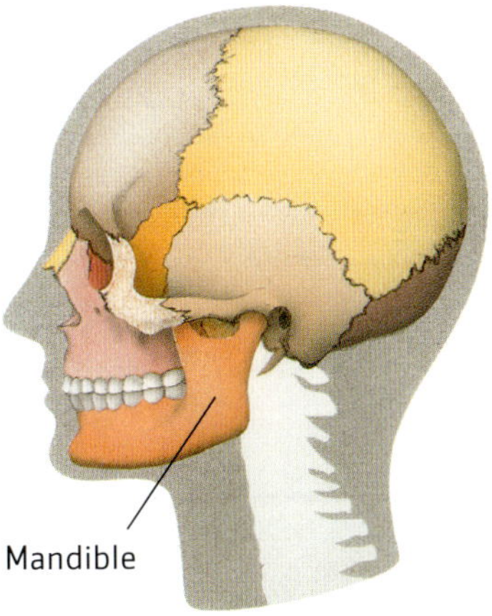

The mandible is the lower jawbone. It is shaped like a horseshoe. The chin is like the center part of the horseshoe. The "arms" of the horseshoe turn up along the side of the face. They end at the *temple*, on the side of the head near the eye.

The mandible works like a hinge. It allows the mouth to open and close. It helps in talking and eating.

Special chewing muscles are attached to the sides of the mandible. These muscles help in chewing food. Most tongue muscles are also connected to the mandible.

Other articles to read include: **Bone; Digestive system; Mouth; Skull; Teeth; Tongue.**

The *mandible* is the lower jawbone. It helps the mouth chew food.

Manganese

Manganese *(MANG guh neez)* is a brittle, silvery metal. Plants and animals need small amounts of manganese. It is used in steel and has many other industrial uses.

In nature, manganese is always found mixed with other elements. It is found in Earth's crust in such minerals as braunite and manganite. It was first *isolated* (separated from a mixture) by the Swedish chemist Johan Gottlieb Gahn in 1774.

Living things use manganese in *enzymes* and other proteins. An enzyme is a protein that speeds up chemical reactions. A lack of manganese can cause problems with bones and the central nervous system. People can get manganese by eating beans, green vegetables, nuts, grains, and cereals.

Other articles to read include: **Enzyme; Food; Nutrition.**

Nuts are a good source of dietary manganese. People need a small amount of manganese in their diet for good health.

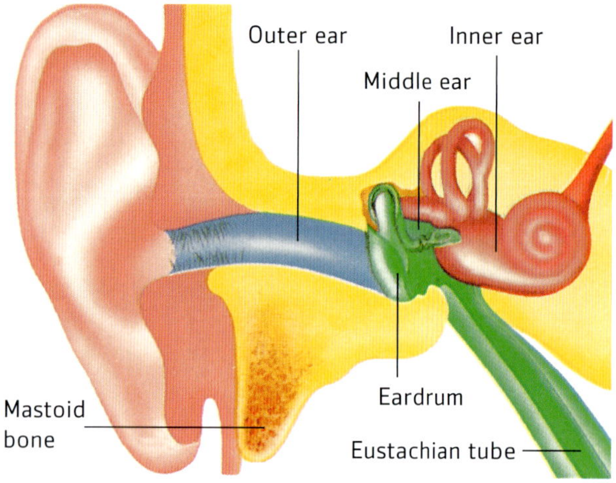

The *mastoid bone* is the hard area just behind and below the ear.

Mastoid bone

The mastoid *(MAS toyd)* bone is part of the skull. It is not actually a separate bone. Instead, it is part of the larger *temporal bone*. There is a temporal bone on each side of the skull.

The mastoid is the hard area just behind and below the ear. It is *porous (POHR uhs)* (filled with tiny holes), like a sponge. The *pores* (hollow spaces) are called the *mastoid cells.* People have different sizes and numbers of mastoid cells. The mastoid cells connect with a large opening, or cavity. This cavity opens into the middle ear. Infections in the middle ear can spread to the mastoid bone. This problem is called *mastoiditis (MAS toy DY tihs).*

Other articles to read include: **Bone; Ear; Ear infection; Skull.**

Margaret Mead (above right) studied the culture of people of the Pacific Islands.

Mead, Margaret

Margaret Mead (1901-1978) was an American *anthropologist (AN thruh PAHL uh jihst),* a scientist who studies groups of people and their ways of life. She studied people in the Pacific Islands.

Mead was born in Philadelphia, Pennsylvania. She earned a Ph.D. degree from Columbia University. For many years, she worked at the American Museum of Natural History in New York City.

To learn about people of the Pacific Islands, Mead lived with them. Two of her books are *Coming of Age in Samoa* (1928) and *Growing Up in New Guinea* (1930). They compare teenagers in these places to teenagers in Western countries.

Other articles to read include: **Anthropology.**

Measles

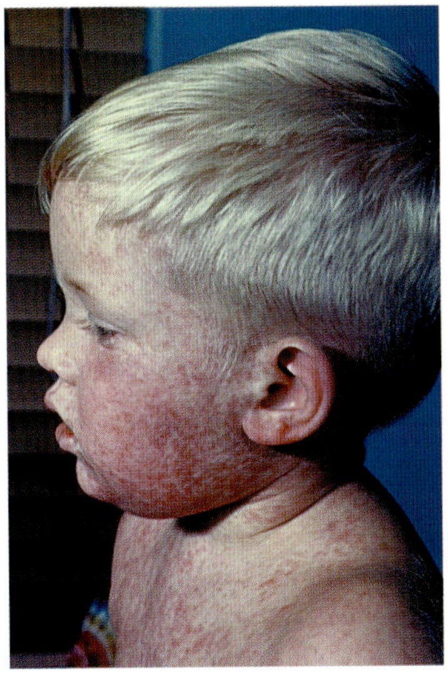

Measles is a disease that makes the skin break out in a pink rash.

Measles is a disease that causes a pink rash all over the body. Most people who get measles get the disease when they are children.

Measles is caused by a tiny particle called a *virus.* It spreads through the air when someone coughs or sneezes. People who catch measles have a fever, a runny nose, watery eyes, and a cough. Then small pink spots appear. After the coughing stops, the rash fades away.

Children should receive a shot of the measles *vaccine (VAK seen).* This shot can protect most people from getting measles.

Other articles to read include: **Disease; Immunization; Skin; Virus.**

Medical technology

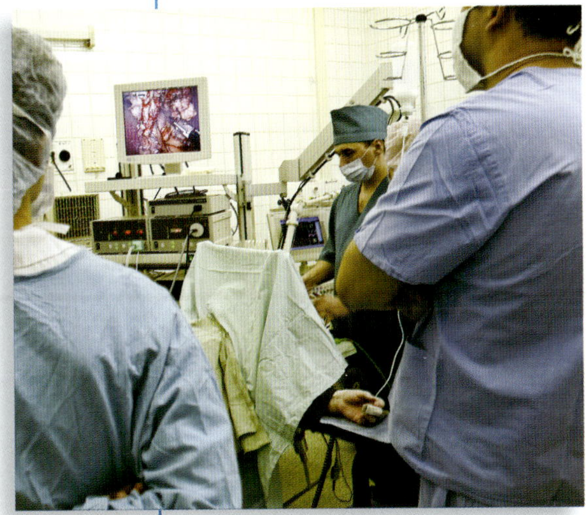

A modern operating room makes use of a wide variety of medical technology to help surgeons in operations.

Medical technology includes the tools that health workers use to learn how a person is sick or injured. Health workers also use medical technology to help make a patient feel better.

People who study medical technology are called medical *technicians (tehk NIHSH uhnz).* After graduating from school, most medical technicians work in hospitals and *laboratories (LAB uhr uh TAWR eez).* They help doctors find out what disease a person has.

Medical technicians work in various areas of science. They use electronic instruments and high-powered microscopes. They may use X rays or other technology to make images of various body parts, such as the head, chest, and abdomen. They also help cure diseases by running tests on blood and other body fluids to find certain chemical substances.

Other articles to read include: **Angiogram; Magnetic resonance imaging; Medicine; Positron emission tomography; Radiology; Ultrasound.**

Medicine

A doctor examines a series of X-ray images with a patient as she explains her diagnosis and possible treatments.

Medicine is the science and art of healing. It is a science because people learn it by studying and doing experiments. It is an art because it depends on the way doctors and other workers use their skills to heal people. People who visit doctors are called *patients.*

Doctors do three important things. First, they make a *diagnosis (DY uhg NOH sihs).* They figure out the cause of a patient's illness or injury.

Second, doctors *treat,* or help, patients. They *prescribe,* or order, medicines. They may also do surgery or order other treatments.

Third, doctors help prevent disease. They give *vaccinations (VAK suh NAY shuns)* against some diseases. They try to find and treat diseases early to keep them from getting worse. That is why doctors want people to get regular checkups.

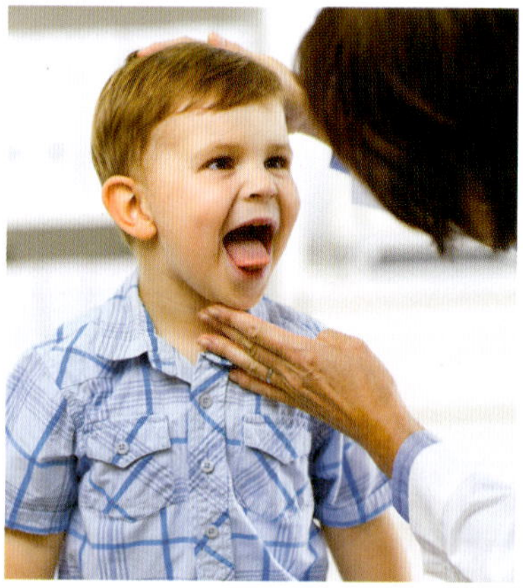

A doctor examines a young patient's throat as part of a medical checkup. Such checkups are usually done in a doctor's office.

Doctors make decisions about the care a patient gets. Many doctors can take care of most of a patient's needs. For serious illnesses, they send patients to a *specialist.* Specialists have training in a certain field, such as allergies or heart disease.

Most doctors care for people in their offices. They may work alone or in a group. Doctors also work in hospitals and in clinics.

People who want to be doctors take science and mathematics courses in college. Then they go to medical school. After they graduate, they work in a hospital and train under experienced doctors. Then they pass examinations before they can treat people on their own.

Other articles to read include: **Alternative medicine; Dentistry; Genetics; Health; Herbal medicine; Holistic medicine; Internal medicine.**

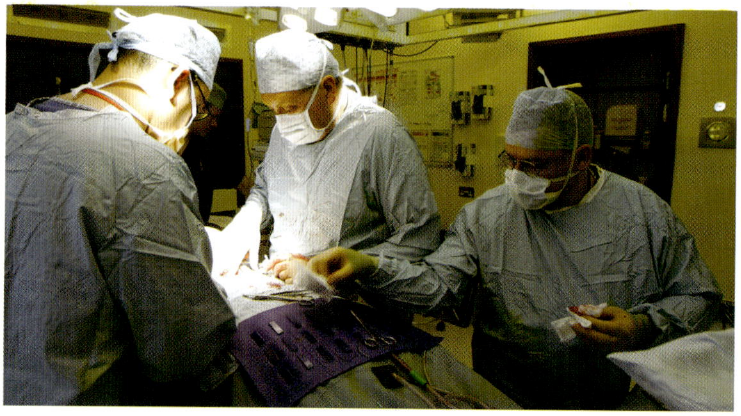

An operating room contains all the equipment and supplies needed for surgery, such as scalpels, gauze bandages, and machines for delivering oxygen to the patient. Nurses and other doctors assist during the operation.

Meiosis

Meiosis *(my OH sihs)* is a kind of *cell division*. In cell division, one cell splits apart to become two cells. Meiosis takes place in *sex cells*. Sex cells are the cells involved in *reproduction*, the production of young.

Chromosomes (KROH muh sohmz) are structures in cells. They carry *genes*, which act as chemical instructions for how the body grows. Chromosomes occur in pairs in most body cells. However, a male sex cell carries only half of each pair. The female sex cell carries the other half.

Before meiosis, the cell creates a copy of each chromosome. The cell then divides. This division leaves two cells with an equal number of double-stranded chromosomes. These two cells are called *daughter cells*.

Each daughter cell then divides. As the cells divide, the double-stranded chromosomes separate. This results in a set of four sex cells. Each sex cell has half of a complete set of chromosomes.

In reproduction, a male sex cell and a female sex cell merge. They form a single cell with a complete set of chromosomes. The cell develops into a new living thing.

Other articles to read include: **Cell; Chromosome; Mitosis; Nucleus; Reproduction, Human.**

Meiosis

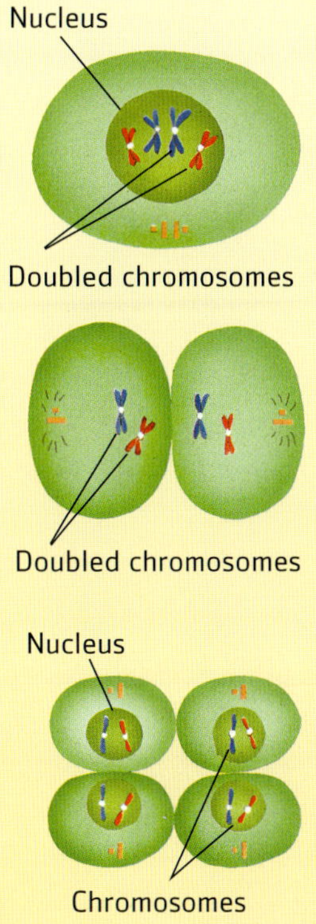

Before meiosis takes place, the *chromosomes* in a sex cell duplicate. The *nucleus* is the central part of the cell.

The cell then divides, leaving two cells with half as many chromosomes.

The cells divide again. The four cells each have one chromosome from each of the original doubled pairs.

Melanin

Melanin *(MEHL uh nihn)* is a brownish-black *pigment* (coloring material) in the body. Melanin gives color to skin, hair, and eyes. Dark-skinned people have more melanin in their skin than do light-skinned people. Freckles are also caused by melanin. Most people's hair turns gray or white as they grow older. This happens because melanin no longer forms in the hair.

Strong sunlight makes the skin produce more melanin. Melanin helps protect the skin from damage by the sun's rays.

Some people have no melanin. They have a condition called *albinism (AL buh nihz uhm)*. People with albinism have milky-white skin, white hair, and blue or pink eyes.

Other articles to read include: **Albinism; Freckle; Mole; Skin; Sunburn.**

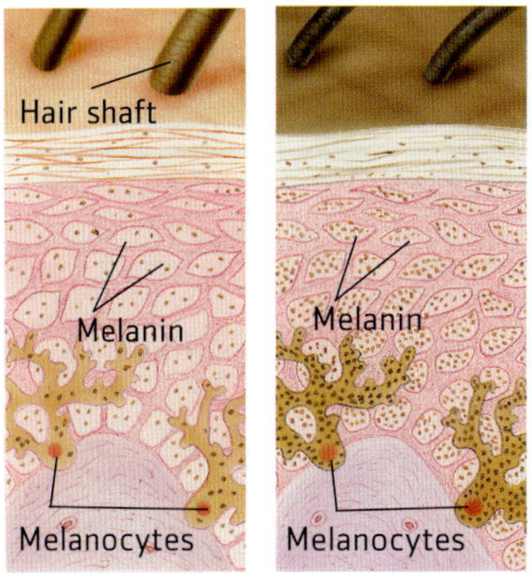

Skin color depends mainly on the pigment *melanin*. In light skin (above left), cells called *melanocytes* produce little melanin. In dark skin (above right), they produce more melanin.

Melatonin

Melatonin *(MEHL uh TOH nihn)* is a *hormone* (body chemical). It is made by a wide variety of living things. In people, it is mainly made by the *pineal gland*. The pineal gland is a tiny organ in the brain. In people, melatonin causes sleepiness.

Darkness causes the body to make melatonin. Light stops the making of melatonin. Melatonin helps control the body's natural cycle of waking and sleeping. People who have trouble sleeping may take melatonin pills. Scientists think such pills may have other health benefits.

Other articles to read include: **Biological clock; Gland; Sleep.**

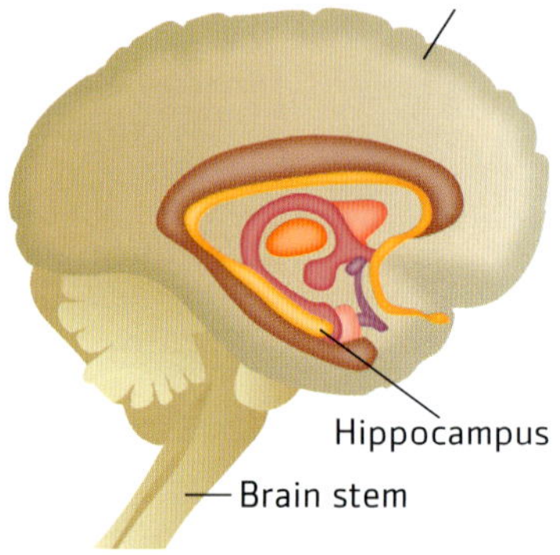

The part of the brain that is most involved in memory is called the *hippocampus.*

Memory

Memory is the ability to remember things we have learned or that have happened to us. It is the brain's ability to store information. The part of the brain that is most involved in memory is called the *hippocampus (HIHP uh KAM puhs).*

Memory is one of the most important parts of learning. Without memory, we would have to keep learning the same things over and over again. Reading a word, adding a number, or meeting a person would always be a brand-new event. We would not be able to build on what we had experienced before.

Psychologists (sy KOL uh jihsts) (experts who study how people behave) have learned that there are three kinds of memory. *Sensory memory* is the shortest kind. It is just a quick picture in the mind of something we have seen. It disappears in seconds. *Short-term memory* lasts a little longer, up to half a minute. We use short-term memory when we repeat back something we have just heard. *Long-term memory* is the memory that stores things we have experienced or learned and keeps it for a lifetime.

Some people can remember many things for a long time. Other people have trouble remembering things. There are tricks to help make a person's memory work better. For example, many people remember the number of days in the month by using a poem that starts, "Thirty days has September. . . ."

Other articles to read include: **Alzheimer's disease; Amnesia; Brain; Learning.**

Meningitis

Meningitis *(MEHN ihn JY tihs)* is a disease that affects the brain and the spinal cord. The spinal cord runs down the inside of the backbone and connects most of the nerves in the body to the brain.

Meningitis is usually caused by tiny germs called *bacteria* or *viruses*. People with meningitis may get a fever, feel sick to their stomach, or have a stiff neck. Most people get completely well in time. But in some people, meningitis can make the brain *swell* (become bigger). Even after they are no longer sick, such people may have hearing problems or other difficulties.

Doctors can give people medicine for the meningitis that is caused by bacteria. But there are no medicines against the meningitis caused by viruses.

Other articles to read include: **Bacteria; Brain; Disease; Nervous system; Spine; Virus.**

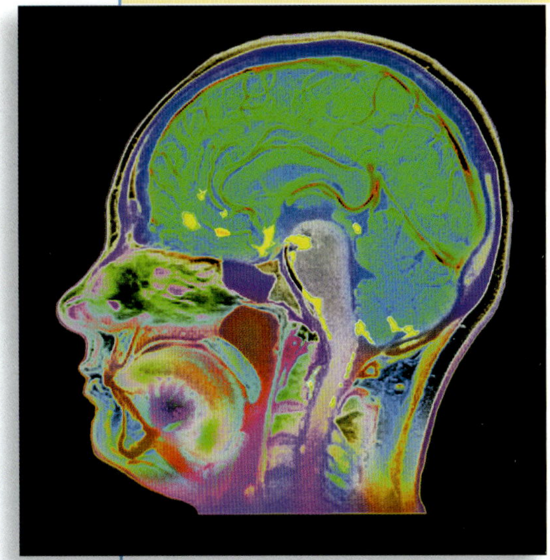

Meningitis appears as yellow spots in this magnetic resonance imaging (MRI) scan.

Menstruation

Menstruation *(MEHN stru AY shuhn)* is a loss of blood and cells that occurs about once a month in most women. The process of menstruation lasts from three to seven days. This time is called the *menstrual period*. Most girls experience their first menstrual period between the ages of 10 and 16.

During each month, blood and cells build up in the lining of a woman's *uterus* (womb), the organ that holds a baby during pregnancy. The thickening of the lining prepares the uterus for pregnancy. If pregnancy does not occur, the lining breaks down. The blood and cells are released through the vagina. The vagina is a canal that leads from the uterus to the outside of the body.

A woman stops having menstrual periods during a time of life called *menopause*. Menopause occurs between the ages of 45 and 55 in most women.

Other articles to read include: **Pregnancy; Reproduction, Human; Uterus; Vagina.**

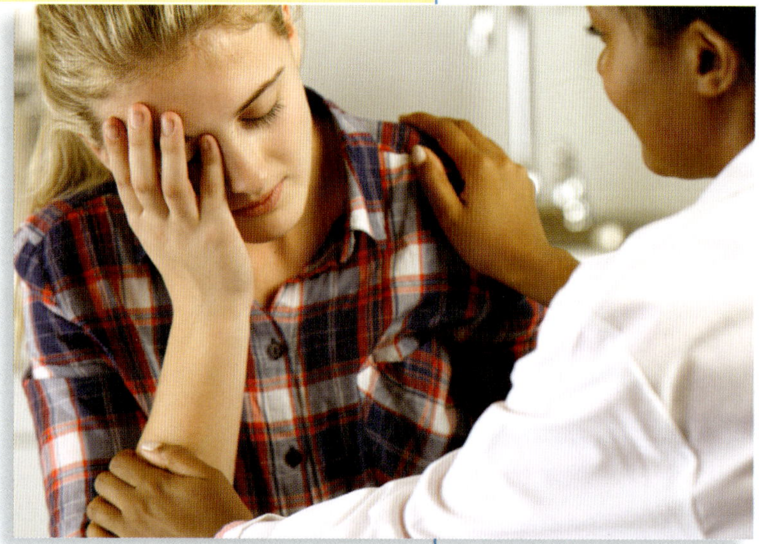

Depression is the most common form of mental illness. All people feel sad at times. Depression is considered a mental illness when feelings of sadness last for an extended period.

Mental illness

Mental illness is a disease of the mind or brain that affects a person's thoughts, emotions, personality, or behavior. In everyday language, people may call a mental illness that occurs suddenly a *nervous breakdown*. But doctors and others who help treat mental illness do not use this term. Mental health professionals sometimes refer to mental illnesses as *mental disorders* or *psychiatric illnesses*.

There are many kinds of mental illness. Signs of mental illness include extreme changes in moods, such as sadness or worry. A person may also have difficulty thinking clearly. Almost everyone has mood changes or finds it difficult to think clearly from time to time. But a person who is mentally ill usually has symptoms that are more severe. The symptoms usually damage the person's ability to conduct everyday activities.

Mental illnesses have various causes. Some mental illnesses are due to physical changes in the brain resulting from illness or injury. Chemical imbalances in the brain may cause other mental illnesses. Social factors also play a role in certain mental illnesses.

Mental illness affects people in all countries and in all parts of society. In many cases, the mental illness is mild and may not need treatment. But people with severe mental illness need treatment by doctors or mental health professionals. People with severe mental illness are sometimes called *insane*.

People with mental illness often feel shame and embarrassment about their illness. In the past, people reacted to the mentally ill with fear and disgust. Treatment methods used today usually help people recover from their symptoms more quickly than in the past. Most people with mental illness can return to leading normal lives with treatment.

Other articles to read include: **Alcoholism; Amnesia; Anorexia nervosa; Anxiety disorder; Autism; Brain; Bulimia; Clinical psychology; Depression; Disability; Eating disorder; Freud, Sigmund; Mind; Phobia; Psychiatry; Psychology; Schizophrenia; Suicide; Tranquilizer.**

Metabolism

Metabolism *(muh TAB uh lihz uhm)* is the chemical processes inside living cells. Cells are the tiny building blocks of life. Through metabolism, they make the materials and energy necessary for life.

Metabolism changes food into energy, water, or waste. People and other animals eat many times their own weight in food each year. But they do not gain that much weight. This is because metabolism converts most of the food to energy and waste.

Metabolism works in two ways. On one hand, it breaks down some compounds to make energy. On the other, it builds up compounds that the body needs to work and grow.

Other articles to read include: **Cell; Life; Thyroid gland; Weight control.**

Microbiology

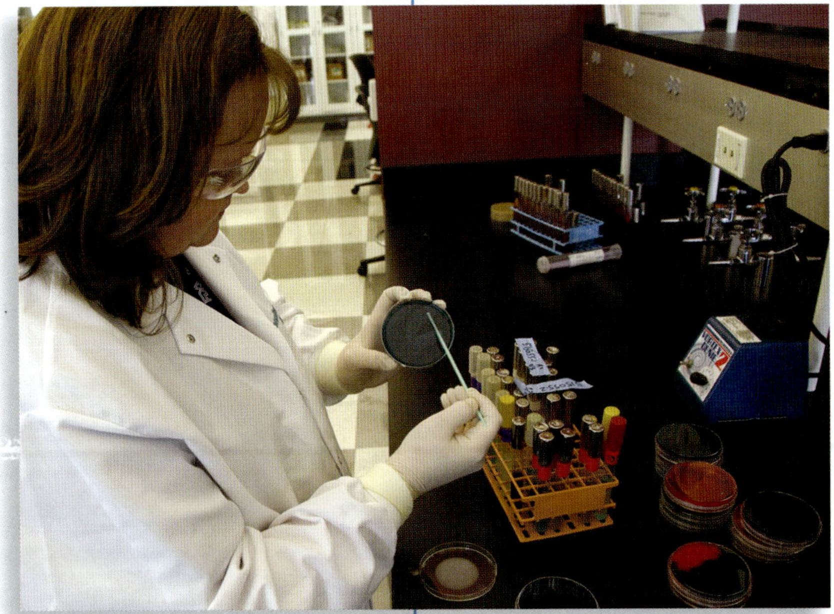

This microbiologist is working with bacteria in a laboratory.

Microbiology *(MY kroh by OL uh jee)* is the study of tiny living things. These living things are known as *microbes* or *microorganisms*. These tiny *organisms* (living things) cannot be seen without a microscope. People who study microbiology are called *microbiologists.*

Microbiologists study organisms such as bacteria, fungi, protists *(PROH tihsts),* and viruses. Many microbiologists specialize in certain types of organisms. Bacteriologists (*bak TIHR ee OL uh jihsts*) study bacteria. Virologists (*vy ROL uh jihsts*) study viruses.

Many microbiologists study the relationships between microbes and other living things. For example, they may study how microbes cause disease in people. *Dental microbiologists* study the role of microorganisms in the mouth, especially in

Continued on the next page

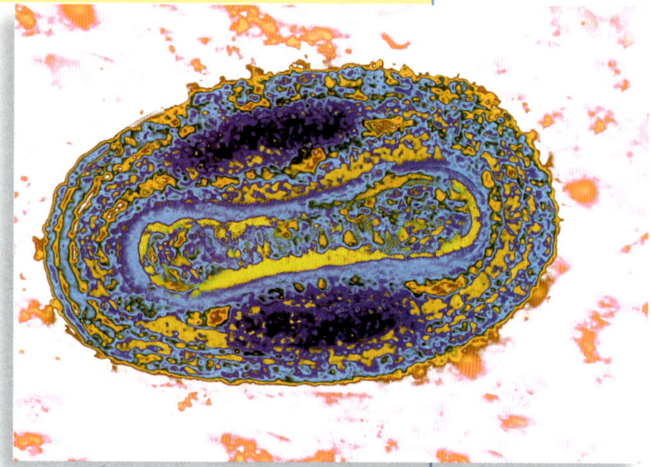

Microbiologists called *virologists* study viruses. This image of the smallpox virus was produced using an electron microscope.

Microbiology *Continued from the previous page*

tooth decay. *Agricultural microbiologists* study microorganisms in plants and soil.

Although some microorganisms can cause disease, others are helpful. Bacteria that live in the human gut help people to digest food. Some microorganisms, such as yeast, are used to make or flavor foods. Others are used to treat sewage or clean up pollution. People use some microbes to make medicines or vitamins.

Microorganisms are generally less than 4/1000 inch (0.1 millimeter) across. They are so small that they can be seen only with powerful microscopes that can magnify an object many thousands of times.

Other articles to read include: **Antibiotic; Bacteria; Biology; Disease; Germ; Penicillin; Virus.**

Middle-aged people tend to place increasing value on their friendships and family life.

Middle age

Middle age is a time in a person's life between early adulthood and old age. This period usually lasts from about the age of 40 to 65.

Middle age is often a time when adults "settle down." Middle-aged people tend to place increasing value on their family life and friendships. Many people may feel closer to their own elderly parents. Parents often become more open with their children.

Some middle-aged people may not enjoy this part of life because they fear old age. But studies show that many people still feel they can live a full life. Their happiness is often increased by the skills and experiences gained over the years.

Other articles to read include: **Adult; Aging.**

Migraine

A migraine *(MY grayn)* is a bad headache. During a migraine, the head may hurt on only one side. People with migraines may also feel sick to their stomachs. Some people who get migraines first see an *aura (AWR uh),* a shimmering light or blind spot, before the headache begins.

Doctors have found that certain foods, such as chocolate, may trigger migraines in some people. Certain activities, such as seeing bright lights, may act as triggers, too. If people who get migraines avoid such triggers, they may get fewer headaches.

Doctors think that migraines are caused by a chemical in the brain called *serotonin (sihr oh TOH nuhn).* Certain medicines can help people with migraines by stopping the headaches after they have started.

Other articles to read include: **Brain; Headache.**

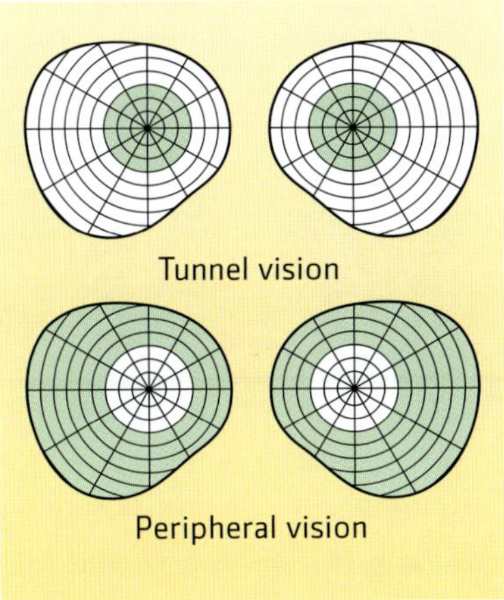

Migraines may cause visual problems, such as *tunnel vision* or the ability to see *peripheral* (side) vision only. The shaded area shows the area of vision.

Mind

Mind is a word generally used to describe an individual's thoughts and ways of understanding the world. The mind is related to the brain. However, the mind is not a physical object. People have disagreed for centuries about the best way to define the mind.

Scientists and thinkers of all kinds have contributed to our knowledge of the mind. Philosophers, psychologists, and computer scientists have all made contributions.

Many scientists say the mind has three distinct parts. These parts are called (1) the *base level*, (2) *self-awareness*, and (3) *theory of mind*. The base level helps events fit into an individual's thoughts. Self-awareness is the ability to keep track of one's own thoughts. Theory of mind refers to the fact that minds can know that other minds exist.

Most complex animals also have what can be described as a mind. A mind enables animals to react to their surroundings. It also allows them to make sense of the world around them.

Other articles to read include: **Brain; Consciousness; Intelligence; Memory.**

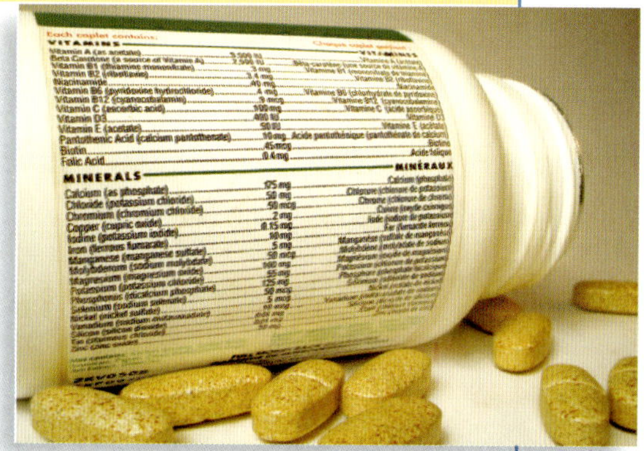

The minerals in a multivitamin can help the body to maintain good health if a person is unable to eat a balanced diet.

Mineral

Minerals are natural substances needed by the bodies of human beings and other living things. Minerals help the body grow. They also help the body's cells and organs work properly. People need only small amounts of minerals each day.

Minerals are not created by living things. Plants get minerals from the water or soil. Animals get minerals from eating plants or eating animals that eat plants. Minerals needed by the body include calcium, phosphorus, potassium, sodium, and magnesium. Calcium, magnesium, and phosphorus help form the bones and teeth. Milk and milk products provide calcium. Cereals and meats provide phosphorus. Whole-grain cereals, nuts, beans, and green leafy vegetables are good sources of magnesium.

Other articles to read include: **Calcium; Diet; Food; Manganese; Nutrition; Vitamin.**

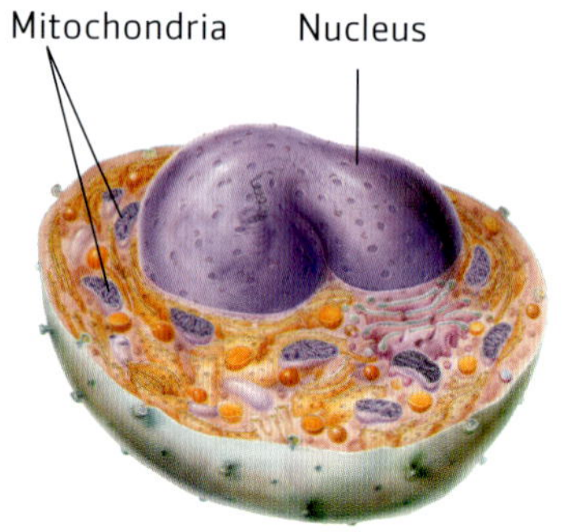

Mitochondria are the parts of a cell that turn chemical energy from food into energy the cell can use. This drawing shows a cross section of a cell and its mitochondria.

Mitochondria

Mitochondria *(MY tuh KAHN dree uh)* are one of many different parts inside a *cell.* Cells are the tiny building blocks that all living things are made of. Mitochondria can be round or rod-shaped. They can also form a network of small tubes.

The job of mitochondria is to take chemical energy from food and turn it into energy the cell can use. Mitochondria use energy that comes from substances in foods called *carbohydrates* and *fats.* Carbohydrates are found in foods such as rice, bread, and potatoes. Fats are found in foods that include meats and oils.

Mitochondria use the energy that is released when carbohydrates and fats are broken down. The energy is used to make a new substance that cells use as fuel to grow and to perform other important tasks in the body.

Other articles to read include: **Carbohydrate; Cell; Fat; Food.**

Mitosis

Mitosis *(mih TOH sihs)* is a kind of *cell* division. In cell division, one cell splits apart to become two cells. Mitosis happens in most kinds of cells. In mitosis, one cell splits to form two identical cells. Mitosis enables the body to grow and maintain tissues. Mitosis is different from *meiosis*. Meiosis happens only in sex cells.

Cells contain *chromosomes (KROH muh sohmz)*. Chromosomes carry *genes*, which act as chemical instructions for how a living thing develops. Before mitosis, each chromosome has two identical strands held together. These strands are called *sister chromatids*.

The chromosomes then line up along the middle of the cell. The sister chromatids split apart, becoming chromosomes themselves. The body of the cell splits to form two cells, called *daughter cells*. Each daughter cell contains a complete set of chromosomes. These chromosomes are identical to those in the original cell.

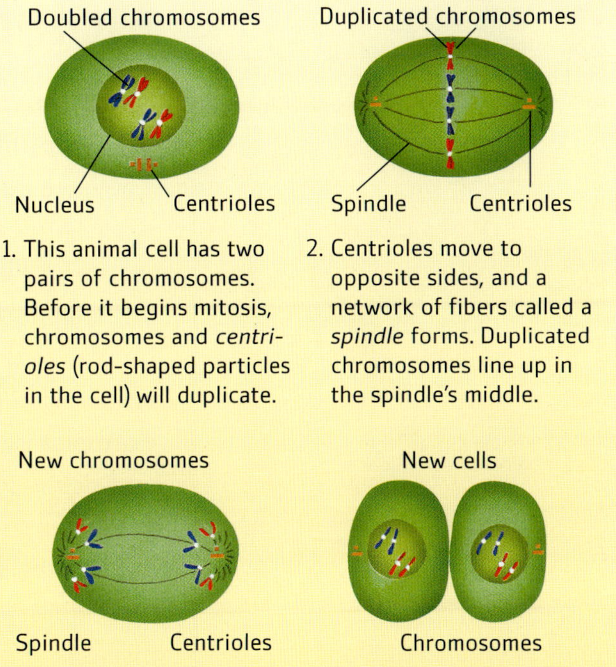

1. This animal cell has two pairs of chromosomes. Before it begins mitosis, chromosomes and *centrioles* (rod-shaped particles in the cell) will duplicate.
2. Centrioles move to opposite sides, and a network of fibers called a *spindle* forms. Duplicated chromosomes line up in the spindle's middle.
3. The duplicated chromosomes separate and become new chromosomes. The separated chromosomes move to opposite sides of the cell.
4. The main body of the cell divides, and the cell splits. Each new cell receives chromosomes that are duplicates of those of the parent cell.

Other articles to read include: **Cell; Chromosome; Meiosis; Nucleus; Reproduction, Human.**

Mole

A mole is a colored growth on the skin. Its cells contain a *pigment* (coloring material) called *melanin (MEHL uh nihn)*. Moles may be on the skin at birth. These moles are sometimes called *birthmarks*. Most moles appear during childhood or teenage years.

Moles are common. They may be on any part of the body. Moles vary in size, but most moles are small. They may be flat or raised. They range from light brown to bluish-black in color. Some moles have long, dark hairs.

Most moles are harmless. But in rare cases, a mole can turn into a cancerous tumor. Any mole that changes should be checked by a doctor. Moles can be removed by surgery.

Other articles to read include: **Freckle; Melanin; Skin; Skin cancer.**

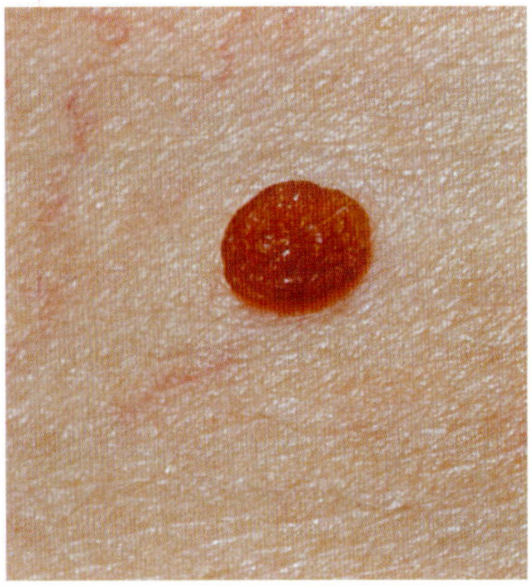

A mole is a colored growth on the skin.

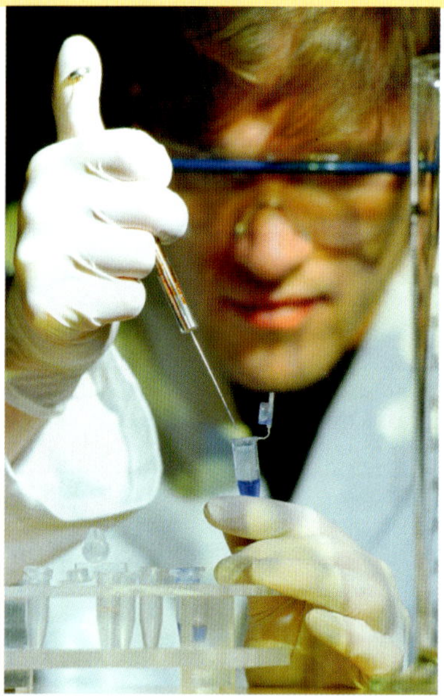

A researcher in molecular medicine prepares blood samples for gene therapy experiments.

Molecular medicine

Molecular medicine is a field of science in which researchers use basic knowledge about the biology of cells and diseases. They use this knowledge to develop treatments, therapies, and drugs. Molecular medicine often focuses on developing treatments for diseases that result from *abnormal* (not normal) genes or the abnormal function of genes.

Scientists know that certain diseases are passed from one generation to the next. These are called *hereditary diseases.* Some examples of hereditary diseases are cystic fibrosis, hemophilia, and sickle-cell anemia. They are all caused by a single abnormal gene. Researchers in molecular medicine are also working to identify the genes associated with complex diseases. Some of these illnesses are cancer, heart disease, and diabetes. Complex diseases are not caused by abnormalities of a single gene.

Other developments in molecular medicine include the use of *gene therapy* to correct defective genes. Gene therapy also includes the creation of artificial *chromosomes* (tiny structures inside cells). However, most techniques in molecular medicine today are experimental.

Other articles to read include: **Cell; Chromosome; Disease; Gene; Gene therapy; Heredity; Medicine.**

Mononucleosis

Mononucleosis (*MON uh NOO klee OH sihs*) is a mild disease that is easily spread from person to person. It is often called *mono.* It is usually caused by a microbe called the Epstein-Barr virus. Mononucleosis is most common in young adults. But it also strikes children and older people. The disease can spread through direct contact between people, such as kissing.

People often feel very tired when they have mononucleosis. They may have chills, fever, and sore throat. Most doctors recommend mild to complete bed rest, depending on the seriousness of the case. The disease is not fatal. Most patients recover within three to six weeks.

Other articles to read include: **Disease; Fever; Virus.**

Motion sickness

Some rides in amusement parks can cause motion sickness.

Motion sickness is an uncomfortable feeling some people get when they travel in ships, cars, buses, trains, or planes, or when they go on certain rides in an amusement park. It is also called *seasickness, carsickness, trainsickness*, or *airsickness.*

People with motion sickness become pale and sweaty. They feel sick to their stomachs and may throw up. Sometimes they burp, get a headache, or become dizzy or sleepy.

People get motion sickness because the movement they are experiencing upsets their sense of balance. Such a person may feel better by keeping his or her head still or by looking straight ahead to the *horizon*. The horizon is the line where the land and sky seem to meet. Some medicines can prevent motion sickness if they are taken before a person travels.

Other articles to read include: **Aerospace medicine; Nausea.**

Motivation

Motivation is anything that causes people to behave as they do. Most people know what it feels like to be motivated to do something. But it is difficult to figure out an exact scientific definition for motivation.

In studying motivation, scientists sometimes concentrate on the *arousal* of behavior. Arousal means being "stirred up" or "ready for action." For example, the sensation of thirst may arouse a person to drink.

A person's behavior can also be directed by their *motives* (reasons for doing things). For example, imagine a coach whose football team is playing against a much stronger team. The coach might be most strongly motivated by the desire to win. In that case, the coach might try everything to get an upset victory. A different coach might be motivated more by the feelings of the players. That coach might worry more about keeping the team from becoming discouraged.

Other articles to read include: **Behavior; Emotion.**

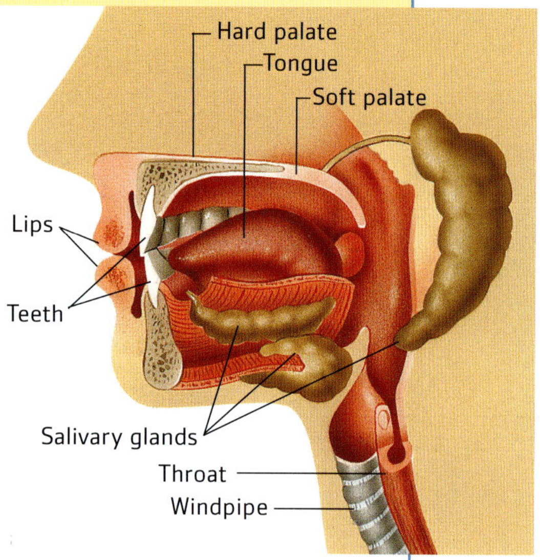

The mouth is adapted for taking in food. Food is ground by the teeth and moistened and partly digested by *saliva.* The tongue tastes and mixes the food and aids in swallowing. The tongue, teeth, and lips also help form the sounds of human speech.

Mouth

The mouth is the part of the body that takes in food. The lips at the mouth opening help us drink and pick up our food. Inside the mouth are two rows of teeth, one above the other, and a tongue. The teeth grind and crush food into little pieces so that it can be swallowed. The tongue helps us eat, swallow, and taste food. The tongue, teeth, and lips also help us to talk.

The inside of the mouth gives off a watery liquid called *saliva (suh LY vuh).* As the teeth chew food, saliva mixes with the food and makes it wet. That softens the food and makes it easier to swallow. The saliva also contains chemicals that start to break down some of the food.

Other articles to read include: **Digestive system; Esophagus; Palate; Saliva; Taste; Teeth; Tongue; Trachea.**

Mucus

Mucus *(MYOO kuhs)* is a clear, slimy fluid. It is found in the body, on surfaces called *mucous membranes (MEHM braynz).* Mucous membranes line the mouth, the nose, and other body organs and passages. Mucus is mostly a mixture of protein and sugar.

Mucus helps things pass easily over mucous membranes. For example, mucus helps food slide down the *esophagus (ee SOF uh guhs),* the tube that leads to the stomach.

Mucus also catches dirt and other foreign matter. It helps keep this matter out of the body. For example, mucus and hairs in the nose trap dust and other unwanted particles.

Other articles to read include: **Esophagus; Germ; Nose.**

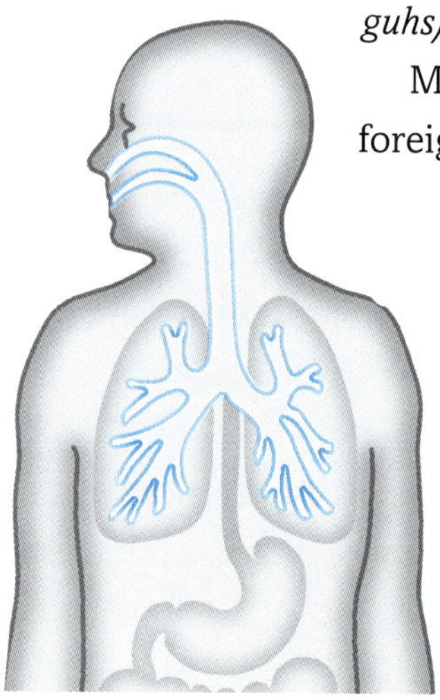

Mucous membranes (outlined in blue) produce sticky *mucus* that traps germs. Tiny, hairlike *cilia* push mucus from the lungs and trachea up to the mouth.

Multiple birth

In *identical twins,* both babies come from a single egg and share the same physical traits.

A multiple birth is the birth of more than one baby from the same mother at about the same time. *Twins* (two babies), *triplets* (three babies), *quadruplets* (four babies), and *quintuplets* (five babies) are all multiple births. Many animals give birth to more than one offspring at a time. However, human beings usually have only one baby at a time.

Most multiple births in humans are twins. There are two most common kinds of twins: *fraternal* and *identical.* Fraternal twins may be of the same sex or they may be a brother and a sister. They form when two separate eggs are fertilized. Each baby looks different. Identical twins are always of the same sex and they look alike. They form when a single fertilized egg splits.

Other articles to read include: **Baby; Childbirth; Pregnancy.**

Multiple sclerosis

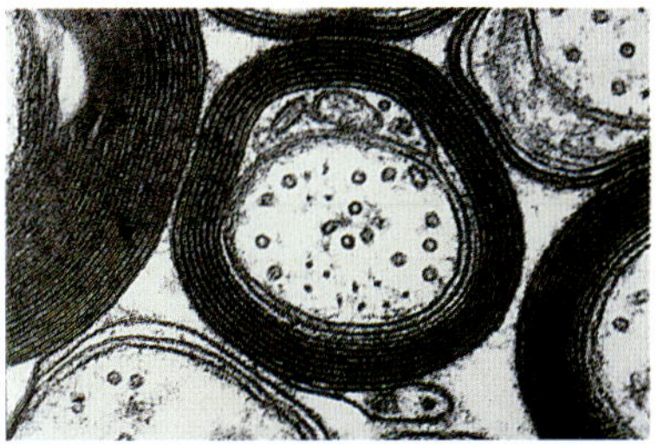

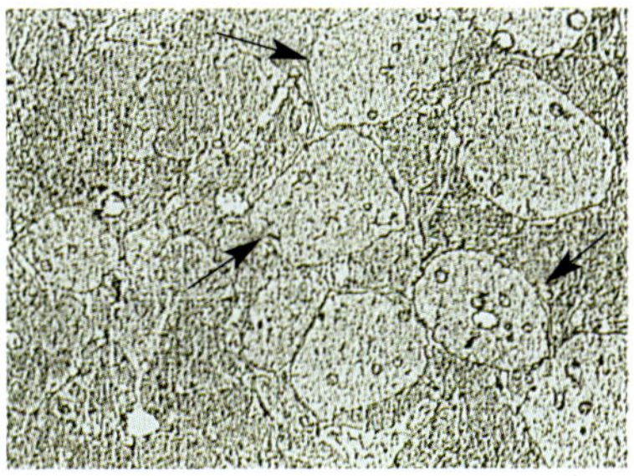

Normal nerve cells (top) have fatty protective layers surrounding the cells. Multiple sclerosis can destroy these layers, exposing parts of the cells (arrows, above).

Multiple sclerosis *(sklih ROH sihs)* is a disease that damages the brain and the *spinal cord.* The spinal cord is a bundle of nerves that runs down the inside of the backbone and connects all of the nerves in the body to the brain. Multiple sclerosis is often called MS. The disease is more common among women, but men also get MS.

MS usually strikes between the ages of 20 and 25. People with MS begin to have trouble walking, to feel weakness or tingling in their arms or legs, or to have problems seeing. These problems usually go away for a while and then come back again. Over time, the person may become *disabled* (unable to perform daily tasks).

There is no cure for MS. But there are some medicines that can keep people feeling better longer before the problems return.

Other articles to read include: **Brain; Disability; Disease; Nervous system; Paralysis; Spine.**

Mummy

Mummies are dead bodies that have been preserved for hundreds or thousands of years. The most famous mummies are from Ancient Egypt. Many museums have at least one Egyptian mummy. The term *mummy* refers to any dead body preserved for a long time.

The early Egyptians believed that the dead lived on in the next world after they died. They believed that a person had the same body in the next world. So they wanted to keep the body in good condition. They worked hard to keep bodies from decaying, or rotting. Thousands of years later, scientists found the bodies.

Scientists have learned how the early Egyptians made mummies. Ancient books say that it took 70 days to make a mummy. First, most of the inside body parts were taken out. Usually, the inside of the body was filled with pieces of cloth or sawdust. Then the Egyptians placed the body in special chemicals to dry it out. Finally, they wrapped the body in many layers of cloth and placed it in a coffin. The coffins were made of wood or stone. Some were rectangular. Others were shaped like the mummy. The mummy in its coffin was then placed in a tomb. Along with the mummy, the Egyptians placed objects of daily living, such as clothing, food, and jewelry. The ancient Egyptians believed that the dead would need these things in the next world.

Other articles to read include: **Death; Human body.**

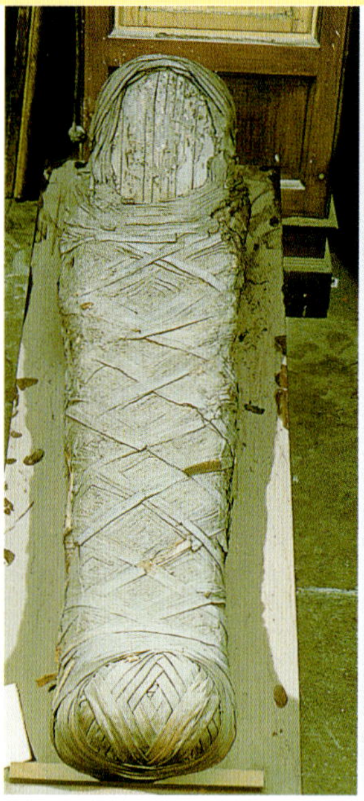

Mummies reveal how the people of ancient Egypt cared for the dead. The mummies were wound tightly with linen and then laid out in coffins. In some periods, the coffins were painted (above right).

An Egyptian mummy undergoes a computed tomography (CT) scan (below). The scan (below right) can reveal information on the person's diet, general health, age, and gender.

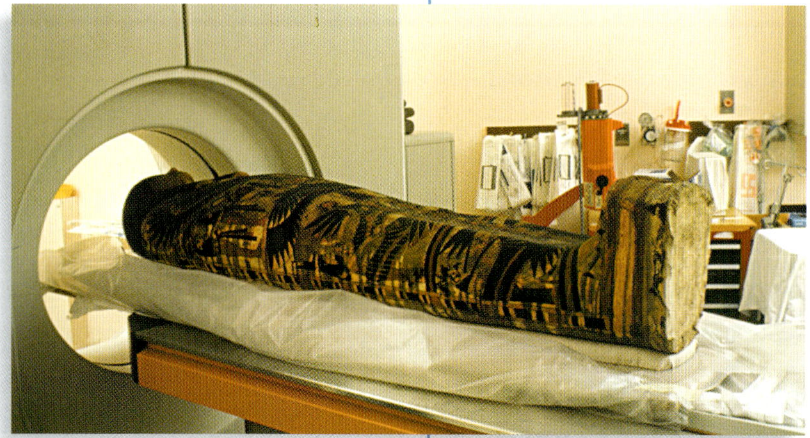

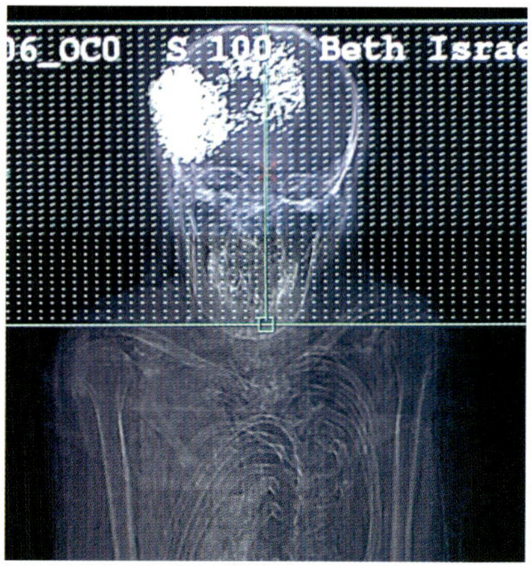

Mumps

Mumps is a disease that spreads easily from person to person. It causes painful swelling below and in front of the ears. Mumps is caused by a virus, or tiny germ, in the saliva of a person with mumps.

A person shows the first signs of mumps about 18 days after coming in contact with the mumps virus. These signs include fever, headache, muscle aches, and sometimes vomiting. Then the swelling begins. Pain in the swollen area may make it hard for the person to chew or swallow. The swelling lasts about a week.

Today, there is a *vaccine (vak SEEN)* for mumps. It is a shot that protects people from the disease.

Other articles to read include: **Disease; Immunization; Virus.**

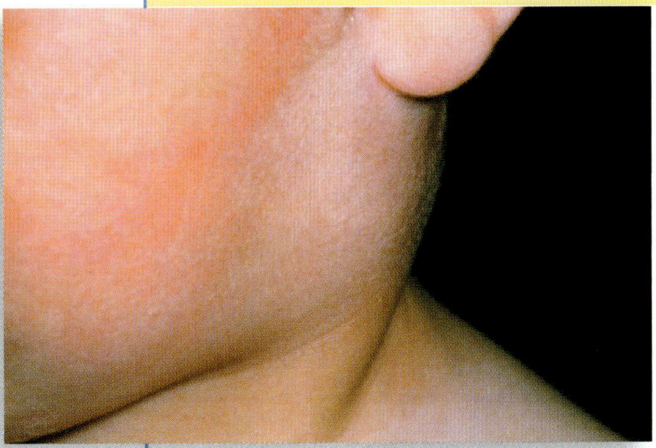

Mumps causes a painful swelling below and in front of the ears.

Muscle

The human body has more than 600 major muscles. About 240 of these muscles have specific names.

Muscle is the tough, elastic tissue that makes body parts move. The human body has more than 600 major muscles. We use muscles to walk, jump, and throw. We use muscles in the jaw to help us chew food. There are some muscles in the body that work all the time, even when we are resting. Muscles in the heart and blood vessels push blood into the body. Muscles in the chest help us breathe. Muscles help move food through the stomach and intestines and help digestion.

There are three main types of muscles. *Skeletal (SKEHL uh tuhl) muscles* hold the bones of the skeleton together and give the body shape. They also make the body move. They make up a large part of the legs, arms, chest, abdomen, neck, and face. Some skeletal muscles are tiny, such as the small, weak muscles of the eye. Other skeletal muscles are large and strong, such as the muscles of the thigh.

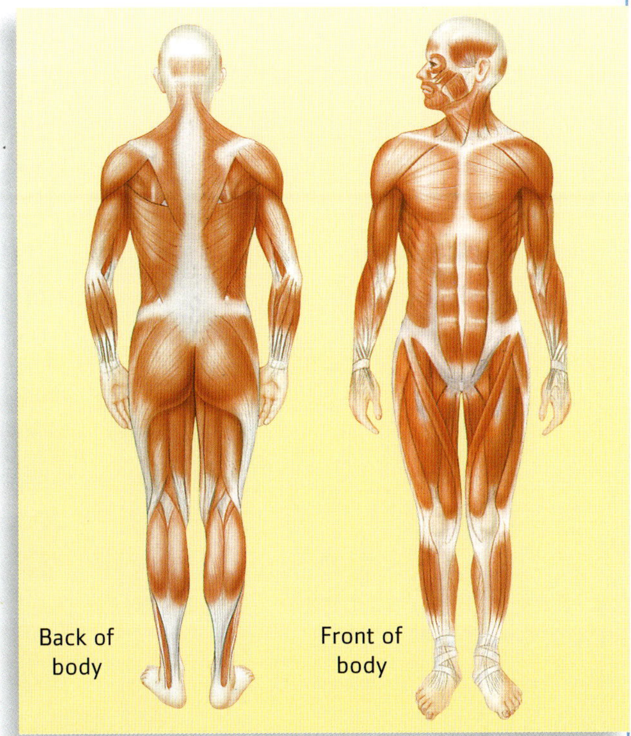

Continued on the next page

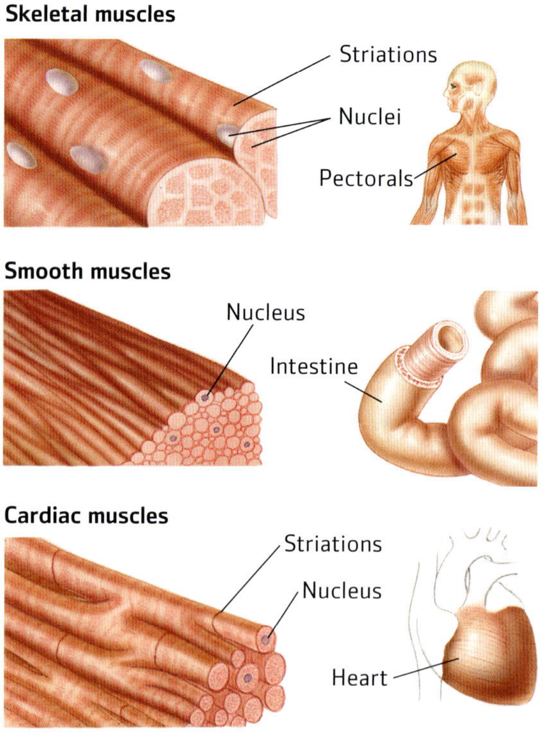

Muscle *Continued from the previous page*

Smooth muscles are in various organs of the body. They are in the walls of the stomach, intestines, blood vessels, and bladder. Smooth muscles are smaller than skeletal muscles. They work slowly and automatically.

Cardiac muscles make up the walls of the heart. These muscles help push blood out of the heart and into the *arteries* (tubes that carry blood away from the heart). The blood then carries nourishment to the body's cells. Cardiac muscles work automatically, like smooth muscles.

Other articles to read include: **Cramp; Diaphragm; Heart; Human body; Muscular dystrophy; Paralysis; Skeleton; Tendon; Tongue.**

The human body has three kinds of muscle: (1) *skeletal* muscle (2) *smooth* muscle, and (3) *cardiac* muscle. Skeletal muscle fibers have bands called *striations.* Each fiber also has many core elements called *nuclei.* Smooth muscles have no striations and only one nucleus in each fiber. Cardiac muscle has striations and a single nucleus in each fiber.

Muscular dystrophy

Muscular dystrophy *(DIHS truh fee)* is a name for certain kinds of muscle diseases. These diseases weaken the muscles that hold the bones of the body together. Muscular dystrophy makes it hard for a person to move, hold the body up, and even breathe.

Some types of muscular dystrophy begin when a person is still a child. Other types of the disease begin in adulthood. But all of them are inherited. That means that the diseases are passed on in families, from parents and grandparents to children.

Continued on the next page

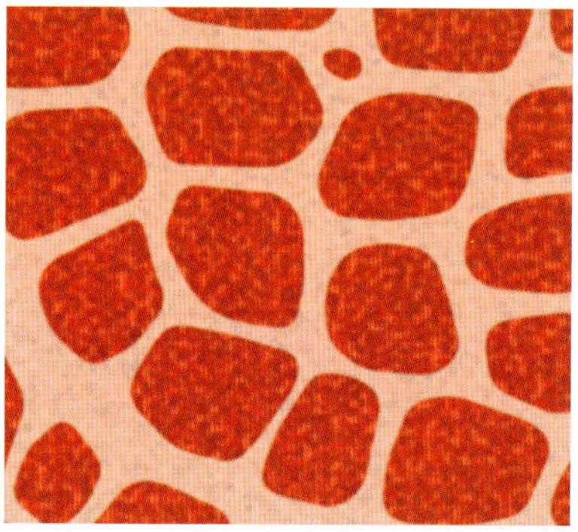

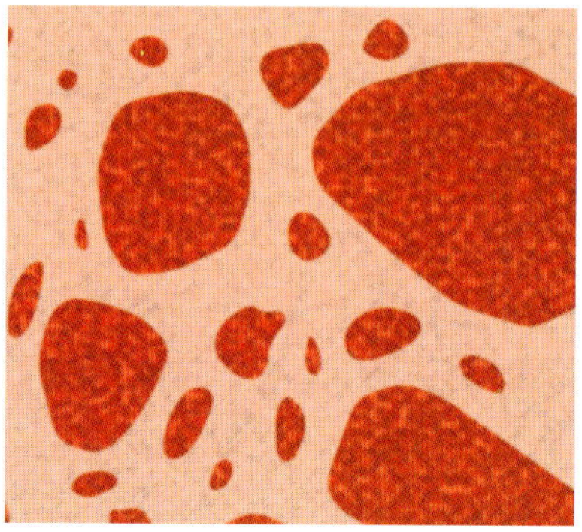

The muscle tissue of a person with muscular dystrophy (far right illustration) may appear wasted and irregular compared with normal muscle tissue (near right).

Doctors have not yet found a way to cure any of the kinds of muscular dystrophy. They use stretching exercises and braces to keep muscles normal for as long as possible. They use medicines to make breathing easier.

Other articles to read include: **Disease; Muscle; Paralysis.**

Mutation

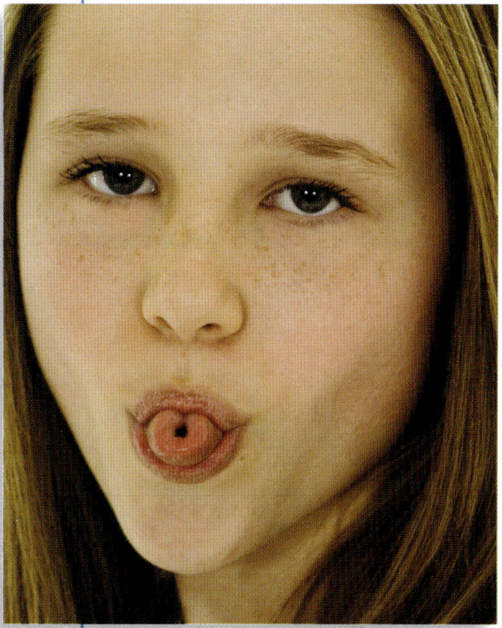

The ability to roll the tongue is a trait based on a single gene. A mutation in this gene may prevent a person from rolling the tongue.

A mutation is a change in the genetic material of a living *cell.* Cells are tiny building blocks of life. Genetic material is made up of genes and *chromosomes (KROH muh sohmz).* Genes carry the necessary information for building cells, tissues, organs, and bodies. Chromosomes are tiny, threadlike structures. An organism's genes are found within the chromosomes. When a mutation happens, it can change certain *traits* (characteristics) of the *organism* (living thing). Mutations can be passed on to future generations.

A mutation may or may not have a visible effect on the organism that carries it. Most mutations that cause a visible change are harmful. A mutation can change a single gene or it might change an entire chromosome. Sickle cell anemia is a blood disease caused by a mutation. In a person with this disease, a minor change occurs in a gene that controls the production of red blood cells.

A chromosome mutation occurs if the number or arrangement of chromosomes changes. Down syndrome is a mental and physical disorder caused by a chromosome mutation. The disorder occurs if a person is born with an extra copy of a certain chromosome.

Scientists know that a number of factors often cause mutations in humans. These factors include certain chemicals, X rays, and ultraviolet light.

Other articles to read include: **Cell; Chromosome; Down syndrome; Evolution; Gene; Heredity; Sickle cell anemia.**

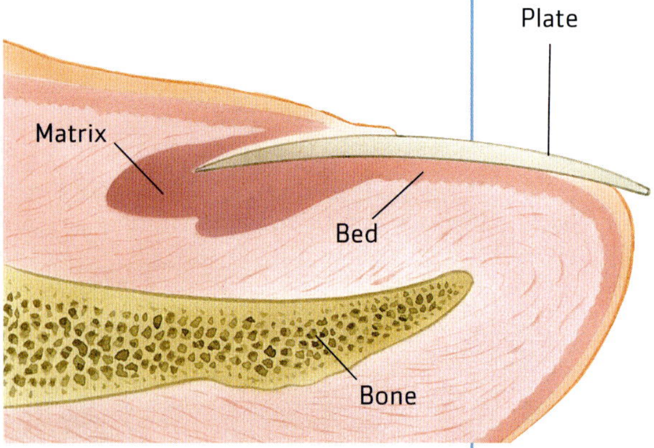

The nails of the fingers and toes are formed from certain cells of the skin. A nail has three parts—the matrix, bed, and plate. The matrix produces the cells of the bed and plate.

Nail

Nails are the tough, hard growths at the ends of the fingers and toes. They are made up of hardened cells. The skin below the nail, from which the nail grows, is called the *matrix (MAY trihks)*. The white, crescent-shaped spot at the base of the nail is called the *lunula (LOO nyuh luh)*.

If a nail is torn off, it will grow back, as long as the matrix is not badly injured. Some illnesses affect nail growth. A doctor sometimes can tell if a patient is sick by looking at the nails. The horns, claws, talons, and hoofs of other animals are made of the same materials as the nails on humans.

Other articles to read include: **Epidermis; Finger; Skin.**

Narcotic

A narcotic *(nahr KOT ihk)* is a substance that has a strong effect upon the human body. Narcotics can cause people to feel no pain. They can also cause people to fall asleep or go into a *coma (KOH muh)*. A coma is like a deep sleep. The term *narcotic* comes from a Greek word that means *to make numb*. When a person is numb, he or she feels no pain.

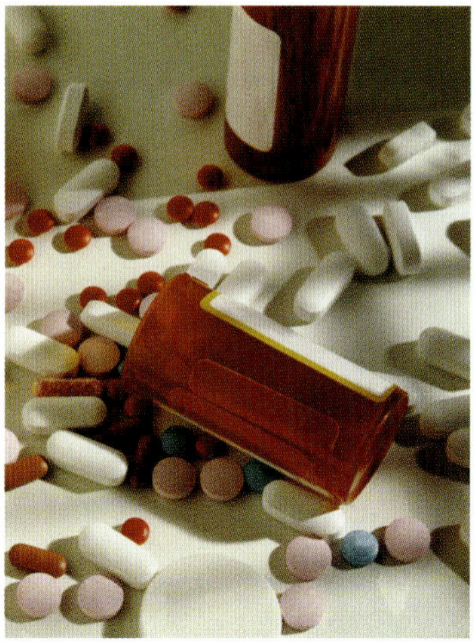

Narcotic drugs should only be used under the care and prescription of a doctor.

Narcotic drugs are useful in medicine, but they can also be dangerous. Large doses of narcotics may cause death. Repeated use may cause *addiction* (physical and mental dependence). A person should only use narcotics under the care of a doctor.

Other articles to read include: **Drug; Drug abuse; Pain.**

Nausea

Nausea *(NAW shee uh)* is an unpleasant feeling in the area of the stomach. It is often followed by vomiting. In nausea, the muscles of the stomach wall slow or stop their movement. This slows or stops digestion of food in the stomach.

Nausea can help prevent the body from absorbing a harmful substance that has been swallowed. If the person vomits, most of the substance will be expelled.

Nausea may result from both mental and physical causes. Mental causes of nausea include unpleasant sights, disgusting odors, and severe worry. Physical causes include dizziness, severe pain, blocking or irritation of the digestive system, too much exercise, and motion sickness. Nausea often accompanies pregnancy, especially in the mornings of the first three months.

Other articles to read include: **Motion sickness; Pregnancy; Stomach; Vomiting.**

Nearsightedness

Nearsightedness is a problem some people have when looking at things that are distant, or far away. People who are near-sighted see things that are near clearly. But things that are farther away look blurry to them. Nearsightedness is also called *myopia (my OH pee uh).*

People usually become nearsighted because they are born with eyeballs that are shaped a little differently than other people's. The eyeballs of nearsighted people are a little longer than normal from front to back.

Doctors can help people who are nearsighted to see better by fitting them with glasses or *contact lenses.* Contact lenses are tiny pieces of specially made plastic that fit right over the eyes. Doctors can also perform surgery that uses lasers to correct nearsightedness.

Other articles to read include: **Contact lens; Eye; Glasses; Farsightedness; Vision.**

Nearsightedness is a condition in which distance vision is blurred, but nearby objects may appear sharp (below). It happens when light rays from distant objects meet before they reach the *retina* (light-sensitive part of the eye). Glasses or contacts with *concave* lenses bring the rays together at the retina, correcting nearsightedness (bottom).

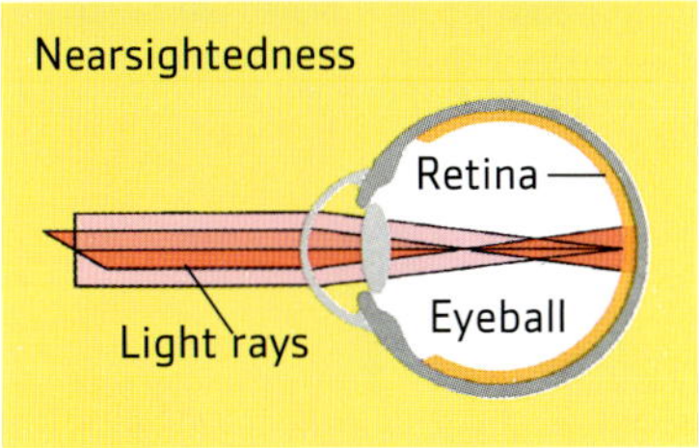

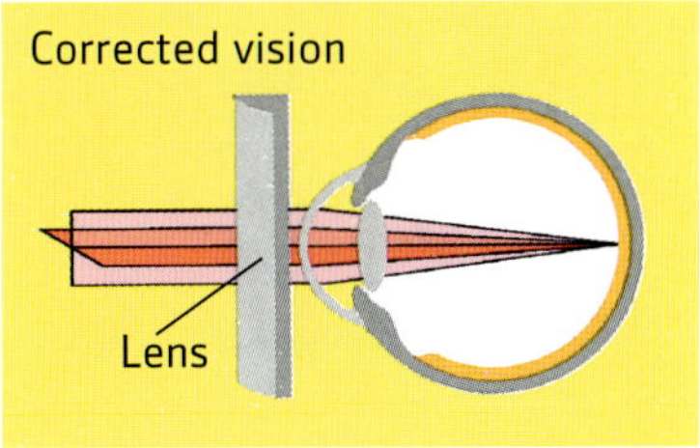

Nervous system

The nervous system helps all the parts of the body work together. Almost all animals have some type of nervous system. In human beings and other animals with backbones, the brain, the spinal cord, and the nerves make up the nervous system.

The nervous system is made up of billions of special cells called *neurons*, or *nerve cells*. Cordlike bundles of neuron fibers are called *nerves*. The nerves form a network of pathways that conducts information rapidly throughout the body. Information from a person's surroundings travels along these pathways to the brain. The brain then sends instructions down other pathways to the muscles to tell them what to do. All of our movements, sensations, thoughts, and emotions happen because of the nervous system. Breathing, digestion, and heartbeat also depend on the nervous system.

The brain and spinal cord form the *central nervous system*. The central nervous system is like the main computer that controls the body and helps its parts work together. A part of the brain called the *cerebrum (SEHR uh bruhm)* directs hearing, sight, touch, thinking, language, and emotions. Another part of the brain, the *cerebellum (SEHR uh BEHL uhm),* controls balance and muscle movements. The *brain stem*, at the top of the spinal column, helps regulate balance, blood pressure, breathing, and heartbeat. The brain stem also relays messages from one part of the brain to another.

The *peripheral (puh RIHF uhr uhl) nervous system* carries all the messages between the central nervous system and the rest of the body. The *autonomic (AW tuh NOM ihk) nervous system* is part of the peripheral nervous system. It controls breathing and digestion.

Other articles to read include: **Amyotrophic lateral sclerosis; Brain; Central nervous system; Cerebellum; Cerebrum; Multiple sclerosis; Narcotic; Neurology; Paralysis; Sleeping sickness.**

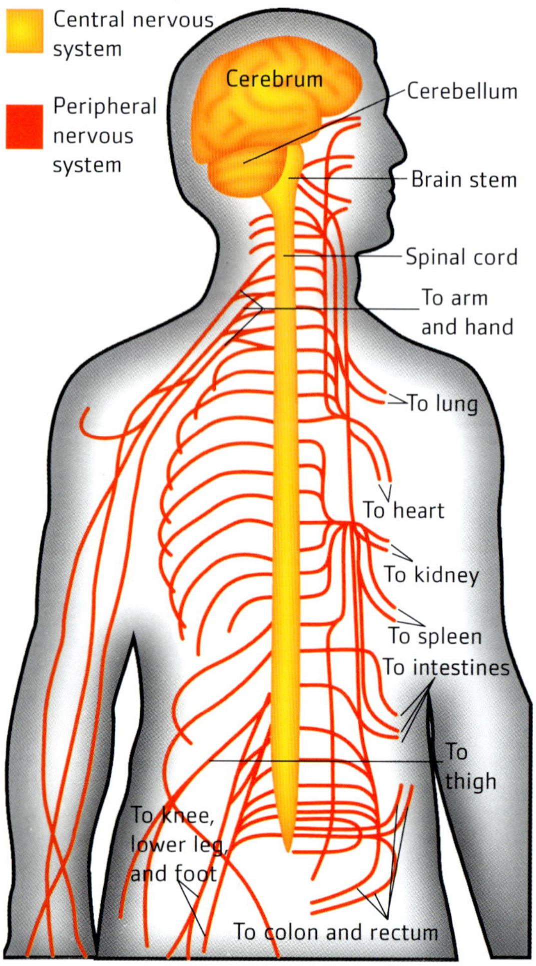

The human nervous system helps all the parts of the body work together. The *central nervous system* (yellow) is made up of the brain and spinal cord. The *peripheral nervous system* (red) carries all the messages between the central nervous system and the rest of the body.

Neurology

Neurology *(nu ROL uh jee)* is the branch of medicine that studies and treats diseases of the muscles and the nervous system. The nervous system includes the brain, the nerves, and the *spinal cord*. The spinal cord is a cable of nerve cells that runs from the brain down the body inside the backbone. Doctors who specialize in neurology are called *neurologists*.

People may go to see a neurologist if they are having such problems as headaches, *paralysis* (inability to move), or neck or back pain. They may also see a neurologist for such diseases as Alzheimer's disease, multiple sclerosis, and Parkinson disease. These diseases may occur if something goes wrong with the brain or nerves.

Doctors may use various techniques in order to learn what the problem might be. One such technique is called *magnetic resonance imaging* (MRI). A doctor may also examine such things as the patient's vision, hearing, strength, and coordination. In addition, a doctor may check how the patient responds to touch, pain, and temperature. After receiving all the information available, the doctor may then treat the patient with medication, *physical therapy* (exercises), or surgery.

Other articles to read include: **Central nervous system; Magnetic resonance imaging; Medicine; Nervous system; Spine.**

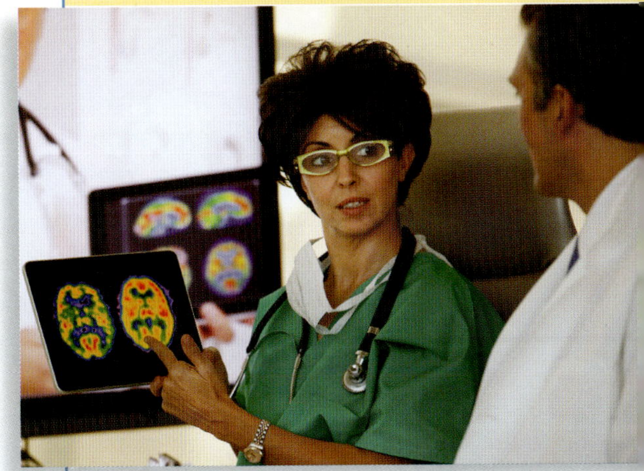

A neurologist reviews a magnetic resonance imaging (MRI) scan of a patient's brain with another doctor. Together, they will determine a plan of treatment for the patient.

Nicotine

Nicotine is a substance found in the leaves, roots, and seeds of tobacco plants. Pure nicotine is poisonous. Even a little can make a person get sick, become very weak, or even die.

Cigarettes and other tobacco products have small amounts of nicotine. When someone smokes a cigarette, the nicotine is quickly taken up by the blood and reaches the brain in a few seconds. People become *addicted* to the nicotine in tobacco. Being addicted means that a person is unable to stop using a substance, even when he or she knows the substance is unhealthy. Doctors know that using tobacco products is unhealthy.

Other articles to read include: **Drug abuse; Poison.**

The nicotine content in cigarettes is tested by machines (above) at a government laboratory. Nicotine causes cigarette addiction.

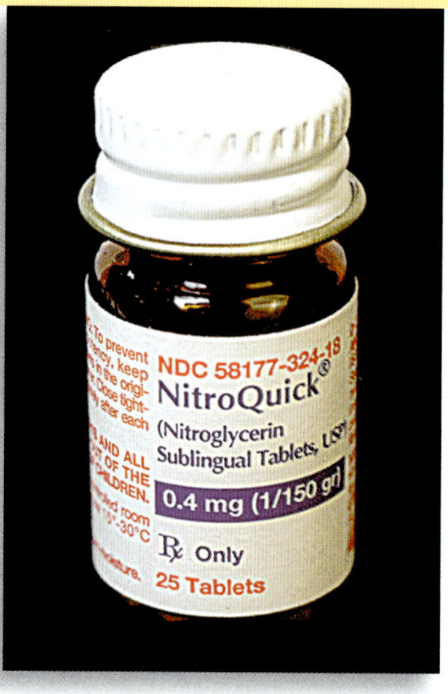

Nitroglycerin tablets can be used to treat certain heart problems.

Nitroglycerin

Nitroglycerin *(NY truh GLIHS uhr ihn)* is a powerful explosive. It is used in dynamite. It is also used as heart medicine.

Nitroglycerin was discovered in 1846 by Ascanio Sobrero, an Italian chemist. But nitroglycerin was not reliable as an explosive. Almost 20 years later, the Swedish chemist Alfred Nobel found a way to use nitroglycerin safely. Nobel called his invention *dynamite*. It became the most widely used explosive until the 1950's.

Sobrero also tasted nitroglycerin. It gave him a terrible headache. Doctors knew of another substance called *amyl nitrite*. It also caused bad headaches. But it helped people with chest pains. This led them to try nitroglycerin as a medicine. Today, doctors treat chest pain with nitroglycerin.

Other articles to read include: **Drug; Heart.**

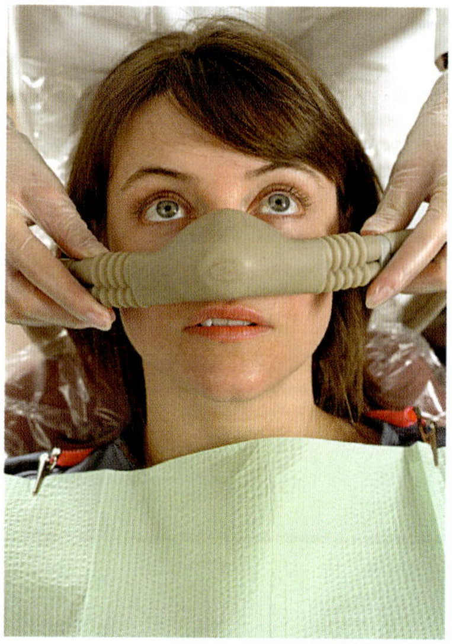

Nitrous oxide can be used to make patients not feel pain during dental treatment. The nitrous oxide may be breathed in through a mask that covers the nose.

Nitrous oxide

Nitrous oxide *(NY truhs OK syd)* is a colorless, odorless gas. Doctors and dentists use it on their patients. It makes the patients not feel pain.

People who breathe nitrous oxide sometimes become excited and silly. For this reason, nitrous oxide is commonly called *laughing gas*. In large enough amounts, nitrous oxide causes unconsciousness.

Nitrous oxide is pleasant to inhale. It takes effect quickly. It also wears off quickly. Doctors always give oxygen when they give nitrous oxide.

Nitrous oxide was first prepared in 1772 by Joseph Priestley, a British chemist. In 1844, the American dentist Horace Wells became the first to actually use nitrous oxide. He inhaled the gas himself before having a tooth pulled. The tooth was pulled painlessly.

Other articles to read include: **Anesthesia; Anesthesiology; Pain.**

Nose

The nose is the organ people use for breathing and smelling. When we breathe, air enters the nose through two openings called *nostrils*. Between the nostrils is the *septum*, a thin wall of tough tissue and bone. Air passes from the nostrils through two openings called *nasal passages*, which lead to the upper part of the throat. Then it moves to the lungs.

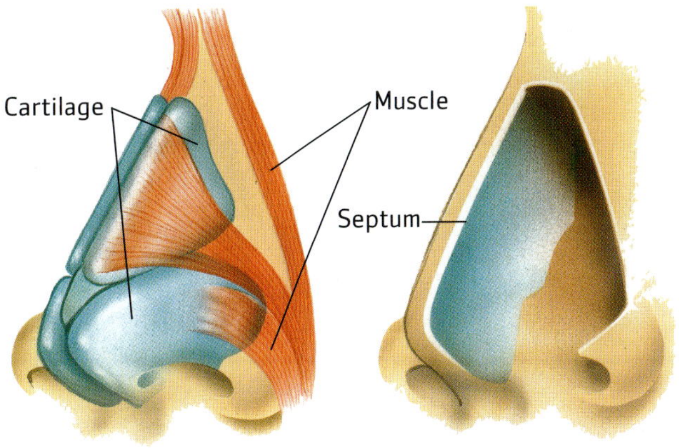

The nose consists mostly of an elastic tissue called *cartilage* (above left). The frontmost part of the *septum,* the wall that separates the nasal passages (above right), is also made up mostly of cartilage.

The nasal passages are covered with *mucous membranes* and tiny hairlike *cilia* that keep dust, germs, and fluids from going into the lungs. At the highest part of the nasal passages, there is a small piece of mucous membrane about as big as a dime. This is where the *olfactory (ol FAK tuhr ee)* nerves are. The olfactory nerves help us smell odors. We sometimes cannot smell when we have a cold, because the infection blocks the passage of air to the center of smell.

Other articles to read include: **Cartilage; Mucus; Nosebleed; Respiration; Smell.**

Nosebleed

A nosebleed is a flow of blood from the nose. Most nosebleeds are a result of some damage to the skinlike layer of mucous membrane that lines the inside of the nose. Nosebleeds may also be a sign of sickness or injury.

Many small tubes called blood vessels carry blood through the mucous membrane inside the nose. If the mucous membrane becomes dry, even tiny scratches can break open the blood vessels.

To stop a small nosebleed, sit down and lean forward. Hold your chin to your chest. Then, pinch your nostrils together for about 10 minutes or until the bleeding stops. If the nosebleed does not stop, get medical help.

Other articles to read include: **Bleeding; Nose.**

To stop a nosebleed, sit down and lean forward. Pinch your nostrils for about 10 minutes or until the bleeding stops.

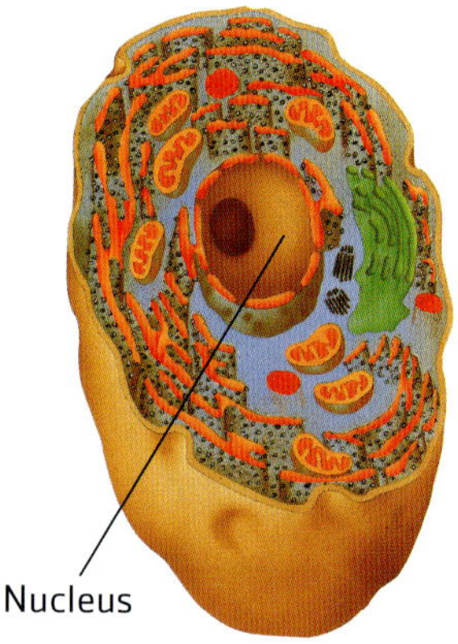

The nucleus is in the middle of the cell. This drawing shows a typical animal cell.

Nucleus

The nucleus is the "control center" of every cell. Cells are tiny building blocks of life. All living things are made of cells. The nucleus is in the center of the cell. The nucleus of each cell has two important parts: *chromosomes (KROH muh sohmz)* and *nucleoli (noo KLEE uh ly).*

The chromosomes are long, thin strands of material. They house chemical instructions called *genes.* Genes tell a living thing how to grow. A living thing inherits its genes from its parent or parents.

Nucleoli are small, round bodies inside the nucleus. The nucleoli help to translate the instructions in genes to a form the cell can use. The translated chemical instructions then pass out of the nucleus and into the larger cell.

Other articles to read include: **Cell; Chromosome; Gene.**

Healthful foods are rich in nutrients. Eating many different kinds of foods is the best way to make sure that the body gets all the nutrients it needs.

Nutrient

A nutrient helps a living thing to grow. Nutrients are chemicals. Food contains certain nutrients. Nutrients give the body the energy to do things and also help fix injuries.

Healthful foods have a lot of nutrients. They can help the body fight off illness. Unhealthful foods have few nutrients. The best way to get nutrients is to eat a variety of healthful foods.

There are six main groups of nutrients: (1) water, (2) *carbohydrates,* (3) fats, (4) *proteins,* (5) minerals, and (6) vitamins. Carbohydrates are sugars and starches. They are the main source of energy for living things. Proteins are used to build body tissues. Water helps the other nutrients move through the body. It also helps remove wastes.

The body breaks down food into nutrients through a process called *digestion.* As food is chewed, a liquid in the mouth begins to break it down into nutrients. After the food is swallowed, it goes to the stomach. In the stomach, the food is broken down

Continued on the next page

even more. The food then passes into the small intestine. The nutrients from the food pass through the walls of the intestine and into the blood.

The blood carries the nutrients throughout the body. Most nutrients change as the body uses them. These changes leave *wastes*, materials that the body cannot use. When a person uses the bathroom, the body gets rid of these wastes.

Other articles to read include: **Carbohydrate; Digestive system; Fat; Mineral; Protein; Sugar; Vitamin.**

This table shows the amount of some chief nutrients recommended in the United States for good nutrition. Nutritional needs vary among men and women and among people of different ages.

Recommended daily dietary allowances of some chief nutrients

	Age	Calcium (mg)	Iron (mg)	Vitamins: A (µg RE)	B_6 (mg)	B_{12} (µg)	C (mg)	D (µg)	E (mg TE)	Niacin (mg NE)	Riboflavin (mg)	Thiamine (mg)
Children	1-3	500	7	300	0.5	0.9	15	5	6	6	0.5	0.5
	4–8	800	10	400	0.6	1.2	25	5	7	8	0.6	0.6
	9–10	1,300	8	600	1.0	1.8	45	5	11	12	0.9	0.9
Males	11–13	1,300	8	600	1.0	1.8	45	5	11	12	0.9	0.9
	14–18	1,500	11	900	1.3	2.4	75	5	15	16	1.3	1.3
	19–30	1,000	8	900	1.3	2.4	90	5	15	16	1.3	1.2
	31–50	1,000	8	900	1.3	2.4	90	5	15	16	1.3	1.2
	51+	1,200	8	900	1.7	2.4	90	10–15	15	16	1.3	1.2
Females	11–13	1,300	8	600	1.0	1.8	45	5	11	12	0.9	0.9
	14–18	1,300	15	700	1.2	2/4	65	5	15	14	1.0	1.0
	19–30	1,000	18	700	1.3	2.4	75	5	15	14	1.1	1.1
	31–50	1,000	8	700	1.3	2.4	75	5	15	14	1.1	1.1
	51+	1,200	8	700	1.5	2.4	75	10–15	15	14	1.1	1.1

mg = milligrams; µg= micrograms; RE = retinol equivalents; NE = niacin equivalents; TE = tocopherol equivalents.
Source: The National Academy of Sciences. Courtesy of the National Academy Press, 2000–2001.

Nutrition

Nutrition is the science that studies how the body uses food. All living things, including people, need food. Food gives the body energy. It also helps the body to grow and to repair itself when it is hurt or sick.

The kind of food a person eats is very important. People who eat a poor diet have less energy and are more likely to get various diseases. Nutrition experts recommend that people eat food from the five main food groups every day. The food groups are (1) grains, including

Continued on the next page

Nutrition *Continued from the previous page*

A 2,000-calorie diet should include the amounts shown below from each group.

Eat 2 ½ cups of vegetables per day. Eat lots of dark-green, leafy vegetables, orange vegetables, and dry beans and peas.

Eat 2 cups of fruit per day. Eat a variety of fresh, frozen, canned, or dried fruit.

Get 3 cups of milk, yogurt, and other milk products per day. Choose milk products that are low-fat or fat-free.

Limit fats, sugars, and *sodium* (salt). Make most of your fat sources fish, nuts, and vegetable oils.

Eat 6 ounces of grain foods—including at least 3 ounces of whole-grain foods—per day.

Eat 5 ½ ounces of meat and beans per day. Choose low-fat or lean meats and poultry. Vary your protein routine by choosing fish, beans, peas, nuts, and seeds

breads, cereals, rice, and pasta; (2) vegetables; (3) fruits; (4) *dairy* (milk and milk products such as yogurt); and (5) meat and beans, including poultry, fish, peas, nuts, and seeds. People should eat only small amounts of fats, sugars, and *sodium* (salt).

Food must be broken down into chemical substances called *nutrients* before the body can use it. Nutrients include vitamins, minerals, and three sources of energy called *proteins*, *carbohydrates*, and *fats*. Water is also a nutrient. The body needs water to cool down, to flush out wastes, and to move other nutrients around.

Food is broken down into nutrients in a process called *digestion*. Digestion begins in the mouth, where saliva wets the food. The food travels through a tube called the *esophagus (ee SOF uh guhs)* into the stomach. There, substances called *digestive juices* break down foods such as meat, eggs, and milk. From the stomach, the food goes to the intestines, where the breakdown is completed. The nutrients then move into the bloodstream, which carries them throughout the body.

It is also important to balance the amount of food you eat with physical activity. Children and teenagers should be physically active for 60 minutes every day or most days.

Other articles to read include: **Carbohydrate; Diet; Digestive system; Eating disorder; Fat; Food; Fruit; Malnutrition; Nutrient; Protein; Vegetarianism; Vitamin.**

ACTIVITY

Eating right

What you need:

- Notebook, diary, or computer for taking notes
- Food plan from ChooseMyPlate.gov

The amount of energy in food is measured in units called *calories.* How many calories you need to eat each day depends on a number of things—including your age and how active you are. The diet shown at the right, for instance, may be good for an 11-year-old boy who is physically active for 30 to 60 minutes each day. No matter what your calorie needs are, a diet high in fruits, vegetables, grains, and dairy but low in sugar and fats will keep you feeling your best.

Keep a list of the kinds and amount of foods you eat in one day. Compare how much you ate from each food group with the amount suggested in the food plan on the website http://www.choosemyplate.gov. What food groups do most of your foods come from? Which group of foods do you need to eat more of? Share your results with a parent or doctor.

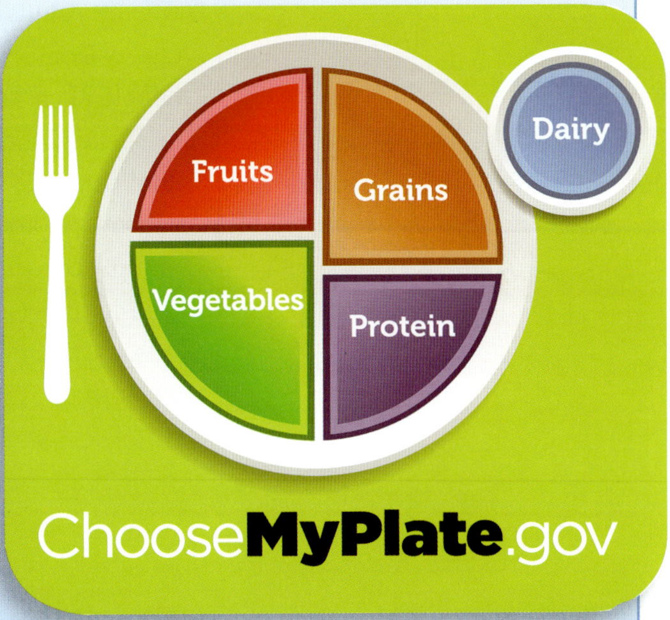

http://bit.ly/YNDWta

Oo

Obesity

Obesity *(oh BEE suh tee)* is a condition in which the body carries too much stored fat. People become obese by eating or drinking more *calories* than their bodies use up in activities throughout the day. The calorie is a measure of the energy in food.

To consider if a person has too much body fat, doctors may use a tool called the *body mass index* (BMI). The BMI is based on a mathematical formula that includes the person's height and weight. Adults who have a BMI greater than 30 are considered obese. Doctors use special charts to check the BMI values of people ages 2 to 20 to decide if a young person is overweight or obese. Other charts are used for people ages 20 to 35 and above age 35.

Doctors are studying why some people become obese and others do not. But they know that being obese is not healthy. Obesity can cause serious medical problems, including heart disease, diabetes, arthritis, and cancer. Doctors try to help people who are obese to lose weight.

Other articles to read include: **Calorie; Diet; Fat; Food; Weight control.**

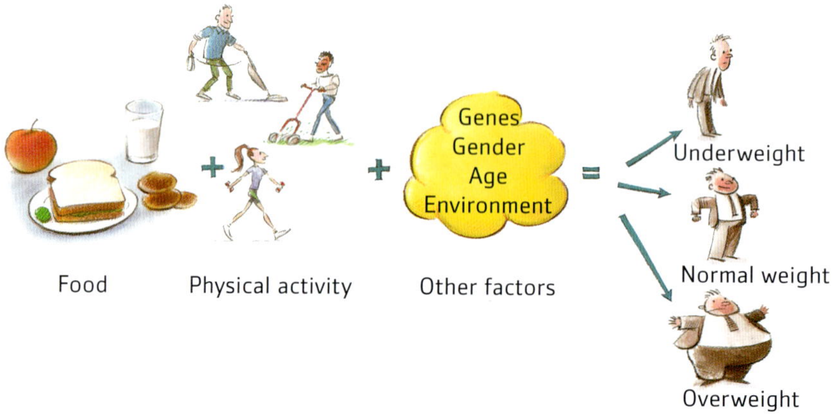

Body weight depends on a number of factors, including the type and amount of food in the diet and the amount of exercise. Age, gender, *genes* (heredity), and environment can also play roles in determining a person's weight.

Obstetrics and gynecology

Obstetrics *(ob STEHT rihks)* and gynecology *(GY nuh KOL uh jee)* are areas of medicine that deal with women's health. Obstetrics deals with pregnancy, childbirth, and the period following childbirth. Gynecology deals with the female reproductive

Continued on the next page

organs. The two areas of medicine are often combined and abbreviated *OB/GYN.*

Doctors who practice obstetrics are called *obstetricians (OB stuh TRIHSH uhns).* During pregnancy, an obstetrician cares for the health of both the mother and the unborn child. During childbirth, the obstetrician helps deliver the baby. The obstetrician also examines the mother over time to make sure she recovers from the pregnancy properly.

Doctors who practice gynecology are called *gynecologists (GY nuh KOL uh jists).* A gynecologist deals with problems of the female reproductive system. Such problems may result from infections, tumors, injuries, or improper balances of *hormones* (body chemicals). The gynecologist may treat a patient by prescribing drugs or performing surgery.

Other articles to read include: **Baby; Childbirth; Medicine; Pregnancy.**

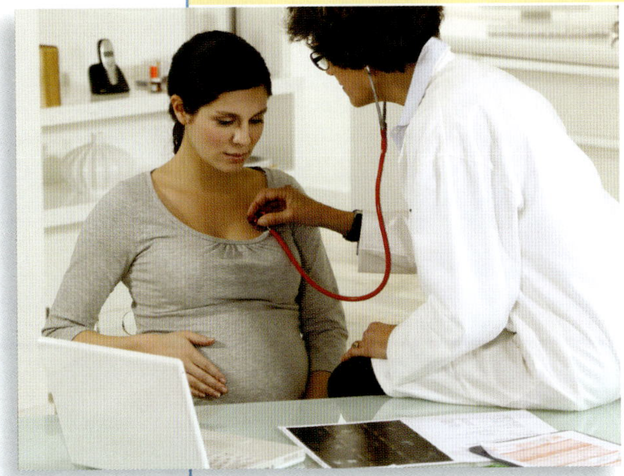

An *obstetrician* listens to the heartbeat of the mother during an examination. During pregnancy, an obstetrician cares for the health of both the mother and the unborn child.

Occupational therapy

Occupational therapy is treatment to help people take part in everyday activities. It can help a person regain skills or learn new ones after an injury or illness. Doctors recommend occupational therapy when health problems interfere with a patient's ability to take part in activities at home, school, or work. For example, a person who uses a wheelchair may need to learn special skills to prepare a meal from a sitting position. A person who has lost sight may need to learn new ways to dress.

People who work in occupational therapy are called *occupational therapists.* Occupational therapists work in hospitals, schools, nursing homes, and day-care centers. Some of them also provide treatment in people's homes.

Other articles to read include: **Disability; Learning; Physical therapy.**

An occupational therapist helps a patient learn how to conduct daily activities from a wheelchair.

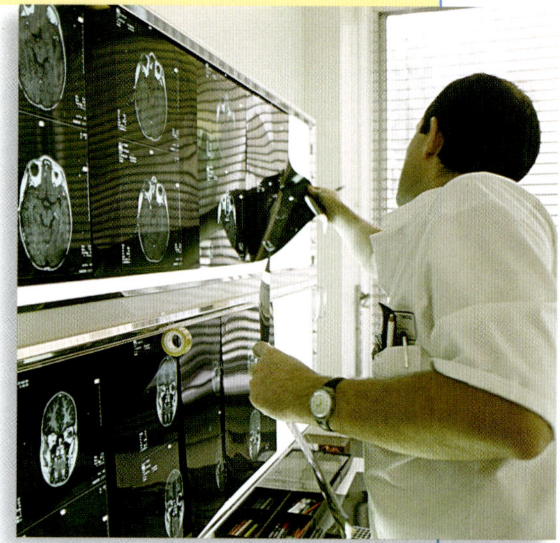

An oncologist examines magnetic resonance imaging (MRI) scans of a patient with a cancerous brain tumor.

Oncology

Oncology *(ong KOL uh jee)* is the study of *cancer.* Cancer is a disease in which cells *multiply* (grow in number) without control. If a cancer is not treated, it can take over healthy parts of the body and cause death. Doctors who study cancer are called *oncologists (ong KOL uh jihsts).*

By comparing normal cells with cancer cells, oncologists can learn how normal tissues grow. With this information, they can figure out how cancerous tissues grow and perhaps find ways to control this growth.

A mass of abnormal cells is called a *tumor.* Oncologists can remove a piece of the tumor and study it under a microscope to determine if it is cancerous. This procedure is called a *biopsy (BY op see).*

Other articles to read include: **Biopsy; Cancer; Chemotherapy; Tumor.**

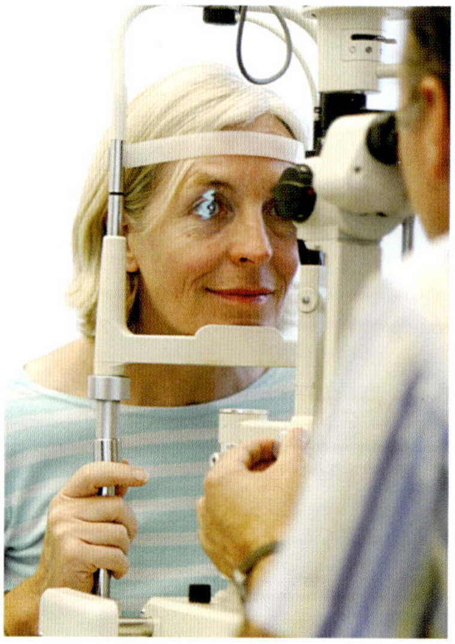

An ophthalmologist shines a special light in a patient's eyes during an examination.

Ophthalmology

Ophthalmology *(OF thal MOL uh jee)* is a branch of medicine that specializes in diseases of the eye. A doctor who specializes in ophthalmology is called an *ophthalmologist (OF thal MOL uh jihst).* A person who wants to become an ophthalmologist first becomes a medical doctor, or M.D. The person then studies eye health for another three to five years.

Ophthalmologists check people's eyes with special equipment. For people who have trouble seeing clearly, ophthalmologists can write prescriptions for glasses or *contact lenses*, small disks of specially made plastic that fit over the eye.

Ophthalmologists can also perform operations for people whose vision cannot be corrected with glasses or contact lenses. They can fix problems with the muscles in the eye, which can cause a condition called *cross-eye.* They can also operate to help people with *glaucoma (glaw KOH muh),* in which too much fluid builds up in the eye. Glaucoma is a major cause of blindness.

Other articles to read include: **Contact lens; Eye; Glasses; Glaucoma; Medicine; Optometry; Vision.**

Optical illusion

An optical illusion is something visual that appears to be different from what it really is. It is sometimes called a *trick of the eye.* The eyes have special cells that sense light and send picture signals to the brain. The brain receives the signals and tells us what they mean. This process is called *perception (puhr SEHP shuhn).* Sometimes a perception does not match what is really there. For example, if you look down a long, straight road, the road seems to narrow as it gets farther away. Trees and telephone poles in the distance look smaller than the trees and telephone poles nearby. But they are not really smaller. They just appear that way. These observations are simple optical illusions.

Other articles to read include: **Brain; Eye; Perception; Vision.**

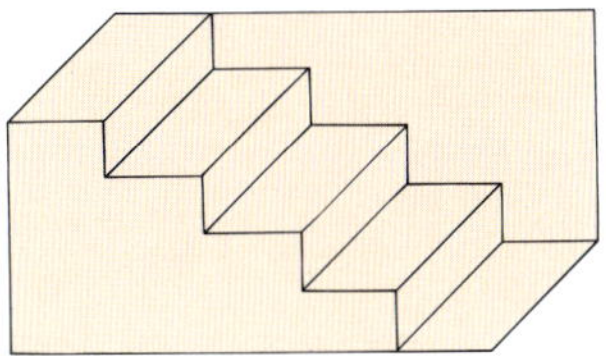

This staircase has stairs that run up from right to left. But the figure can also be seen as an upside-down staircase, with the stairs running "up" from left to right

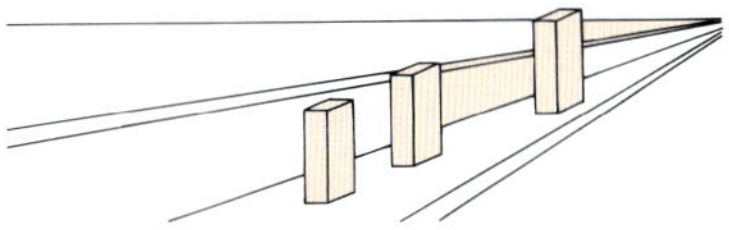

These blocks are all the same size, but the ones drawn to appear farther from the viewer seem larger. This illusion occurs because the blocks are not drawn in perspective.

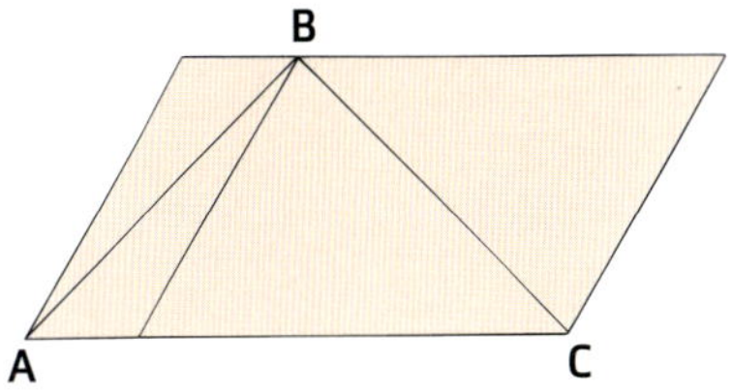

The lines AB and BC in the above figure are equal in length. However, line BC appears longer because of the angles of the other lines in the figure.

How many complete cubes do you see in this drawing? Three or five?

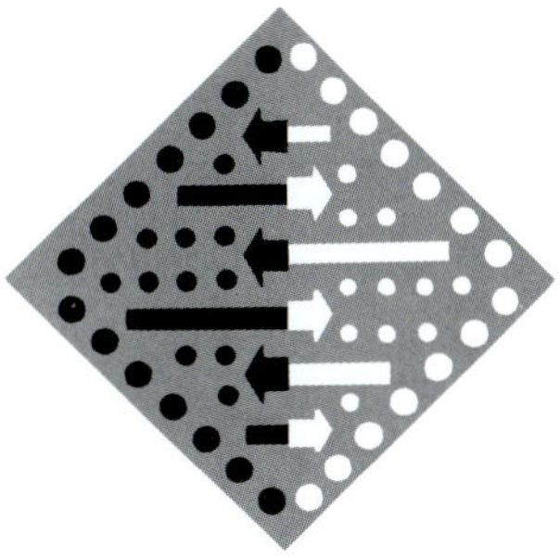

How do these two gray triangles compare in brightness? The gray is actually the same on both sides.

ACTIVITY

Tricking your eyes

You can make an optical illusion that will play a trick on your friends. It will even trick your own eyes.

What you need:

- 2 sheets of paper
- a pencil
- colored pencils or crayons
- scissors
- a ruler

1. On one sheet of paper, using a ruler, draw two lines that are 2 inches (5 centimeters) apart. Using the lines as a guide, draw two animals, people, or plants that are exactly the same height. Color them and cut them out.

2. On the second sheet of paper, draw three slanted lines as shown. Then lay the pictures down on the paper. The bottom of each picture should touch the bottom line.

3. Show the pictures to a friend. Which one does your friend think is taller? Switch the pictures. Which one looks taller now?

http://bit.ly/10OgrOy

Optometry

Optometry *(op TOM uh tree)* is a profession that specializes in the care of *vision* (the ability to see). To become an *optometrist* (doctor who practices optometry), a person must earn a *doctor of optometry* or *O.D.* degree.

Optometrists check people's vision with special equipment. If someone cannot see clearly either nearby things or things that are far away, the optometrist can write a prescription for glasses or contact lenses. Contact lenses are tiny disks of specially made plastic that fit over the eye.

Optometrists can also treat certain diseases of the eyes with medicine. But they cannot perform eye *surgeries* (operations). Eye surgeries are performed by other doctors called *ophthalmologists (OF thal MOL uh jihsts)*.

Other articles to read include: **Contact lens; Eye; Farsightedness; Glasses; Nearsightedness; Ophthalmology; Vision.**

An optometrist tests how well a person can see at a distance using a special chart. The letters of each line are smaller than those in the line above.

Order

An order is a large group of related plants, animals, or other living things. It is one of the categories that scientists use to *classify* (sort) living things. The living things in an order share certain basic qualities because they share a common ancestor.

Living things are divided into groups called *kingdoms, phyla, classes, orders, families, genera,* and *species.* Each order belongs to a larger group called a class. Members of an order are more closely related than are members of a class. Orders can be divided into smaller groups called families. Members of a family are more closely related than are members of an order.

Human beings are in the order Primates. Apes and monkeys also belong to this order. Apes, monkeys, and human beings are similar in many ways because they share a common ancestor.

Other articles to read include: **Class; Classification, Scientific; Family.**

Organ donation

Organ donation is the process in which human organs are obtained for *transplant surgery*. In transplant surgery, organs or tissues are transferred from one person to another. Organs commonly transplanted include the heart, kidney, liver, and lung. Most organs used in transplant operations come from young, healthy people who suffer *brain death* (a permanent end of brain function). Brain death may occur after a serious head injury. Organ donation can save lives and restore health for many people.

The supply of human organs for transplants falls far short of the demand. As a result, doctors must make difficult decisions about obtaining human organs and giving them to people in need of transplants. In most countries, doctors must obtain permission to remove organs from the dead to use for transplant. In the United States, people can mark a space on their driver's license to give permission to donate their organs after death.

Doctors are looking for ways to increase the supply of human organs for transplant. One way is to use living organ donors. Many transplanted kidneys in the United States come from live donors because a person can donate one kidney and remain healthy. Live liver donation is also common. Here, a lobe of the donor's liver is transplanted and grows into a fully functioning organ. Most living organ donors are close relatives of the recipient. But sometimes live organ donations are done between unrelated people.

Other articles to read include: **Kidney; Liver; Surgery; Transplant.**

Orthodontics

Orthodontics *(AWR thuh DAHN tihks)* is a kind of dentistry that involves straightening teeth. The dentists who do this work are called *orthodontists.*

Teeth that are not in the right position can cause such health problems as cavities, gum disease, or difficulty in chewing or speaking correctly. Also, straight teeth look nicer.

Continued on the next page

To straighten the teeth, orthodontists glue metal or plastic bands, called *braces,* to the teeth. The braces are connected with wires. The wires are slowly tightened over a period of months or years to move the teeth into the proper position. Most people get braces when they are 10 to 16 years old. Many adults also get braces.

Other articles to read include: **Dentistry; Teeth.**

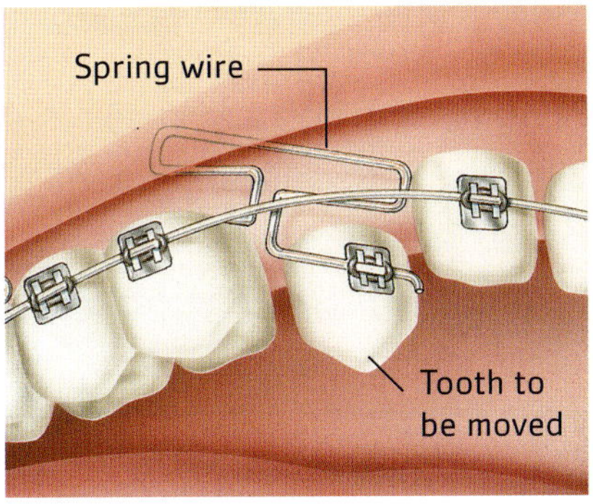

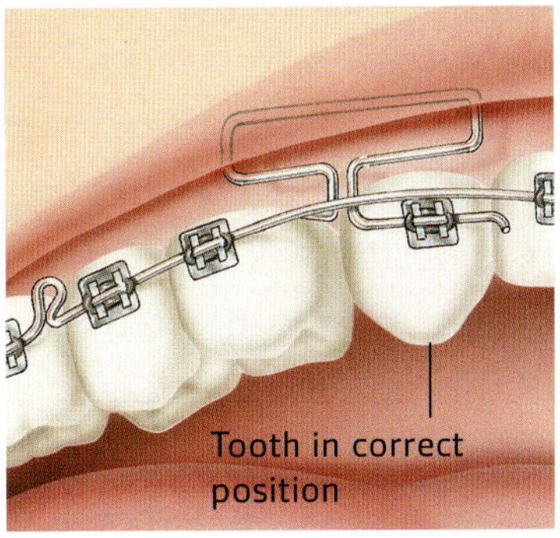

Braces are made of metal brackets and wires. The brackets are glued to the front of each tooth and connected by wires (far left). A *spring wire* is tightened over time until the tooth moves into its correct position (near left).

Orthopedics

Orthopedics *(AWR thuh PEE dihks)* is a branch of medicine that deals with problems with bones and muscles and other body parts that connect them. Doctors who practice orthopedics are called *orthopedists* or *orthopedic surgeons.*

Orthopedists care for people of all ages, from babies to older people. They treat problems that occur because of accidents, such as broken bones and torn muscles. They also treat conditions that people are born with such as problems with the shape of legs or arms or backs.

Orthopedists may treat people with medicine or by prescribing certain exercises, called *physical therapy*. They may also perform surgery. Sometimes orthopedists replace worn body parts, such as hips and knees, with new artificial ones made of plastic, metal, or other materials.

Other articles to read include: **Bone; Exercise; Fracture; Joint; Medicine; Muscle; Physical therapy.**

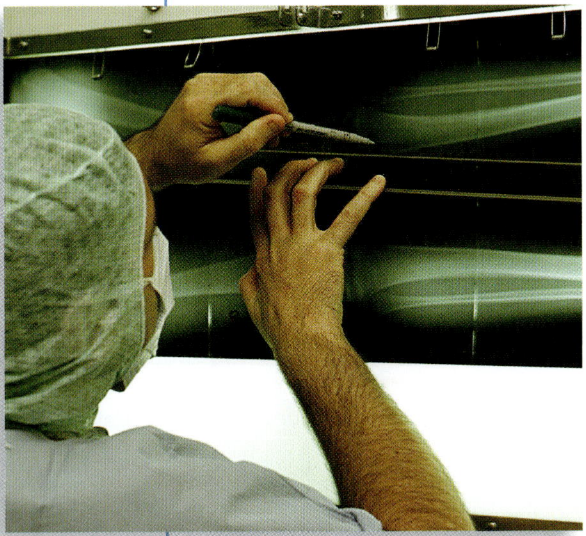

An orthopedic surgeon examines an X-ray image in an operating room.

Osteopathic medicine

Osteopathic *(OS tee uh PATH ihk)* medicine is a system of medical care based on the belief that disease in one part of the body affects other parts of the body. Osteopathic medicine concentrates on the body's system of muscles and bones and their connecting tendons and ligaments. Osteopathic doctors believe the whole person must be considered in providing treatment for any illness.

Because the body's system of muscles and bones is so extensive, osteopathic doctors argue that it has especially important relationships with other body systems. The musculoskeletal system may be affected by many internal illnesses. The condition of the muscles and bones may worsen disease in other body systems, including the circulatory system and the nervous system.

To become an osteopathic doctor, a person must complete four years of training in an approved osteopathic medical college. The graduate receives a *doctor of osteopathy* (D.O.) degree. Osteopathic doctors are considered to have the same skills and responsibilities as other types of medical doctors.

Other articles to read include: **Bone; Holistic medicine; Medicine; Muscle.**

Osteoporosis is a condition in which bones become fragile. Healthy bone (below) has a honeycomblike microscopic structure that is smooth and dense. Bone affected by osteoporosis (bottom) is weakened by loss of bone tissue, leaving pits.

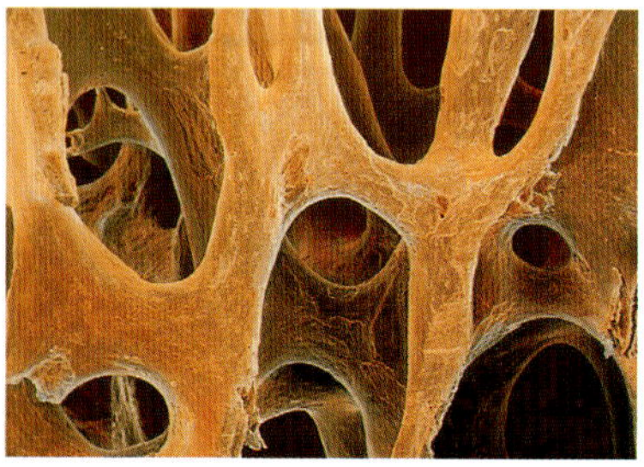

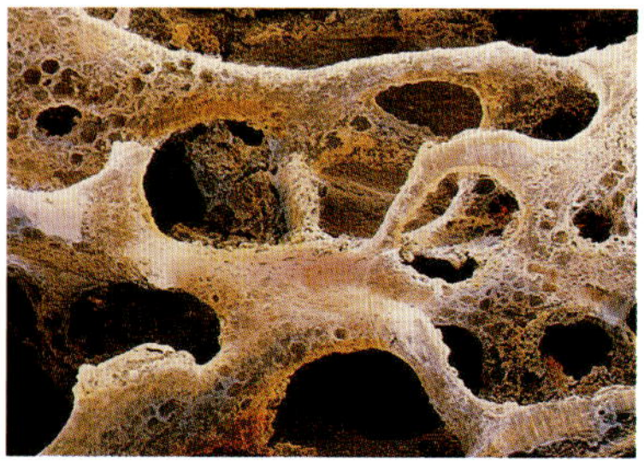

Osteoporosis

Osteoporosis *(OS tee oh puh ROH sihs)* is a condition in which bones become fragile. People with osteoporosis have an increased risk of breaking bones throughout their bodies, especially in their wrists, spine, and hips. Breaks may result from minor falls or injuries that would not harm normal bones. Osteoporosis is a major cause of pain and disability in older adults.

Osteoporosis occurs as certain bone cells are worn out and removed by the body faster than new bone is formed. As a result, bone density gradually drops and bones become weaker.

Certain minerals and vitamins, especially calcium and vitamin D, are important for bone health. Regular exercise also helps keep bones strong. Scientists have also developed drugs that help preserve bone and treat osteoporosis.

Other articles to read include: **Arthritis; Bone; Calcium; Disease; Mineral; Vitamin.**

Otoscope

An otoscope *(OH tuh skohp)* is an instrument for looking inside the ear. It is used by doctors. It helps them see if a patient has an ear infection, illness, injury, or other ear problems.

The otoscope contains a *magnifying lens*. The lens is a piece of glass that makes things look bigger. The otoscope also has a light. The light shines into the ear.

A doctor uses the otoscope to check the *eardrum*, a thin piece of tissue inside the ear. A normal eardrum looks pearly-white or light gray. If the eardrum looks red, there may be an infection.

Other articles to read include: **Ear; Ear infection.**

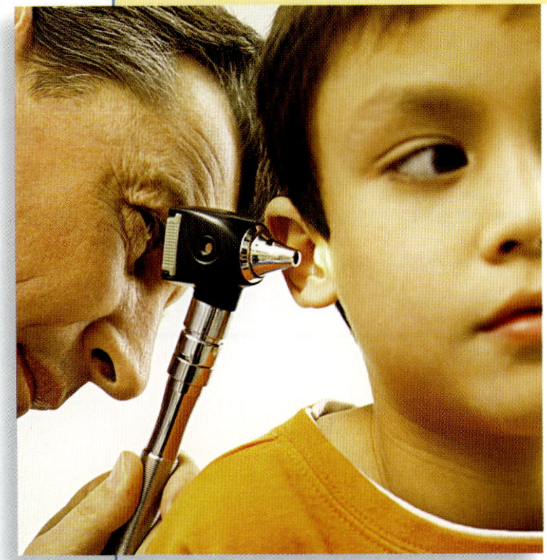

The *otoscope* is a medical instrument used to examine a patient's eardrum.

Ovary

The ovary *(OH vuhr ee)* is a female sex organ. Females have two ovaries. Ovaries store and release egg cells and make chemical substances called *hormones*. A human ovary is oval-shaped and about the size of a walnut. The ovaries are in the abdomen.

When a girl is born, her ovaries have about 400,000 eggs. Only 400 of these eggs will mature and be released over the woman's lifetime. When an egg is released, the ovaries also release hormones that get a woman's body ready to have a baby. If the egg is *fertilized* by a male sperm cell, the woman becomes *pregnant*. When women get older, usually between the ages of 45 and 55, their ovaries slowly stop working and shrink.

Other articles to read include: **Egg; Fallopian tube; Fertilization; Hormone; Pregnancy; Reproduction, Human; Uterus.**

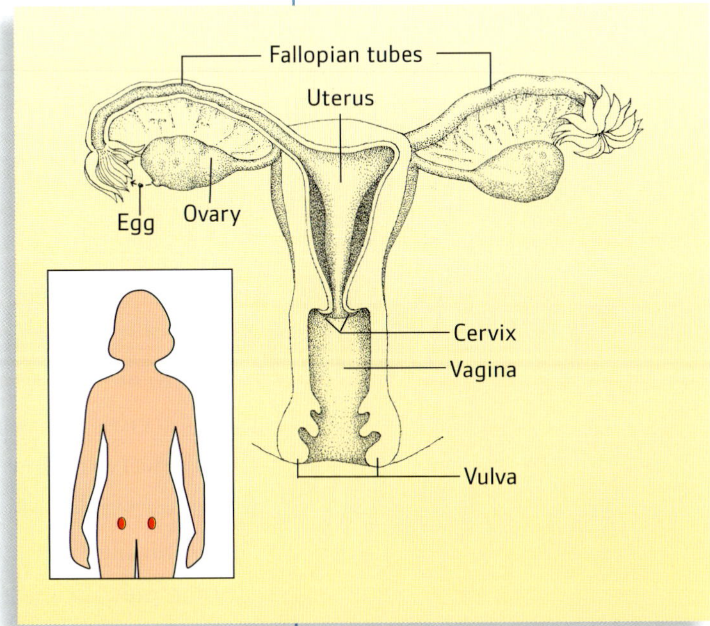

Eggs from the *ovaries* pass through the fallopian tubes to the *uterus* (womb).

Pp

Pacemaker

An *artificial pacemaker* can be seen inside a person's chest in this X-ray image. The device uses electrical signals to help control the beating of the heart.

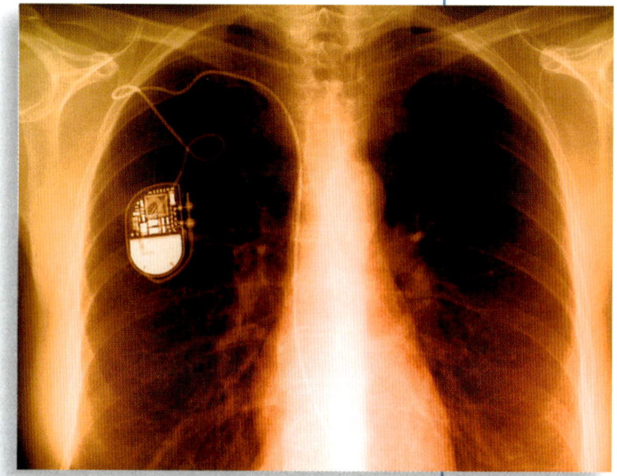

A pacemaker is a small device that helps people with certain kinds of heart problems. The pacemaker is *inserted* (put into) in a person's chest, just under the skin, during an operation.

The hearts of human beings and many other living things beat in a certain *rhythm* (pattern). That rhythm is controlled by electrical signals that are sent by a system that doctors call the heart's natural pacemaker. But sometimes, an illness or certain kinds of medicine can make people's hearts beat too slowly or too quickly. If an operation cannot fix the heart's natural pacemaker, doctors may insert an artificial one.

An artificial pacemaker makes use of a battery. The battery sends electrical signals that control the beating of the heart.

Other articles to read include: **Heart; Pulse; Surgery.**

Pain

Pain is a bad feeling that a person's body gets when it is hurt or sick. It is the body's way of telling us that something is wrong.

There are different kinds of pain. Some pain—called *acute* pain—comes on suddenly and then goes away. An example of this kind of pain is when you accidentally stick your hand in a flame. Other pain—called *chronic* pain—lasts for a long time. Many people with long-term diseases, such as cancer, have chronic pain. Sometimes pain hurts a lot. Other times, we only feel pain a little.

The body feels pain because of special *nerves* called *receptors*. Nerves are pathways that connect all parts of the body to the brain. Receptors change certain chemicals released by the body's cells into *electrical signals*. These electrical signals travel along nerves to the brain, telling the brain which part of the body hurts.

Continued on the next page

Then the brain can tell us what to do to stop the hurt, such as moving our hands away from fire.

Doctors can treat acute pain by removing its cause and giving relief while the body heals. For example, doctors treat a broken leg by setting the bone and giving drugs intended to stop acute pain. *Aspirin* is a common drug that people use to stop acute pain. Aspirin works mainly by blocking the formation of certain chemicals that lead to pain. *Narcotics* are powerful drugs that doctors often give to patients who are suffering from chronic pain.

Other articles to read include: **Acupuncture; Anesthesia; Anesthesiology; Aspirin; Drug; Narcotic; Nervous system.**

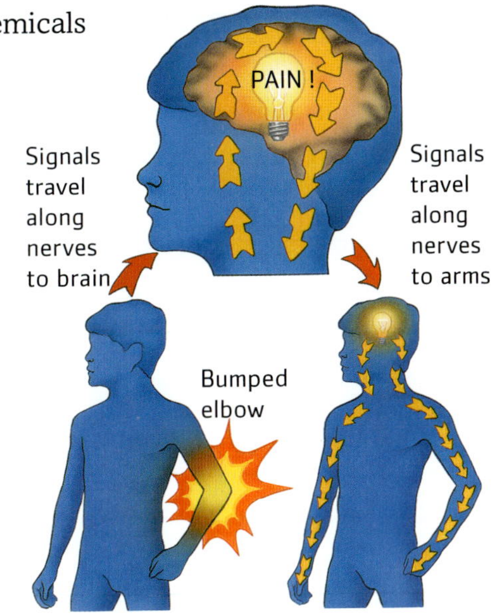

You feel pain when you bump your elbow because electrical signals travel along nerves from your elbow to your brain. The brain tells you that your elbow hurts, and it sends electrical signals to your arms. These signals might cause you to move your elbow away from the blow and rub it.

Palate

The palate *(PAL iht)* is the roof of the mouth. It has two different parts: the *hard palate* and the *soft palate.* The hard palate is the hard, bony part in the front of the mouth. The soft palate is the muscular area behind the hard palate. Both parts are covered by a thin sheet of tissue called a *mucous membrane.* A small flap hangs from the middle of the soft palate. It is called the *uvula (YOO vyuh luh).*

The palate separates the mouth and the nasal cavity. During swallowing, the soft palate blocks off the nasal passage.

Some children are born with a split or *cleft* in the palate. The cleft can be fixed with surgery.

Other articles to read include: **Bone; Mouth; Mucus; Nose; Teeth.**

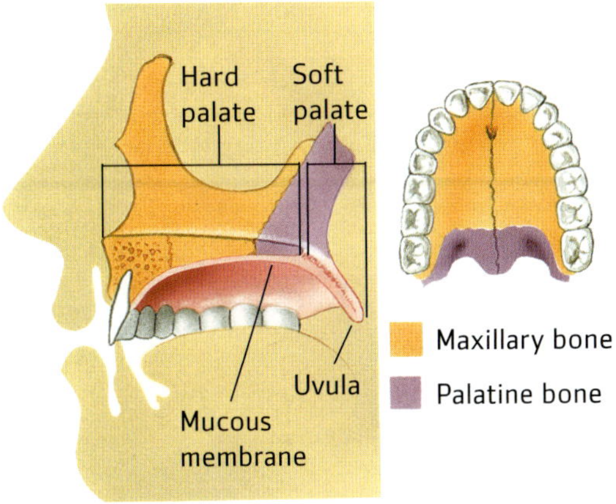

The palate has two parts: the *hard palate,* in front, and the *soft palate,* in back. The hard palate is formed by the maxillary and palatine bones.

Palliative care

Palliative *(PAL ee AY tihv)* care is medical care for people dying of incurable illness. The goal is to provide comfort for the patient and a peaceful death. In palliative care, caregivers try to relieve the symptoms of the illness, especially pain. They also provide mental, social, and spiritual support.

Palliative care is not intended to cause death. But in palliative care, dying is recognized as part of life. Once doctors know that the patient is going to die, they stop trying to cure the illness. They try to make sure the patient is comfortable and ready to die peacefully.

Family members are often able to help care for the patient in their home. This lets patients die surrounded by family and loved ones, rather than in a hospital.

Other articles to read include: **Death; Pain.**

Pancreas

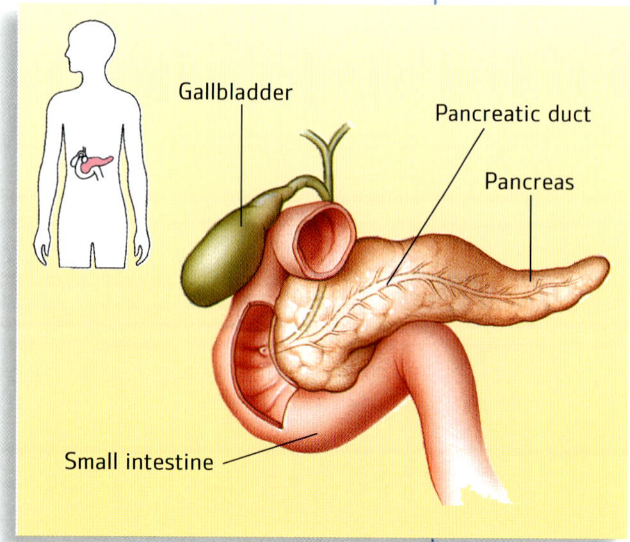

The *pancreas* produces juices that flow through a tube called the *pancreatic duct* into the small intestine. There, the juices help *digest* (break down) food.

The pancreas *(PAN kree uhs)* is an organ in the bodies of humans and other animals with back-bones. It makes juices that help in the *digestion* (breakdown and use) of food. It also makes certain *hormones (HAWR mohnz).* Hormones are chemicals that help bodies grow and develop.

The human pancreas is pinkish-yellow. It is about 6 to 8 inches (15 to 20 centimeters) long, and it lies crosswise behind the stomach.

Digestive juices from the pancreas flow through a tube into a part of the small intestine, where they break down food. *Insulin (IHN suh lihn)* and *glucagon (GLOO kuh gon)* are two hormones the pancreas makes. They work together to help the body use *glucose (GLOO kohs),* a sugar.

Other articles to read include: **Digestive system; Gallbladder; Glucose; Hormone; Insulin; Intestine.**

Pap test

A Pap test is a medical test used to detect cancer in the *cervix*. The cervix is part of a woman's *uterus* (womb). The Pap test has helped prevent many deaths from cancer of the cervix.

Before cancer develops in the cervix, the cells of the cervix go through many changes. These changes can take several years. A Pap test can detect cancer in its early stages. It can then be treated more easily.

Women 21 years of age or older should have a Pap test every two years. The test can be done in a doctor's office. It causes no pain and little discomfort. The doctor collects a sample of cells from the cervix with a cotton swab, wooden scraper, or small brush. If unusual cells are found, the doctor orders other tests and decides on any treatment needed.

Other articles to read include: **Cancer; Uterus.**

Paralysis

Paralysis *(puh RAL uh sihs)* is a condition in which someone is unable to move the muscles in his or her body. Muscles are the body parts that help other parts move.

People can be *partly paralyzed (PAR uh lyzd)*—that is, unable to move an arm, a leg, or one side of the body. They can also be *totally paralyzed*—unable to move any part of the body. Sometimes paralysis goes away after a while. Other times it does not.

People become paralyzed when an accident or illness damages the muscles, brain, or *nerves*. Nerves are the pathways that connect all parts of the body to the brain. Doctors and workers called *physical therapists* can help some people with paralysis. Sometimes, healthy parts of the brain can take over the work of a damaged part.

Other articles to read include: **Amyotrophic lateral sclerosis; Brain; Disability; Muscle; Nervous system; Occupational therapy; Physical therapy; Poliomyelitis; Stroke.**

Partial paralysis need not prevent a person from having a good job and a full life. This partially paralyzed man works in an office.

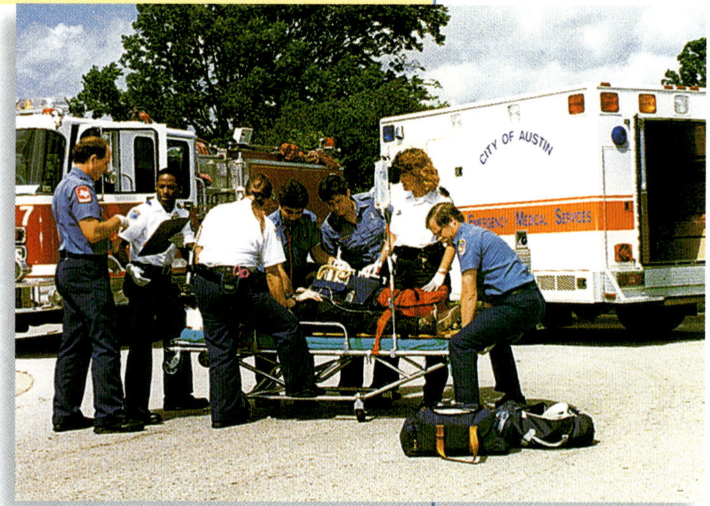

Fire department paramedics treat a person needing emergency medical care. Paramedics often have to rush people to the hospital in an ambulance.

Paramedic

A paramedic *(PAIR uh MEHD ihk)* is a type of trained medical worker. Paramedics take the place of doctors in certain situations.

There are different kinds of paramedics. The most well-known kind are called *emergency medical technicians* (EMT's). EMT's help people who have been in an accident or who have become suddenly and seriously ill.

Most EMT's travel in an ambulance with many kinds of medicine and special medical equipment. EMT's use a two-way radio to talk with doctors at a hospital. The doctors help the EMT's decide how to treat the patient before bringing the person to the hospital.

People who want to become paramedics go through a training program at a hospital or college. They take more training every year to learn the latest life-saving procedures.

Other articles to read include: **First aid; Medicine; Physician.**

Ambroise Paré

Paré, Ambroise

Ambroise Paré *(ahm BRWAZ pa RAY)* (1510?–1590) was a French doctor. He developed new methods of surgery.

Before Paré, most doctors poured boiling oil on wounds. Paré stopped this practice. He developed a special substance used with bandages. He covered the wounds and allowed them to heal. During operations, he sewed blood vessels shut to stop bleeding. This and other work helped to improve surgery.

Paré learned medicine in the French army. In 1552, Paré became surgeon to King Henry II of France. He later became first surgeon to King Charles IX and King Henry III.

Other articles to read include: **Medicine; Surgery.**

Parent

Parents are the most important influence on the lives of their children. Parents provide care, love, and training for children.

A parent is a father or mother. People have two types of parents, *biological parents* and *social parents*. Biological parents are the man and woman who physically produce a baby. They provide the child's *genetic* (inherited) characteristics. Social parents are the ones who raise the child. They may or may not be the same as the biological parents.

The role of parents is to provide care, love, and training for their children. Children need years of physical care, including food, shelter, and protection from harm. Love and affection are also necessary for healthy growth and development. Parents teach children right from wrong by encouraging good behavior, discouraging bad behavior, and providing good examples of how to act.

Other articles to read include: **Baby; Child; Heredity.**

Parkinson disease

Parkinson disease is a medical problem that slowly destroys cells in certain parts of the brain. These cells are involved in moving the body. Signs of Parkinson disease include shaking hands, stiff muscles, slow movement, and balance problems. The most common form of Parkinson disease normally affects people between 50 and 70 years of age.

The effects of Parkinson disease can be crippling. People with the disease often walk with a shuffle. They may find it hard to write clearly or button clothing. Muscles of the face may grow stiff, causing a "masklike" expression. Patients may have trouble starting movement, such as rising from a chair.

Doctors do not know what causes most cases of Parkinson disease. Some cases are caused by certain drugs or poisons. Doctors treat Parkinson disease with drugs. In some cases, they may use surgery to destroy areas of the brain that produce the effects of the disease.

Other articles to read include: **Brain; Muscle; Nervous system.**

Louis Pasteur made many discoveries that still play important roles in health and medicine. Most of his work involved preventing the growth of germs called bacteria.

Pasteur, Louis

Louis Pasteur *(lwee pas TUR)* (1822–1895) was a great French scientist. His work has saved many lives.

Pasteur was born in Dole, France. Early on, he showed a talent for art. He later studied chemistry in Paris. By age 26, he was famous for his work in chemistry. However, he soon started studying tiny living things called *bacteria*.

Pasteur was the first to show that living things come only from other living things. Before that, many scientists believed that life could come from things that are not alive, such as dirt. Pasteur also showed that the spread of bacteria can be controlled.

In the early 1860's, Pasteur discovered that germs could be killed with heat. This use of heat became known as *pasteurization (PAS chuhr uh ZAY shuhn).* Pasteur used this method to control the growth of germs in wine, milk, beer, and food.

In 1865, a disease was killing a lot of silkworms, which spin the fibers used in silk cloth. Pasteur proved that a germ that attacks silkworm eggs caused the disease. He then showed that killing the germ would get rid of the disease.

Pasteur proved that many diseases are caused by germs. He then showed that germs can be made weak in a laboratory. When the weak germs are placed in an animal's body, the animal can fight off the germs without getting sick. This method of fighting off germs is called *vaccination (VAK sih NAY shuhn).*

Other articles to read include: **Bacteria; Disease; Germ; Food; Immunization.**

Pathology

Pathology *(puh THAHL uh jee)* is the study of diseases. Doctors who study diseases are called *pathologists (puh THAHL uh jists).*

Most pathologists work in laboratories. They use special equipment, such as *microscopes.* Microscopes can help pathologists see very tiny things, such as *germs.* Germs are living things that can make people sick.

Continued on the next page

Some pathologists study animal diseases. They hope that by learning how a disease makes animals sick, they will understand how the same disease can make people sick.

Other pathologists do tests that help doctors take care of people. Some tests can tell doctors exactly what sickness a person has. Other tests can tell if a certain body part or fluid, such as blood, is healthy or not.

Other articles to read include: **Disease; Germ; Medicine; Public health.**

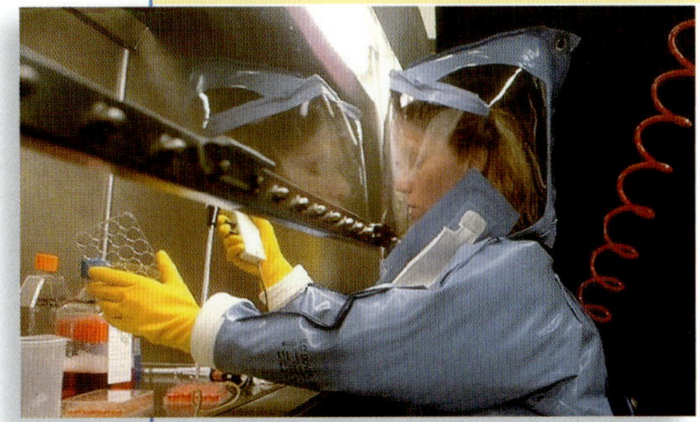

Pathologists working for the United States Centers for Disease Control and Prevention run tests in laboratories to solve many mysteries about diseases.

Pavlov, Ivan Petrovich

Ivan Petrovich Pavlov *(ih VAHN peh TRAW vihch PAV lov)* (1849–1936) was a Russian *physiologist.* Physiologists study how living things function. Pavlov won the 1904 Nobel Prize in physiology or medicine. He won for his research on *digestion,* the way the body breaks down and uses food. Pavlov showed how different parts of the body add different chemicals to food to break it down. For example, certain glands in the mouth area add *saliva (suh LY vuh)* to food to begin digestion. Saliva is a sticky fluid that helps the body break down food. The *stomach, pancreas,* and *liver* are some of the other body parts that make chemicals to digest food.

Pavlov also studied how the brain works. Through his experiments, Pavlov learned that animals could be trained to react to a *stimulus.* A stimulus is something that causes the body to perform a certain action.

Pavlov experimented with dogs. He rang a bell each time a dog was fed. After a while, the dog began to make saliva whenever it heard the bell ring, as if food was coming. The dog had learned to connect the stimulus of the ringing bell with the food, even though the bell and food were originally unrelated. Pavlov believed that people learned many things in the same way.

Other articles to read include: **Digestive system; Gland; Learning; Physiology; Reflex action; Saliva.**

Ivan Petrovich Pavlov's experiments with dogs revealed insights not only into animal behavior, but also into human behavior. Pavlov rang a bell each time a dog was fed. The dog learned to associate the bell with food.

A pediatrician uses an *otoscope* to examine a young girl's ear. Infections of the ear are common among children.

Pediatrics

Pediatrics *(PEE dee AT rihks)* is the area of medicine concerned with children's health. Doctors who practice pediatrics are called *pediatricians (PEE dee uh TRIHSH uhns)*. To become a pediatrician, a person must graduate medical school and complete at least three years of special training. Pediatricians care for children from birth through the teenage years.

Children have different health problems than adults do. For example, far more children than adults get chickenpox. Children also grow rapidly. Pediatricians do not just treat injuries and illnesses. They must also work to ensure children's physical and emotional development.

Other articles to read include: **Baby; Child; Medicine.**

Pelvic inflammatory disease

Pelvic inflammatory disease is an irritation of the *pelvic cavity* in women. The pelvic cavity is the part of the body between the legs and the abdomen. In women, it surrounds the bladder, the end of the large intestine, and the reproductive organs.

Pelvic inflammatory disease is often called PID. It affects the lining of the *uterus* (womb), the fallopian tubes, and the lining of the lower abdominal cavity. The disease is caused by the spread of bacteria from the vagina into the pelvis.

Signs of PID include lower abdominal pain, release of fluid from the vagina, fever, nausea, and vomiting. But many patients have few or no signs. In these cases, doctors may not discover the disease until much later.

PID can cause a woman to lose the ability to become pregnant. PID is usually spread through sexual intercourse. Doctors can treat PID with drugs such as antibiotics.

Other articles to read include: **Abdomen; Bacteria; Bladder; Disease; Pelvis; Pregnancy; Sexuality; Vagina.**

Pelvis

The pelvis *(PEHL vuhs)* is the set of bones that form the hips. The pelvis has two big hipbones. They join together in the front. They join at the back with a bone called the *sacrum (SAK ruhm)*. Inside the pelvis are the bladder and part of the large intestine.

Each hipbone is made of three bones that grow together. The wide, flat bone you can feel on your hip is called the *ilium (IHL ee uhm)*. The *ischium (IHS kee uhm)* is the bone you feel when you sit on a hard chair. The *pubis (PYOO bihs)* bones form two arches in front. They join together in the middle.

Other articles to read include: **Bladder; Bone; Hip; Intestine; Pelvic inflammatory disease; Skeleton.**

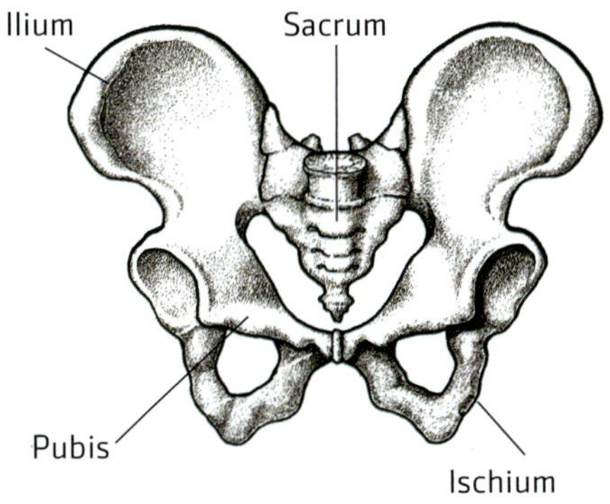

The bones of the pelvis form a structure something like a shallow dish. You can feel a bone called the *ilium* when you put your hand on your hips.

Penicillin

Penicillin *(PEHN uh SIHL ihn)* is a strong medicine called an *antibiotic.* It is usually given as an *injection* (shot). Doctors use penicillin to treat serious diseases caused by *bacteria.* Bacteria are tiny living things that can make people sick.

Penicillin was the first major antibiotic developed by scientists. It was discovered by accident in 1928 by the British scientist Sir Alexander Fleming. Fleming had a dish in his laboratory with bacteria on it. In the middle of the dish, he saw some *mold.* Mold is the cottony, often green, growth you might find on bread or other food that has spoiled. Fleming noticed that the bacteria around the mold had died.

A few years later, other scientists figured out how to get penicillin from the mold. Doctors gave the penicillin to a man who was very sick, and he got better. After that, penicillin was used for many years. It was used so much that today many bacteria have become resistant to penicillin, and penicillin can no longer kill them.

Other articles to read include: **Antibiotic; Bacteria; Drug; Fleming, Sir Alexander.**

The mold that makes penicillin looks like a tiny forest when seen under a high-powered microscope. The greenish "treetops" carry tiny structures called *spores,* which the mold uses to reproduce.

Penis

The penis *(PEE nihs)* is the organ on the outside of a man's body that is involved in reproduction. The penis is shaped like a finger. It hangs between the legs. In people and most other mammals, both urine and *semen* leave the body through the penis. Semen is the fluid that carries sperm.

The penis is covered in thin, hairless skin. An opening in its tip leads to the *urethra (yu REE thruh)*. The urethra is the passageway for semen and urine. The tip of the penis is slightly enlarged and very sensitive. A fold of skin called the *foreskin* covers the tip. In many males, the foreskin has been removed in a surgery called *circumcision*.

The penis is usually soft and limp. Sexual excitement increases the flow of blood to the organ. This fills its tissues, making it stiff. The stiffened penis is called an *erection*. An erection enables the male to have sexual intercourse.

Other articles to read include: **Reproduction, Human; Sexuality; Testicle; Urinary system; Urine.**

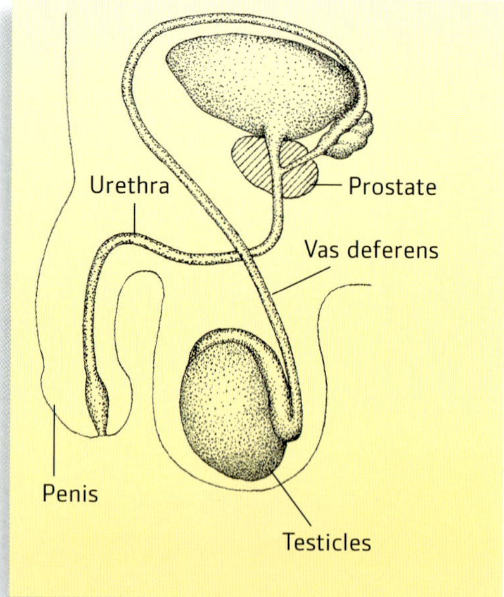

Sperm cells from each testicle travel through ducts called the *vas deferens.* There, they mix with a fluid called *semen* from the prostate. Semen and urine are released from the penis through the *urethra.*

Perception

Perception—or being able to *perceive*—is the way in which humans and other living things sense, know, and understand the world around them. Our knowledge of the world comes through our sense organs. These organs react to various physical energies in the world around us.

The eye, for example, perceives certain kinds of energy as light. Noses and tongues perceive chemical changes in surroundings as smell and taste. Sense organs in the skin respond to such things as temperature changes and pain. The ears react to certain kinds of vibrations.

Part of what is perceived comes through the senses from an object, but another part is made by the brain. The brain makes sense of the messages sent from the eye, for example, as light and color and messages from the ear as sound.

Other articles to read include: **Brain; Ear; Eye; Hearing; Senses; Smell; Taste; Touch; Vision.**

Personality

Personality is the individual quality that makes one person act differently from another. To a *psychologist* (a person who studies the mind), personality is an area of study that deals with human behavior, including actions, emotions, and thought processes. Psychologists study the patterns of behavior that make individuals different from one another. They try to learn how these patterns develop, how they are organized, and how they change.

There are several things that contribute to the development of an individual's personality. Childhood and social experiences, emotional reactions, environment, learning, and observation all affect personality. Some personality patterns remain from childhood into adulthood. But personality continues to develop as a result of new experiences and changes in environment.

Other articles to read include: **Behavior; Emotion; Mind; Psychology.**

Perspiration

Perspiration helps the body to cool itself during intense physical activity. People also *perspire,* or sweat, when they are nervous.

Perspiration *(PUR spuh RAY shuhn)* is water that comes out of the skin. It is also called *sweat.* The water is mixed with other substances. People perspire or sweat when they are hot or nervous. They also perspire when they exercise.

Perspiration is made by long, coiled structures inside the skin. These structures are called *sweat glands.* The human body has more than 2 million sweat glands all over its surface. Certain parts of the body may have more and larger sweat glands than others. These include the armpits, palms of the hands, and soles of the feet. These areas often perspire more than others. Sweat travels to the skin's surface through the sweat glands. It comes out of the skin through tiny holes called *pores.*

Sweating is an important way for the body to cool itself. As the perspiration evaporates, it removes heat from the skin.

Other articles to read include: **Exercise; Gland; Pore; Skin.**

Pharmacology

Pharmacology *(FAHR muh KOL uh jee)* is the study of drugs and their effect on living things. People who study these effects are known as *pharmacologists (FAHR muh KOL uh jihsts)*. Pharmacologists consider any chemical a drug if it affects living things. This includes medicines and poisons.

Some pharmacologists study how the body uses and eliminates drugs. Others study poisons and their effects, detection, and treatment. Pharmacologists may work for universities, hospitals, government agencies, or drug companies.

Other articles to read include: **Drug; Medicine; Poison.**

A pharmacist counts out pills to fill a doctor's prescription, while another pharmacist enters information about a prescription into the pharmacy's computer.

Pharmacy

A pharmacy *(FAHR muh see)* is the place where *drugs* (medicines) are made and sold. It is often called a *drugstore*. Pharmacies usually also sell other things besides medicines. The person who makes the medicines is called a *pharmacist*, or *druggist*.

When a person is sick, a doctor often writes out a form called a *prescription*. The prescription gives the name of the medicine the person needs. The prescription also tells how much medicine to take and how many times a day to take it. The pharmacist's job is to fill the prescription. Today, many prescriptions are sent by phone or email.

A pharmacist counts out the number of pills a person needs and prints a label with the doctor's directions. Sometimes, a pharmacist makes the medicine by mixing a liquid or a cream.

People who want to become pharmacists go to a special school called a *college of pharmacy*. They study biology, chemistry, and mathematics. They must pass a test to earn a pharmacist's license.

Other articles to read include: **Drug; Medicine.**

Pharynx

The pharynx *(FAR ihngks)* is a cone-shaped tube in the throat. It joins the nose and mouth to the *larynx (LAR ihngks)* (voice box) and *esophagus (ee SOF uh guhs)*. The esophagus is a tube from the mouth to the stomach. The pharynx is about 5 inches (13 centimeters) long. Both air and food pass through it.

When you breathe in, air from the nose or mouth goes into the pharynx. The air then goes through the larynx and windpipe into the lungs.

When you eat, food passes from the mouth into the pharynx. As you swallow, muscles in the throat cover the larynx. This keeps food from going into the windpipe. Instead, the food goes down the esophagus to the stomach.

Other articles to read include: **Digestive system; Esophagus; Larynx; Mouth; Respiration; Trachea.**

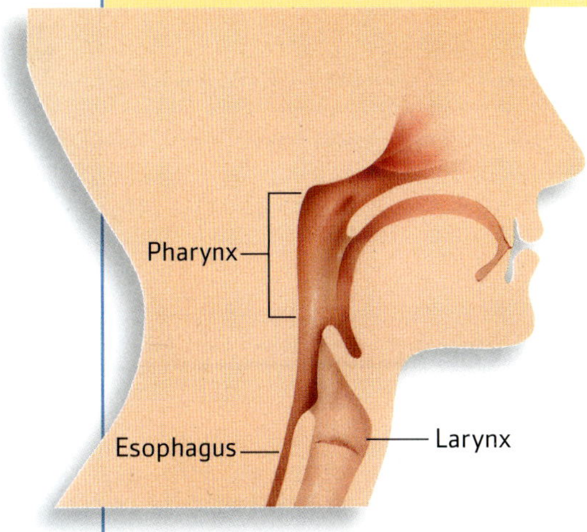

The *pharynx* connects the nose and mouth with the *larynx* (voice box) and esophagus.

Phobia

A phobia *(FOH bee uh)* is a strong, unreasonable fear of some object or situation. About half of all people say they have a phobia. Common phobias include fear of crowds, darkness, heights, and snakes or spiders. Most people try to avoid the object of their phobia.

Most phobias develop in middle to late childhood. But they can also form later in life.

Phobias are unreasonable because they exaggerate the danger of an object or situation. For example, a person is not likely to fall while looking out the window of a tall building. But a person with a phobia of heights would still feel fear in this situation. People with phobias usually know that their fears are unreasonable.

People can overcome phobias. Good experiences with the object of the phobia can help. For example, imagine a person who has a fear of cats. The person might be helped to overcome that fear by petting a tame cat in safe surroundings.

Other articles to read include: **Anxiety disorder; Mental illness.**

Phylum

The phylum *(FY luhm)* is one of seven chief levels of groups that scientists use to *classify* (sort) all living things. The largest level of classification is called a *kingdom*. Each kingdom is divided into several *phyla* (the plural of *phylum*). Members of a phylum are more closely related than are members of a kingdom. Phyla are further divided into *classes*. Members of a class are more closely related than are members of a phylum.

All of the living things in a phylum have certain basic features in common because they share a common ancestor. In the animal kingdom, for example, animals with backbones and their close relatives make up the phylum Chordata *(kawr DAY tuh)*. All amphibians, birds, fish, mammals, and reptiles belong to this phylum. Human beings also are members of the phylum Chordata. These animals share a common ancestor that had a backbone.

Other articles to read include: **Class; Classification, Scientific; Kingdom.**

Running is a great way to maintain physical fitness.

Physical fitness

Physical fitness is having a strong, healthy body. Physical fitness helps people to look and feel their best.

The body is made to bend, stretch, run, jump, and climb. The more a person does these things, the stronger and fitter the body will become. Being fit means having stamina *(STAM uh nuh)*, strength, and flexibility.

Stamina means having the energy, or power, to be able to keep doing something for a long time. It takes time to build stamina. Regular exercise is the best way to develop stamina.

Strength means having strong muscles and strong bones. People can increase their muscle and bone strength in three ways. One way is to exercise regularly. A second way is to get the right amounts of sleep and rest. A third way is to eat many kinds of healthy foods.

Continued on the next page

Physical education classes are an important way for children to develop physical fitness. Most schools provide 20 to 30 minutes of exercise each day.

Muscles, like other parts of the body, need exercise to grow. Exercise makes muscles grow bigger and work better. Strong muscles help a person do more without getting tired as fast. They also give a person firm arms and legs.

Flexibility means being able to bend and move easily. Small children are flexible because their muscles and some of their other body parts are *elastic,* or stretchy. Older people are not as flexible. Older adults may need to do exercises that require bending if they want to stay flexible.

Flexing and stretching exercises help us all to be flexible. These kinds of exercises also strengthen our muscles and make us feel relaxed. People with flexible bodies can bend, stretch, twist, and turn easily.

To be physically fit, we need to eat many kinds of healthful foods. We need fresh fruits and vegetables, low-fat milk, bread, rice, pasta, fish, and lean meats. Fried foods and sweets do not strengthen our bodies like healthful foods. They should be eaten only in small amounts.

Most schools offer *physical education* classes, sometimes called *PE* or *gym,* to help children develop good fitness habits. Schools should provide at least 20 to 30 minutes of exercise each day. A good school program also offers team sports and classes in health.

For adults, health experts recommend one of two kinds of exercise. One kind, called *light exercise,* includes biking, walking, or gardening. The other is called *aerobic (air OH bihk) exercise. Aerobic* means *with air.* An aerobic exercise is an activity that makes you breathe more deeply than usual. Health experts recommend either 30 minutes or more of light exercise at least five days a week or 20 minutes or more of aerobic exercise three to five times a week.

Other articles to read include: **Exercise; Food; Health; Muscle; Posture.**

A physical therapist helps a patient rebuild strength through exercise in a pool. The water helps support weakened muscles.

Physical therapy

Physical therapy is the use of exercise, special equipment, and other methods to treat disease, injury, or disability. Physical therapy is done by health care professionals called *physical therapists*. They work in clinics, hospitals, schools for people with disabilities, private offices, and nursing homes.

Physical therapy is often used to treat paralysis and muscle weakness. These conditions can result from strokes, fractures, and other injuries. Physical therapists also help people learn to use braces, crutches, and wheelchairs. With the aid of physical therapy, a person with disability can often lead a more normal life.

Other articles to read include: **Disability; Exercise; Occupational therapy.**

A *primary care physician* listens to a young patient during a checkup. Primary care physicians take care of basic health needs.

Physician

A physician *(fuh ZIHSH uhn)* is a medical doctor. A person who goes to see a physician is called a *patient.*

Physicians first make a *diagnosis (DY uhg NOH sihs).* That is, they figure out what is wrong with the patient.

Then, physicians *treat* (help) patients. They may *prescribe* (order) certain medicines. Or they may perform an operation, set a broken bone, or give some other form of treatment.

Physicians also help prevent disease. They give *vaccinations (VAK sihn AY shunz),* or shots, against some diseases. They also do checkups. In a checkup, they may find an illness early. They can treat it to keep it from getting worse.

Some physicians work in offices. Others work in hospitals or in clinics.

Some physicians see patients with all kinds of problems. Others are *specialists*. Specialists have special training in one

Continued on the next page

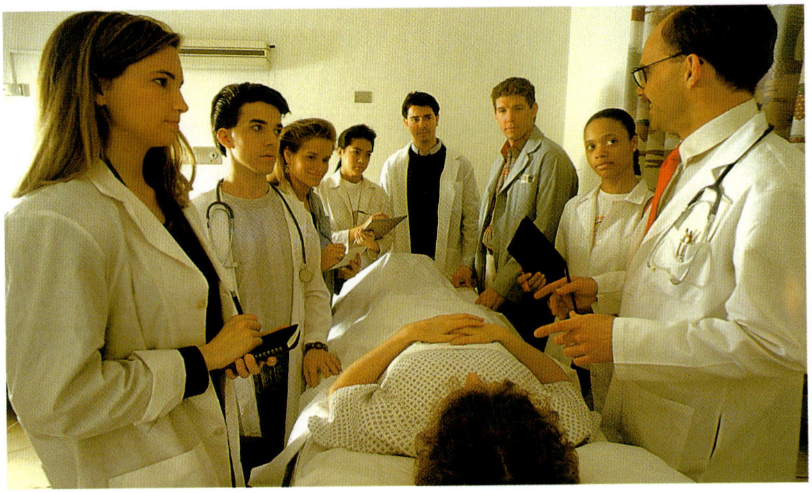

Doctors in training listen carefully and take notes as an experienced physician discusses a patient's treatment.

kind of medicine. For example, *pediatricians* specialize in treating children. *Ophthalmologists* specialize in treating the eyes. *Cardiologists* specialize in heart disease.

People who want to become physicians usually study science and mathematics in college. Then they go to medical school. After medical school, they work in a hospital. There, other doctors help them with patients. Physicians must pass an *examination* (test) before they can care for patients of their own.

Other articles to read include: **Anderson, Elizabeth Garrett; Blackwell, Elizabeth; Medicine; Neurology; Oncology; Ophthalmology; Obstetrics and gynocology; Orthopedics; Psychiatry; Radiology.**

Physiology

Physiology *(FIHZ ee OL uh jee)* is the study of how living things function. Scientists who study physiology are called *physiologists (FIHZ ee OL uh jihsts).* They study things as basic as cells and as complicated as the human body. Physiologists study how the parts or organs of a living thing work together. For example, they may study how muscles work or how nerves carry signals.

Doctors and others study physiology to learn how the body functions normally. This helps them understand what happens when the body has problems. For example, studies of the circulatory system help doctors understand and treat heart disease, stroke, and high blood pressure.

Other articles to read include: **Biology; Human body; Pavlov, Ivan Petrovich.**

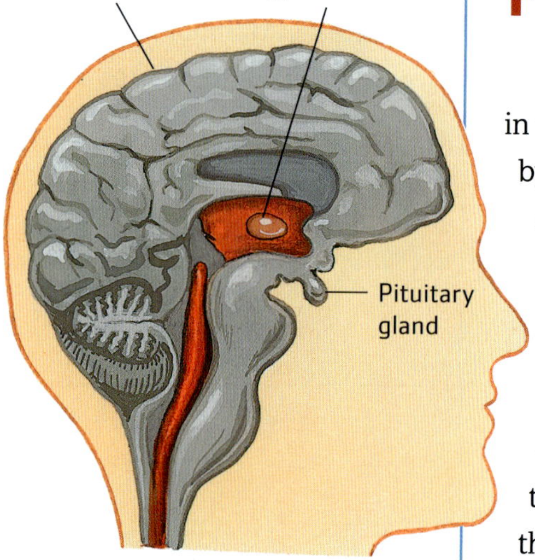

The *pituitary gland* is connected to a part of the brain called the *hypothalamus.* The hypothalamus signals the gland when to start and stop releasing certain hormones.

Pituitary gland

The pituitary (*pih TOO uh TEHR ee*) gland is an important organ in the body. Glands produce special chemical substances needed by the body. The pituitary gland produces substances called *hormones*. Hormones control a wide range of body functions.

The pituitary gland lies under the brain. It is connected to a part of the brain called the *hypothalamus (HY puh THAL uh muhs)*. The pituitary gland is about the size of a pea.

Hormones from the pituitary gland control growth in children. Other pituitary hormones control the use of food by the body or the production of milk in mothers. Still others help the kidneys keep water for later use. Certain hormones from the pituitary gland control the production of other hormones by other glands.

Other articles to read include: **Brain; Gland; Hormone; Hypothalamus.**

Placenta

The placenta *(pluh SEHN tuh)* is a disk-shaped organ in pregnant women. It forms on the wall of the *uterus*. The uterus, also called the *womb*, is the organ in which a baby develops. The placenta provides the unborn baby with food and oxygen. It also carries away the baby's waste products. In addition, the placenta makes chemicals called *hormones*. The hormones help the baby to develop and the mother to have a normal pregnancy.

A flexible tube connects the unborn baby to the placenta. This tube is called the *umbilical cord*. The umbilical cord carries food, oxygen, and wastes between the baby and the placenta. The blood of the baby and of the mother do not mix.

The placenta begins to form after the first week of pregnancy. It is made up of cells from both the mother and the unborn baby.

Minutes after the baby is born, the placenta separates from the uterus. Muscles of the uterus then push the placenta out of the mother's body. When this happens, the placenta is called the *afterbirth*.

Other articles to read include: **Baby; Childbirth; Hormone; Pregnancy; Umbilical cord; Uterus.**

Plague

Plague *(playg)* is a terrible sickness that in the past usually caused death. One widespread outbreak of plague happened in Europe in the 1300's. This outbreak has been called the Black Death. Throughout history, outbreaks of plague have killed many millions of people. Today, doctors usually can cure plague with medicines called *antibiotics*.

Plague is caused by tiny living things called *bacteria*. These bacteria live in rats and other small animals. The disease is usually spread to human beings and large animals by fleas.

There are different kinds of plague. Bubonic plague is the most common kind. With this sickness, the bacteria cause painful swellings on the body. Other kinds of plague cause sickness in the blood or in the lungs.

Other articles to read include: **Antibiotic; Bacteria; Disease.**

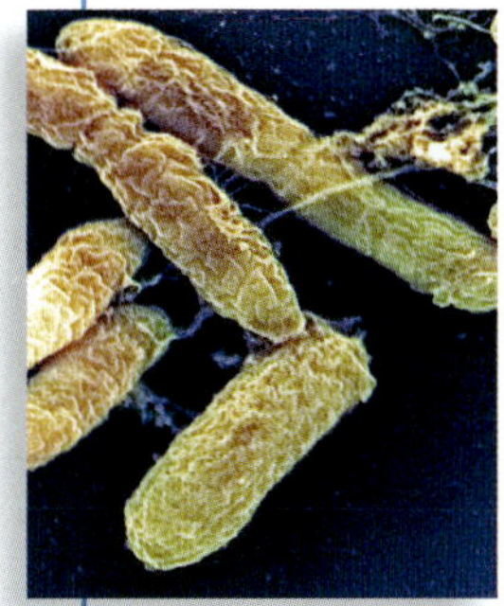

Plague bacteria

Rat

Flea

Plague can spread to human beings in a series of steps. First, the plague bacterium infects a rat or other rodent. Fleas may then spread the bacterium from rat to rat. A flea may also spread plague to a human through a bite. An infected person can spread the bacterium to other people by sneezing or coughing.

Plasma

Plasma *(PLAZ muh)* is the liquid part of blood. More than half of the blood in people and animals is plasma.

Plasma carries the three types of cells found in blood. The three types of cells are (1) *red blood cells,* (2) *white blood cells*, and (3) *platelets*. Plasma carries blood cells through the body. It also carries tiny bits of sugar and other important chemicals to the cells of the body.

Doctors sometimes give plasma to people with bleeding disorders and certain other illnesses. Doctors also often use plasma during operations.

Other articles to read include: **Blood; Circulatory system; Red blood cell; White blood cell.**

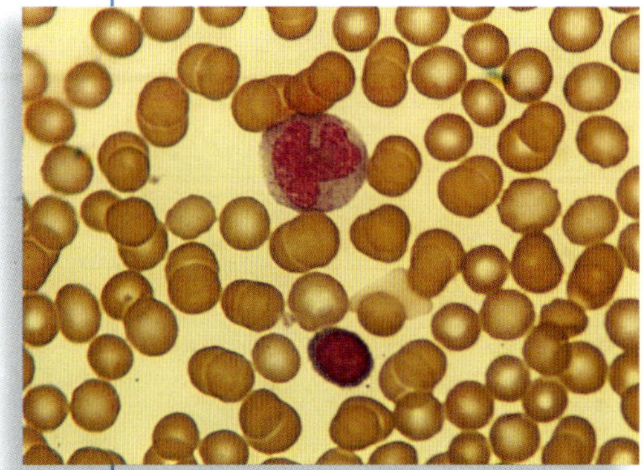

Blood consists of cells suspended in a watery liquid called *plasma.*

Plastic surgery

Plastic surgery is an operation to change the shape of a body part. Most plastic surgery is either *reconstructive* or *cosmetic.* In reconstructive plastic surgery, doctors repair a missing or damaged body part. In cosmetic plastic surgery, doctors reshape undamaged body parts to change appearance.

In reconstructive surgery, damaged tissue is often replaced with healthy tissue from another area of the body. This procedure is often used to treat severe burns, gunshot wounds, and injuries from automobile accidents. Plastic surgery can also correct birth defects of the face, ears, hands, and other body parts.

Cosmetic surgery is most often used to reverse signs of aging. A *facelift* operation removes some skin from the face to make a person look younger. *Liposuction (LIHP uh SUHK shuhn)* can remove fat from the hips, stomach, and legs. In this operation, fat is sucked out through a tube inserted under the skin. Cosmetic surgeons may also use *implants* (materials put into the body) to improve appearance. Implants can be used to change the shape of the nose, cheeks, or chin. A common plastic surgery is the use of implants to change the size or shape of a woman's breasts.

Other articles to read include: **Aging; Burn; Skin; Surgery.**

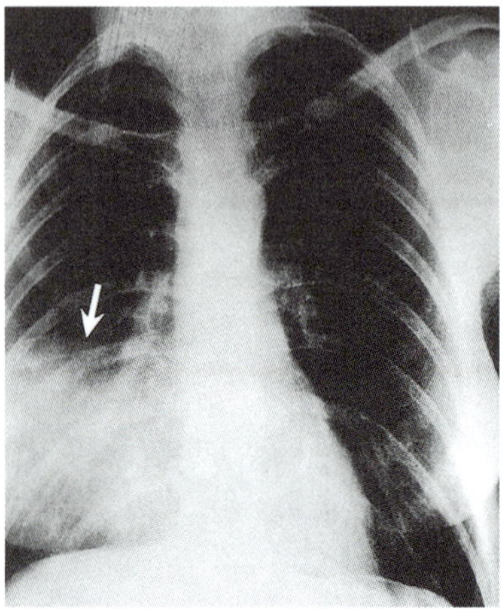

A person with pneumonia gets a build-up of liquid in the lungs, seen as a light area in this X-ray image.

Pneumonia

Pneumonia *(noo MOHN yuh)* is a disease of the lungs, the parts of the body used to breathe. Usually, pneumonia is caused by tiny living things called *bacteria, viruses,* or *fungi (FUHN jy).*

Pneumonia germs get into the air when someone who has pneumonia coughs or sneezes. Other people catch pneumonia by breathing in the germs. The germs grow in a person's lungs and may make the lungs fill with liquid.

Most people who catch pneumonia from bacteria have sudden chills, high fever, and chest pain. They may cough up thick liquid called *mucus (MYOO kuhs).* Pneumonia caused by viruses is usually milder. People with pneumonia often need bed rest. Pneumonia can also be treated with medicines.

Other articles to read include: **Bacteria; Disease; Fever; Lung; Mucus; Virus.**

Podiatry

Podiatry *(puh DY uh tree)* is the branch of medicine that deals with the human foot, ankle, and related body parts. Podiatry is also called *podiatric medicine*. Doctors known as *podiatrists* provide medical and surgical treatment of problems of the foot and its related body parts. They may *prescribe* (order) medicine and special shoes. They also may fit special devices to people's feet to help correct a problem.

Other articles to read include: **Ankle; Foot; Medicine.**

Poison

Poison is a substance that harms people or makes them ill. People can swallow poisons or breathe them in. They can also *absorb,* or take in, poison through the skin.

The poisons that do the most harm are products that people use around houses and farms, such as insect sprays and cleaning products. Some animals have poisonous bites or stings. Some plants contain chemicals that are poisonous if people eat or touch them.

There are several kinds of poisons. Some poisons, such as acids, destroy skin and flesh. Other poisons cause swelling and soreness in parts of the body, such as the stomach or nose. Some poisons attack the nerves and other parts of the body, such as the heart. Some poisons are eaten in foods. Those poisons can come from chemicals that get in the food, tiny living things called *bacteria,* or foods that are poisonous themselves.

To avoid poisoning, people should never eat wild foods, such as mushrooms and berries, that they do not know are safe. All medicines, cleaning fluids, and other chemicals should be kept out of the reach of children.

Many hospitals have poison control centers that give out emergency information. They tell people about *antidotes (AN tih dohts),* medicines or other things that can be taken to reduce the harmful effects of a poison. Usually people who have been poisoned go to an emergency room for treatment.

Other articles to read include: **Antitoxin; Bacteria; Food poisoning; Toxin.**

Many household products, such as cleaning compounds and insect sprays, are poisons. Such products may be marked with warning labels.

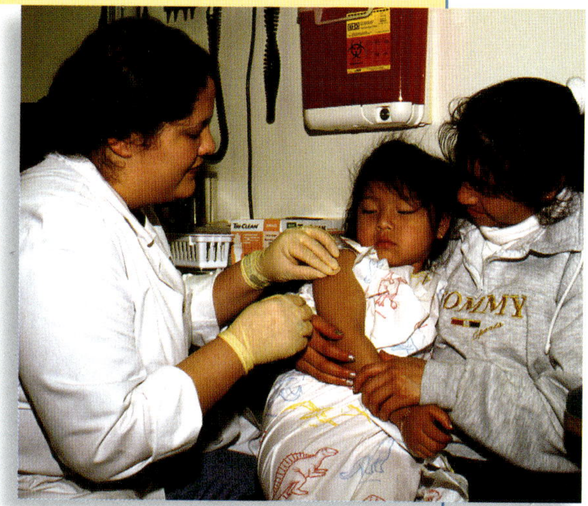

A young girl gets a polio shot at a medical clinic in Guatemala. Since the 1950's, the widespread use of vaccines to prevent polio has nearly wiped out the disease throughout much of the world.

Poliomyelitis

Poliomyelitis *(POH lee oh my uh LY tihs)* is a serious illness caused by tiny germs called *viruses.* The disease is also called *polio* (*POH lee oh*).

A person may get polio if the polio virus gets into the nose or mouth. The virus attacks *nerve cells* in the brain or the *spinal cord.* Nerve cells carry electrochemical signals throughout the body. The spinal cord is a cable of nerve cells that stretches along the backbone.

Some people who get polio get only a fever, headache, or sore throat, or they may vomit. Other people become seriously ill. They may become *paralyzed* (unable to move) or have trouble breathing.

There are no medicines that can kill the polio virus. For many years, polio left many people paralyzed. But in the 1950's, a scientist named Jonas Salk developed the first *vaccine (VAK seen)* (shot) to prevent polio. Today, vaccines given early in life can prevent polio.

Other articles to read include: **Disease; Nervous system; Paralysis; Salk, Jonas Edward; Spine.**

Population

Population is the number of people who live in a particular place, such as a city, a country, or the whole world. Populations are always changing. Sometimes they change because of *immigration* or *emigration.* Immigration is the movement of people into a place. Emigration is the movement out. Populations also change as a result of the difference between the number of births and the number of deaths. Many countries have more births than deaths. So many countries have a constant increase in population.

The world's population totaled more than 7 billion by 2012. The number of people in the world was increasing at a yearly rate of about 1.2 percent in the early 2000's. Experts say that, if this rate continues, the world's population would about double in 60 years.

Continued on the next page

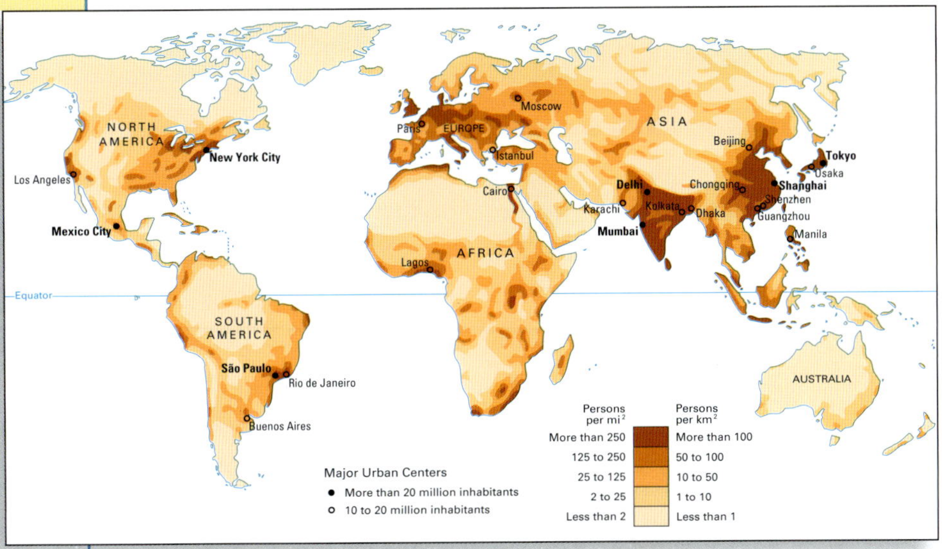

This map shows *population density* (the number of people per square mile or square kilometer) in different parts of the world. The darker the shading, the greater is that area's population density. The map also shows the world's most heavily populated *urban centers* (cities).

The continents with the fastest rates of population growth are Africa and Asia. Asia also has the greatest *population density* (number of people per square mile or square kilometer), and the two countries with the largest populations: China and India.

North America and Australia have slow population growth rates compared with most other continents. In Europe, during the early 2000's, population was actually decreasing.

Other articles to read include: **Death; Life expectancy.**

Pore

A pore is the tiny opening of a skin *gland*. Glands are like little sacs deep in the skin. They collect various liquids for the body to use or get rid of.

Some skin glands make sweat. They are called *sweat glands*. Other skin glands make oil. They are called *sebaceous (sih BAY shuhs) glands*. Sweat glands and sebaceous glands are in skin all over the body.

The human face has a large number of sebaceous glands. Oil from these glands may *cake* (become solid) in the pore. This produces a *blackhead*. The skin around the blackhead can become irritated. This results in *acne* (pimples). Pimples are small, raised swellings on the skin. A person can get a skin rash known as *prickly heat* from blocked sweat glands.

Other articles to read include: **Acne; Gland; Hair; Skin.**

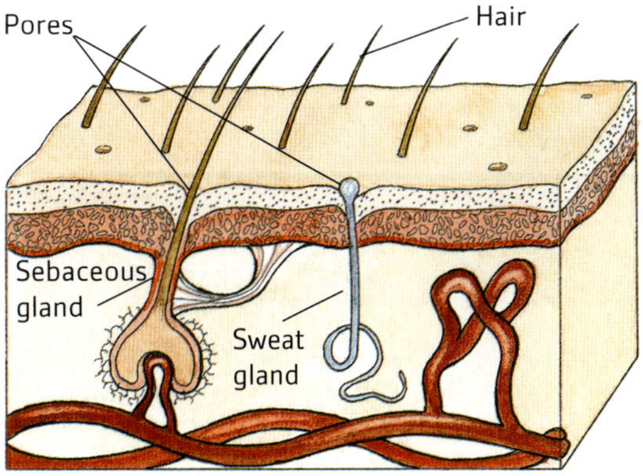

Pores cover much of the skin. They are the openings of two kinds of glands: sweat glands and *sebaceous* (oil) glands.

Red areas in a *positron emission tomography* (PET) scan show the most active parts of the brain (below). The scan is taken using a special machine (bottom).

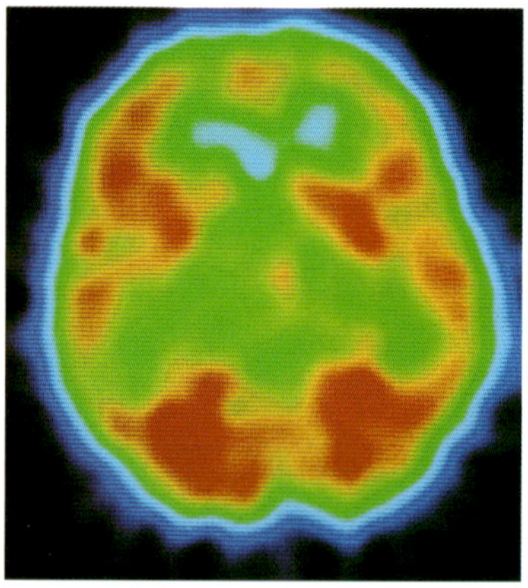

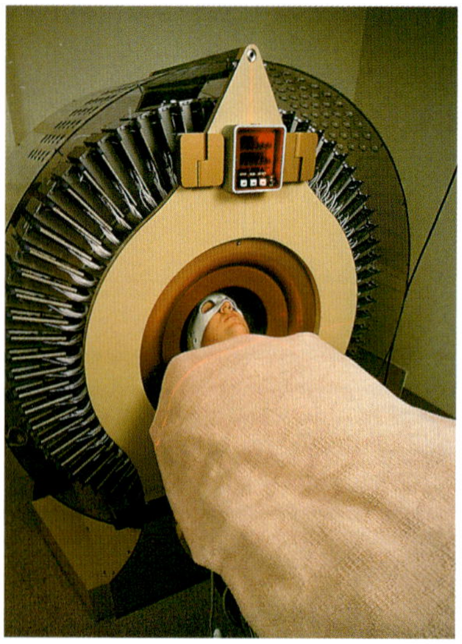

Positron emission tomography

Positron emission tomography *(POZ uh tron ih MIHSH uhn tuh MOG ruh fee),* also called *PET,* is a way of scanning the brain and other body tissues. PET enables scientists to see chemical changes in certain parts of the brain. They can do this while the patient performs various tasks. Such task may include listening, thinking, or moving an arm or leg. Scientists use PET scans to compare brain activity in healthy people with that of people with brain diseases.

Different colors in a PET image show how quickly certain parts of the brain use a sugar called *glucose*. This measure reveals how active these parts are during a particular task. For example, if the person looks at something, the brain region associated with vision will show increased activity.

With a PET scan, it may be possible for doctors to identify the causes of various brain disorders. These disorders include mental illnesses. They also include such conditions as cerebral palsy, epilepsy, and stroke. PET also helps doctors diagnose certain other disorders, including heart disease and cancer.

Other articles to read include: **Brain; Glucose; Mental illness; Radiology.**

Posture

Posture is the position of a person's body while standing or sitting. Certain muscles in the back, hips, and legs keep the body upright. Because of muscle action and the pull of gravity, posture is always changing.

Good posture takes the least amount of muscle activity to breathe well and stay upright. The feet should be placed comfortably apart, with the weight spread evenly over both feet. From a front or back view, the shoulders, the hips, and the fingertips should be even. From a side view, the ear and the shoulder should be in line. The back should not be too curved.

Continued on the next page

Posture is a sign of how a person has stood or sat for much of his or her lifetime. If a person always stands or sits with the head hanging forward, the neck muscles change in length, and good posture becomes difficult. Posture also may show how people feel. If they are tired or depressed, their posture may be poorer than usual. Good posture makes a person seem balanced and confident. It also may allow the body to work at its best.

Other articles to read include: **Exercise; Health; Physical fitness; Spine**

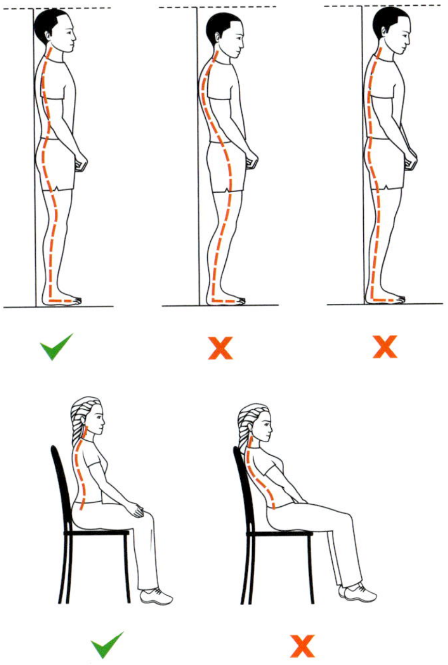

Good posture is maintained in standing or sitting by keeping the head above the backbone and the shoulders back. Poor posture allows the shoulders and head to droop.

Pregnancy

Pregnancy *(PREHG nuhn see)* is the time when a female carries a baby inside her body. A human baby grows inside the mother's body for about nine months. The baby grows in a part of the body called the *uterus (YOO tuhr uhs)*. This part is also called the *womb (woom)*.

Pregnancy begins when a *sperm* (male sex cell) combines with an *egg* (female sex cell) inside a woman's body. The two cells become a single cell that attaches itself to the inside of a woman's uterus. The uterus is made of muscle. It grows larger as the baby grows.

During the baby's growth, all of its inside organs form. When the baby is fully developed, the woman's body will begin *childbirth*. The baby is born by being pushed out of an opening in the mother's body.

Other articles to read include: **Baby; Childbirth; Egg; Embryo; Fertilization; Fetus; Reproduction, Human; Ultrasound; Uterus.**

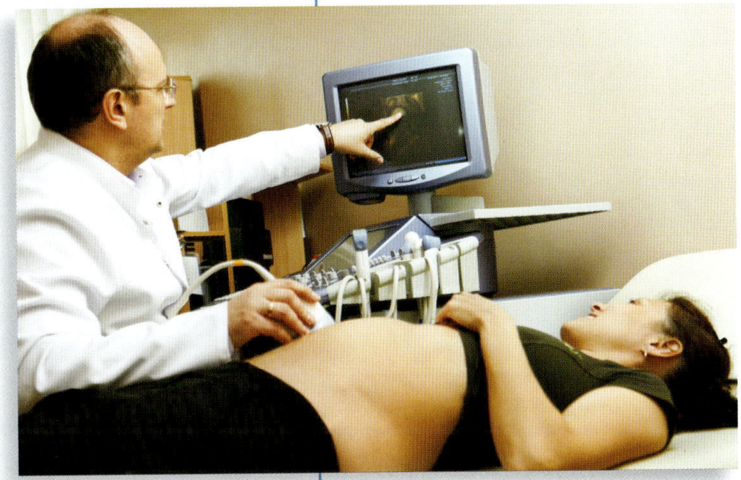

Regular checkups during pregnancy help make sure the baby is born healthy. Here, a doctor examines a pregnant woman using an *ultrasound* device. This device uses high-frequency sound waves to produce an image of the unborn baby.

This illustration shows a scene of prehistoric life in eastern Africa about 1.5 million years ago. A female *Homo erectus*, a type of early human being, holds her infant, while her mate uses a stone tool to cut meat from a dead animal. In the background, plant foods are gathered by three *australopithecines*, more primitive humanlike creatures that lived at the same time.

Prehistoric people

Prehistoric people are human beings who lived more than 5,500 years ago, before people invented writing and began to write down history. Most scientists believe the first human beings lived about 2 million years ago. There are some clues that human beings may have lived as long as 2 ½ million years ago.

Scientists first discovered evidence of prehistoric people in the 1800's, when they dug up sharp-edged stone tools. The scientists later found fossils of the bones of prehistoric people. Fossils are bones, shells, outlines of leaves, and other signs of life that are preserved in layers of rock.

Fossils show that early human beings had smaller brains than most modern people. Scientists developed the theory of evolution, a set of ideas about how living things change over time. This theory says in part that as the environment of the world changed, the ancestors of prehistoric people also went through a series of changes. These changes resulted in the appearance of the first human beings. They, in turn, evolved into modern human beings.

Scientists believe that human beings and apes share a common ancestor. But between 10 million and 5 million years ago, the ancestors of human beings began to evolve separately from the ancestors of apes. This separate evolution was the start of the *hominids*. Hominids include human beings and early humanlike ancestors. Today, they are more commonly called *hominins*.

Scientists who study human evolution are called *anthropologists (AN thruh PAHL uh jihsts)*. Most anthropologists believe that the first hominids included hairy, humanlike creatures called *australopithecines (AWS truh loh PIHTH uh seenz)*. These creatures first appeared about 4 million years ago in Africa. They walked upright and had large faces and jaws.

The first kind of human being, called *Homo habilis*, is thought to have evolved from a kind of australopithecine more than

Continued on the next page

2 million years ago. *Homo habilis* made stone tools. *Homo habilis* also gathered wild plants for food and ate animal meat.

Homo habilis evolved into *Homo erectus*, another kind of human. *Homo erectus* was taller and stood up straighter. *Homo erectus* was probably the first human being to learn to use fire and wear clothing.

Homo erectus evolved into a human being called *Homo sapiens*. This human being had a more rounded skull. The first *Homo sapiens* with modern-looking faces appeared more than 100,000 years ago. Later *Homo sapiens* developed art, spoken language, and farming. Modern human beings are known as *Homo sapiens sapiens*.

Other articles to read include: **Anthropology; Archaeology; Cave dwellers; Evolution; Hominid; Human being; Paleontology; Stone Age.**

A prehistoric rock painting appears to show a human hunter and a bison he has speared. This painting is one of many in the Lascaux Caves of France that date to about 15,000 years ago.

Primate

The primates are a group of mammals made up of apes, monkeys, human beings, and related animals. There are many different kinds of primates. They range in size from 1 ounce (28 grams) to almost 400 pounds (181 kilograms).

Primates share certain traits. Scientists believe that these traits are related to the ability to live in trees. *Grasping* hands let primates hang onto branches and move easily from branch to branch. Most primates can also grab items with their feet. Some primates can even use their tails like an extra hand. Primate eyes face forward, giving the animals excellent vision. Most kinds of primates use their sight more than their senses of hearing or smell.

Most primates have large, complex brains. Many kinds of primates live in large social groups. Primate young usually take a long time to become adults. The young learn much from the adults, including what to eat and how to protect themselves.

Primates live mainly in *tropical* (warm) areas. They are found in Africa, Asia, and Central and South America.

Continued on the next page

There are many different kinds of primates, but they all have bodies that are somewhat similar. The similarity can be seen by looking at the skeletons of primates ranging from lemurs to monkeys, apes, and humans.

Primate *Continued from the previous page*

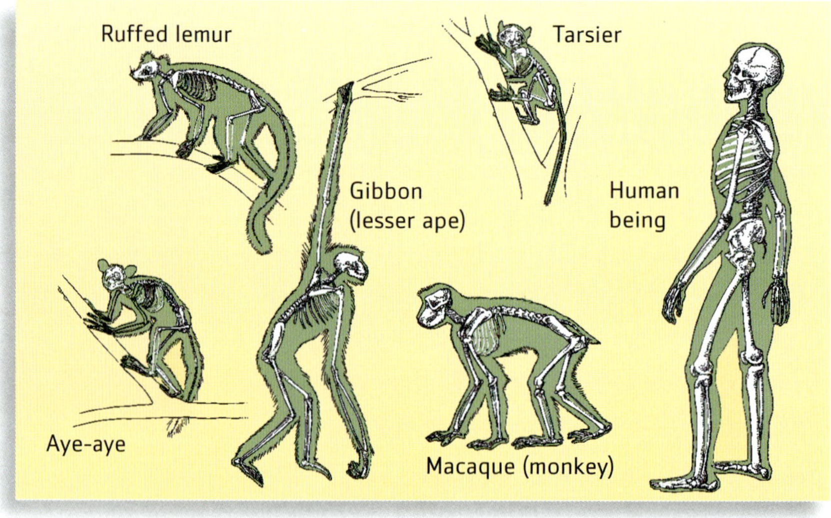

Scientists who study nonhuman primates are called *primatologists (PRY muh TOL uh jihsts).* These scientists have learned a great deal about primates over the years. Jane Goodall, who studies chimpanzees in the wild, is one of the most famous primatologists. She showed that chimpanzees make and use simple tools, among many other discoveries. Scientists can also learn about primate behavior by studying primates in zoos.

Many scientists conduct research using monkeys and other primates in laboratories. Because these animals are closely related to human beings, scientists can use them to study human diseases. Many medicines that help people today were first tested on monkeys. However, some people are opposed to testing medicines on primates.

Other articles to read include: **Animal experimentation; Evolution; Human being; Mammal.**

Progesterone

Progesterone *(proh JEHS tuh rohn)* is a type of *hormone.* A hormone is a chemical substance made in the body. It controls what certain cells or organs do. Progesterone is made mainly by female animals. They make it when they are able to give birth to young. Adult males also make very small amounts of progesterone.

Continued on the next page

Progesterone is important in getting a woman ready for *pregnancy.* Pregnancy is when a woman carries a baby in her body.

At some times during each month, women make more progesterone. This increase can change how a woman's body works. For example, the woman's body temperature can increase.

Doctors use progesterone to treat certain health problems in women. Such progesterone may be used alone or with other drugs.

Other articles to read include: **Estrogen; Hormone; Pregnancy; Reproduction, Human.**

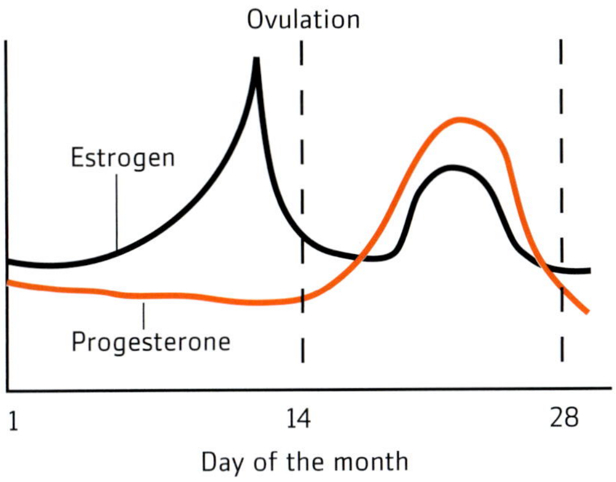

The amount of *progesterone* in a woman's blood increases every month after *ovulation,* the process of releasing an egg. Progesterone prepares the woman's body for pregnancy. The amount of *estrogen,* another hormone, is usually higher just before ovulation.

Prostate gland

The prostate *(PROS tayt)* gland is an organ of the male reproductive system. It makes a thick whitish fluid. The fluid helps carry sperm. In men, the prostate gland sits just below the bladder. It is about the size of a walnut. The *urethra* passes through the prostate gland. The urethra is the tube through which urine leaves the body.

Sperm are produced in a pair of glands called the *testicles.* From there, the sperm travel to the prostate. Fluids from the prostate mix with the sperm to form *semen.* Semen keeps sperm healthy. It also helps carry them out of the body through the urethra.

Other articles to read include: **Reproduction, Human; Testicle; Urinary system.**

Protein

Good sources of protein in the diet include animal foods such as meat, fish, poultry, and eggs. Nuts and beans are good sources of protein from plants.

Protein *(PROH teen)* is one of the three main kinds of food that give the body energy. The others kinds of food are carbohydrates and fats. Plants build proteins from materials they take from the air and soil. Human beings and other animals get proteins from foods. Foods high in protein include eggs, fish, meat, milk, peas, and nuts.

The human body has many millions of cells, and proteins make up a large part of each cell. Proteins are important in building and healing body tissues, such as bone and muscle. Certain proteins have special jobs. For example, blood contains proteins that carry oxygen from the lungs to body tissues. Blood also has proteins that help protect the body from disease.

Other articles to read include: **Carbohydrate; Fat; Food; Hemoglobin; Nutrition.**

Psoriasis

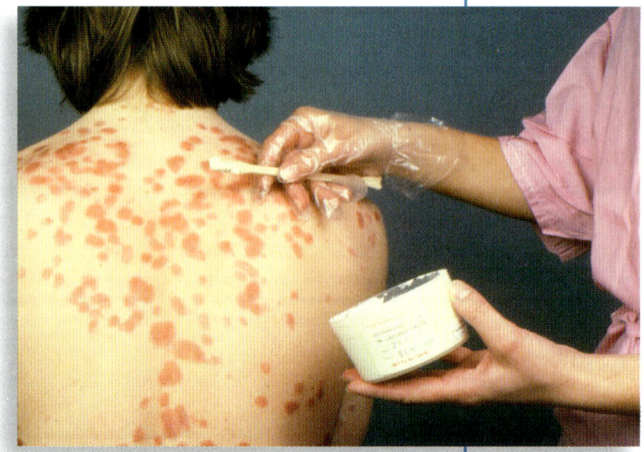

A patient with *psoriasis* on her back gets a special medicine applied to the red, scaly patches. Various lotions and ointments can help control the skin disease.

Psoriasis *(suh RY uh sihs)* is a skin disease. It involves dry, red, scaly patches on the skin. Some people might get only small areas of psoriasis. Others might get it over most of the body.

In the skin, new cells grow beneath older ones. For most people, the old cells flake off as new cells grow. But in people with psoriasis, the new cells grow too quickly. They do not flake off as they grow older. Also, certain chemicals in the body make the skin swell and feel hot and itchy.

Doctors can give medicine to stop the itching. Other chemicals can help the skin cells peel away and slow their growth.

Other articles to read include: **Disease; Skin.**

Psychiatry

A psychiatrist works with a child who has behavior problems.

Psychiatry *(sy KY uh tree)* is a part of medicine that deals with mental health. Most doctors help people when their bodies are sick or hurt. Doctors called *psychiatrists (sy KY uh trihsts)* help people who have problems with their minds.

Psychiatrists work with many kinds of patients. People might visit a psychiatrist if they feel unhappy all of the time, if they see or hear things that are not really there, or if they have other problems that make it hard for them to lead a normal life.

Psychiatrists can help their patients by talking to them about their problems. Psychiatrists can also give the patients medicines that will help make them feel better.

Other articles to read include: **Behavior; Emotion; Freud, Sigmund; Medicine; Mental illness; Mind; Psychology.**

Psychology

Psychology *(sy KOL uh jee)* is the study of how the mind works and of how people and other animals behave. People who study or practice psychology are called *psychologists (sy KOL uh jihsts).*

Psychologists often try to understand why people act the way they do. They study how we see, hear, smell, taste, and feel things. They explore how we learn, think, remember, and forget. They try to figure out what makes people happy, angry, or scared. Psychologists have helped many people learn how to get along better with others and to be happier with their own lives. Some psychologists study the mental abilities of animals, such as chimpanzees, as a way of learning about the development of the human mind.

Psychology is similar to a part of medicine called *psychiatry (sy KY uh tree).* But psychiatrists are doctors who see patients and can *prescribe* (order) medicine. Not all psychologists are doctors.

Other articles to read include: **Behavior; Emotion; Mental illness; Mind; Psychiatry.**

Puberty

Puberty *(PYOO buhr tee)* is a time in a young person's life. It is when a child's body starts to slowly change into that of an adult. Chemical substances in the body trigger these changes. These substances are called *hormones.* The changes help prepare people to become mothers and fathers. Puberty usually starts about the age of 10 to 12.

During puberty, children begin to look more like adults. They become taller and heavier. Boys' voices become deeper. Girls begin to grow breasts. Both boys and girls begin to grow more hair on their body.

Puberty is part of a time called *adolescence (AD uh LEHS uhns).* During this time, children begin to think more like adults. They solve many problems on their own. They may also begin to plan for their adult life.

Other articles to read include: **Adolescent; Child; Gland; Hormone; Reproduction, Human; Sexuality.**

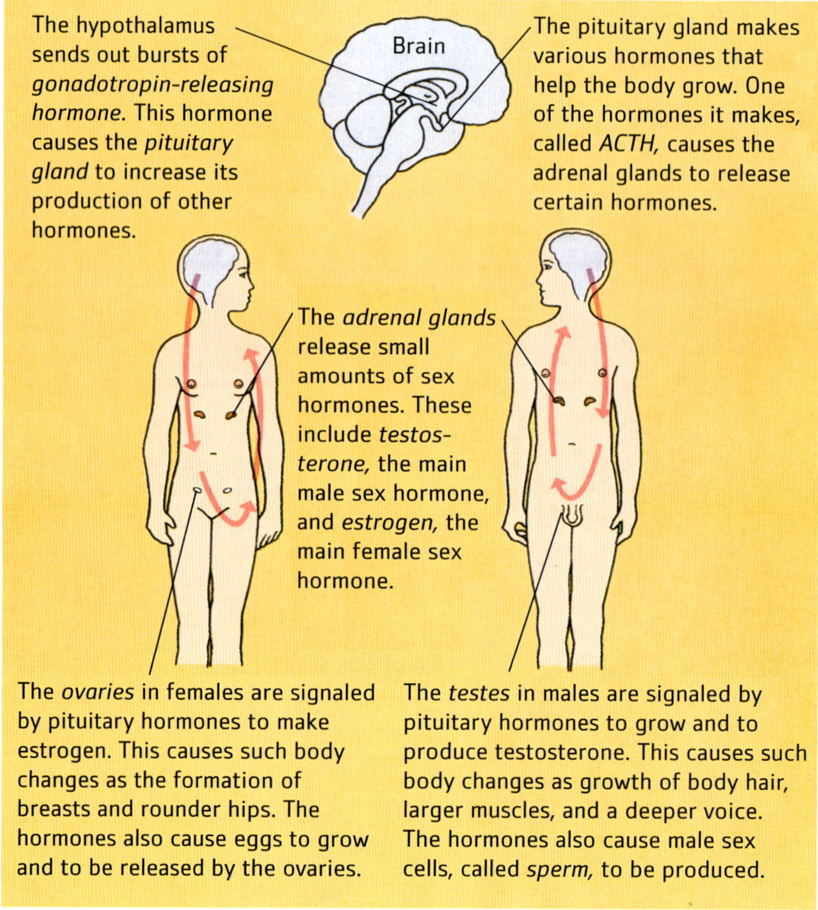

The changes that happen during puberty are caused by the chemical actions of various substances called *hormones.* Hormones are chemical messengers that control the activities of certain tissues in the body. The changes all start in the brain.

Public health

Public health is the general health of all of the members of a community. Public health workers and officials try to stop and cure illness. They work to keep everyone as healthy as possible.

Many countries have public health centers. These centers do different things, depending on the nation's technology, environment, and its health problems. Other groups try to solve public health problems throughout the world.

In the United States, the national, state, and city governments all take part in public health programs. The federal government runs the Public Health Service (PHS), part of the Department of Health and Human Services.

Public health centers do many things to protect people's health. For example, they help make sure drinking water is clean. They also make sure that garbage is thrown out correctly and sewers are working properly. Many hospitals offer special services to aid public health.

Other articles to read include: **Disease; Health; Immunization; Medicine.**

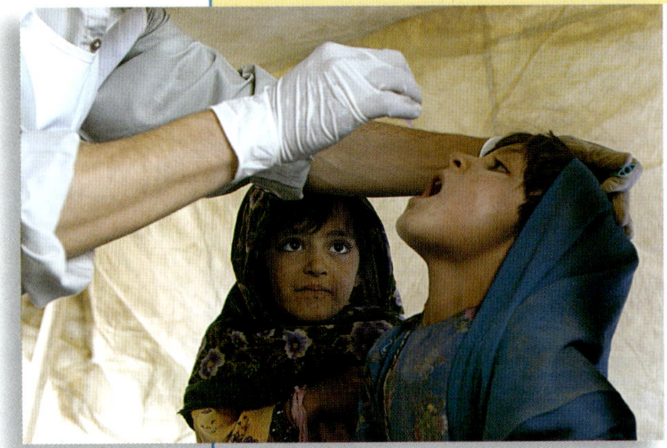

A public health worker in Afghanistan gives a child an oral vaccination to protect the child from the disease polio. Vaccinations against disease are among the most important public health services.

Pulse

A pulse is a slight thumping that can be felt at certain points in the body. This thumping is caused by the beating of the heart.

Every time the heart beats, it pushes blood into blood vessels called *arteries.* With each push, the arteries stretch a little, then relax. Doctors and nurses often take a person's pulse by pressing their fingers on the person's wrist. There they can feel the thumping of an artery after each heartbeat. They count the thumps to make sure that the heartbeat is steady and neither too fast nor too slow.

The normal pulse of a 7-year-old child is about 90 beats per minute. Most adults have a normal pulse rate of about 72 beats per minute.

Other articles to read include: **Artery; Blood; Blood pressure; Heart.**

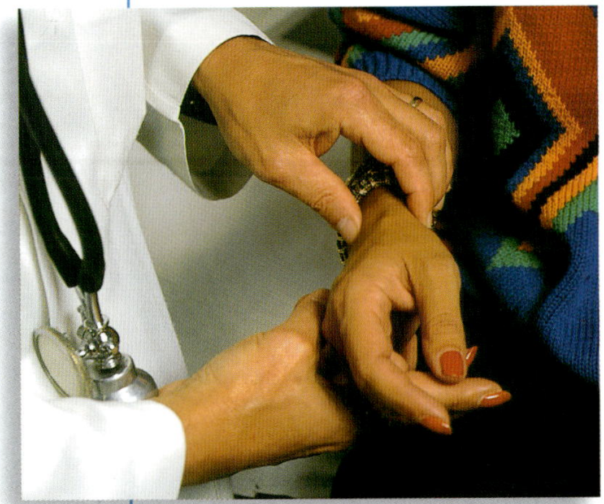

A doctor measures the pulse of a patient by feeling the stretching and relaxing of the arteries in the wrist.

Rr

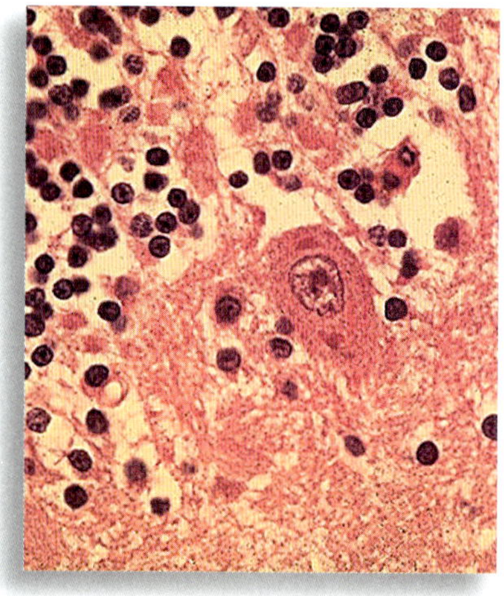

Brain tissue may be analyzed after death to determine if an animal had rabies. Tiny structures called *Negri bodies,* appearing as dark spots, indicate the presence of the rabies virus.

Rabies

Rabies *(RAY beez)* is a serious disease that destroys tissue in the brain. It is caused by a tiny living thing called a *virus.* Human beings and other animals can get rabies.

People usually get rabies from animals such as dogs, cats, bats, and raccoons. Such an animal may carry the rabies virus in its *saliva,* a sticky liquid in the mouth. If the animal bites someone, that person may get rabies.

A person infected with rabies usually notices a headache and finds it hard to swallow. A person can die from rabies if not helped quickly. Doctors give people bitten by infected animals *vaccinations (vak suh NAY shuhnz)* to keep them from getting sick.

Other articles to read include: **Disease; Virus.**

Races, Human

The human races are a way of classifying groups of people. Scientific evidence suggests that all living people are related. But people do not all look alike. Our bodies, noses, lips, and eyes have different sizes and shapes. Our skins, eyes, and hair have different colors. These differences are often used to divide people into different races.

For many years, scholars thought that "pure" races existed in the distant past. These races later bred together, they thought, producing the variety of features we see today. Most modern scientists doubt that "pure" races ever existed. Instead of dividing people into narrow races, they try to appreciate the richness of human diversity.

People generally consider those who "look different" to be members of a different race. As a result, societies continue to divide their members into races.

Some people misuse the idea of race. They suggest that people of different races are born with differences in intelligence, talent, or moral standards. Such claims are not based on firm scientific evidence.

Other articles to read include: **Human being.**

Radiology

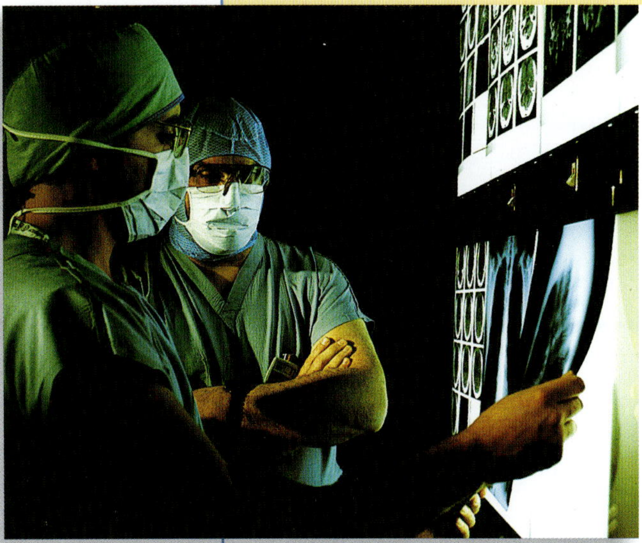

Radiologists examine X-ray images of a patient during an operation. The images can help the surgeon decide how to proceed.

Radiology *(RAY dee OL uh jee)* is a branch of medicine that involves viewing the inside of the body. Doctors who specialize in radiology are called *radiologists.*

One of the first ways scientists learned to see inside the living body was by making use of *X rays.* Later, they discovered how to perform other medical imaging techniques, including *CT* or *CAT scans*, *PET scans*, *MRI scans,* and *ultrasounds.*

X rays are a form of *radiation* (energy given off as waves or particles) that can pass through flesh. X rays can be used to produce images of what lies beneath the skin on a piece of photographic film. X rays are often used to look at bones. A CT scanner uses X rays to produce *cross-sectional images* of organs inside a patient's body. A cross-sectional image is like a slice cut across an object. Computers can put together several CT scans to create a three-dimensional image of an organ. PET scans use a form of radiation called *gamma rays* to produce images of the chemical activity inside the brain and other body tissues. MRI's use *magnetic fields* and *radio waves* to make pictures of tissues inside the body. Ultrasound devices use sound that is too high-pitched for people to hear to create images of normal and diseased tissue inside the body. Ultrasound is also used to make images of unborn babies inside a mother's womb.

All radiology procedures involve using different kinds of complex machines. Doctors usually use the pictures produced with radiology to help them figure out causes of, and treatments for, medical problems.

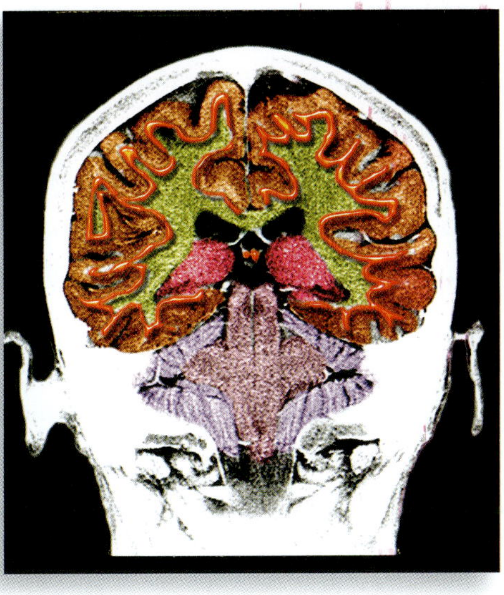

A magnetic resonance imaging (MRI) scan reveals details of the inside of a person's brain. The image has been colored by computer to highlight certain brain regions.

Other articles to read include:
Magnetic resonance imaging; Medicine; Positron emission tomography; Ultrasound.

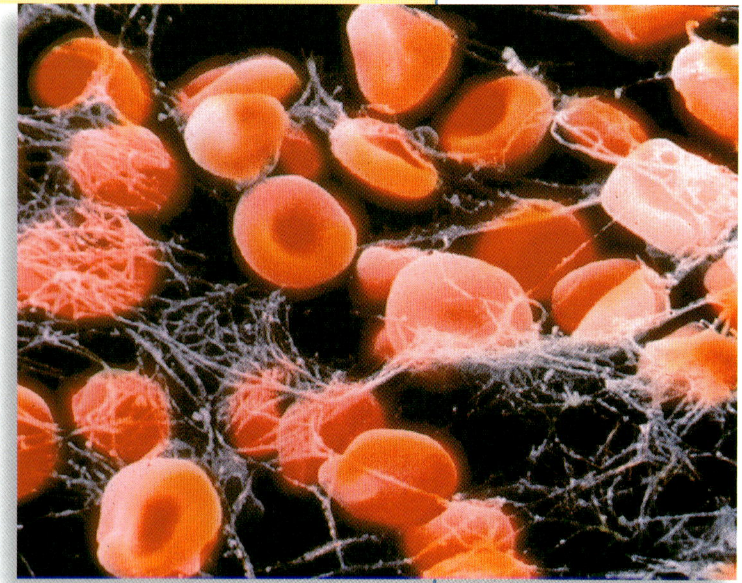

Red blood cells have a somewhat doughnutlike shape. In a blood clot (above), sticky strands of protein tie red blood cells together.

Red blood cell

A red blood cell is a type of cell in blood. It gives blood its red color. Red blood cells deliver oxygen to other cells in the body. They carry waste away from cells, too. Red blood cells are also called *erythrocytes (ih RIHTH roh syts).*

Most red blood cells are round and somewhat flat. They resemble little doughnuts without holes. Red blood cells are everywhere in the blood. They are suspended in a liquid called *plasma.*

Many blood cells wear out and die every day. But the body keeps making new blood cells. New blood cells are made in the *bone marrow,* a material inside bones.

Other articles to read include: **Blood; Bone; Circulatory system; Hemoglobin; Plasma; White blood cell.**

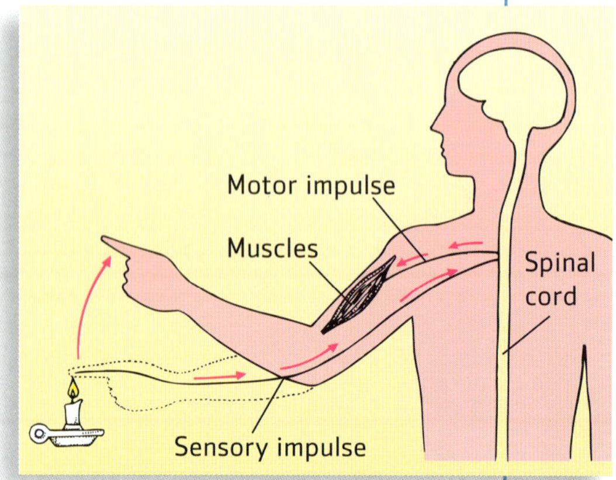

Touching a candle flame can produce a reflex action. It triggers a ***sensory impulse*** that travels along nerve cells to the spinal cord. The spinal cord sends a ***motor impulse*** to the arm muscles, causing the arm to jerk back.

Reflex action

A reflex action is an unplanned response to a *stimulus (STIHM yuh luhs)* (sensation). Imagine your hand accidentally touches something hot, such as a candle flame. You would jerk your hand away without thinking. Jerking your hand away is a reflex action. It is a response to the stimulus of the intense heat.

Most reflex actions do not have to be learned. They occur naturally in human beings and many other animals.

Some reflex actions, however, are learned. A Russian scientist named Ivan Pavlov did an experiment. He rang a bell each time he fed a dog. When the dog got the food, it would naturally *salivate (SAL uh vayt)* (produce saliva in its mouth). Eventually, the dog salivated at the sound of the bell. It did this even when it got no food. This type of learned reflex action is called a *conditioned reflex.*

Other articles to read include: **Learning; Nervous system; Pain; Pavlov, Ivan Petrovich.**

Reproduction, Human

Human reproduction *(HYOO muhn REE pruh DUHK shuhn)* is the way human beings make more of their own kind. A new human being develops from the joining of one cell from a male and one cell from a female. The female cell is called an *egg.* The male cell is called a *sperm.* When the male and female cells join, *fertilization (FUR tuh luh ZAY shuhn)* takes place.

Fertilization is the first step in *pregnancy.* During pregnancy, the fertilized egg develops into a baby inside the female. Pregnancy lasts about nine months.

At the beginning of pregnancy, the fertilized egg is smaller than the period at the end of this sentence. Soon the egg develops into a mass of cells called an *embryo (EHM bree oh).* Over time, the cells rearrange themselves to form *tissues.* A tissue is made up of a large number of cells that are all similar. Different kinds of tissues form different parts of the body.

By the end of the second month of pregnancy, all the major organs have formed. These include the heart and lungs. By this time, the embryo clearly looks human. During the rest of pregnancy, the embryo is called a *fetus (FEE tuhs).* The fetus grows and develops enough to live outside the mother's body. Pregnancy ends when the new baby passes out of the mother's body.

Other articles to read include: **Baby; Cell; Childbirth; Egg; Embryo; Fertilization; Fetus; Multiple birth; Pregnancy; Tissue.**

Human beings reproduce through *sexual reproduction.* In sexual reproduction, a new individual begins to form when a male cell called a *sperm* joins with a female cell called an *egg.* This process is called *fertilization.* Inside the mother's body, the fertilized egg begins to develop into a cluster of cells called an *embryo* and eventually into a *fetus.* When the fetus reaches full development, it passes out of the mother's body as a baby. This event is called *birth.*

Development of a fetus

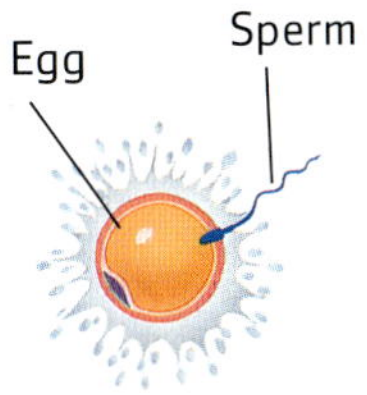

Day 1 The sperm cell joins the egg.

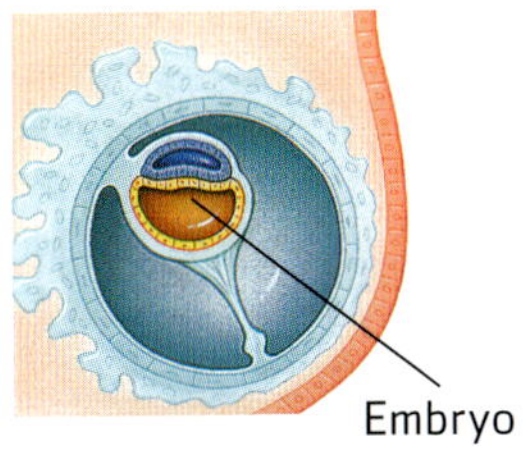

Day 13 Simple parts begin to develop in the embryo.

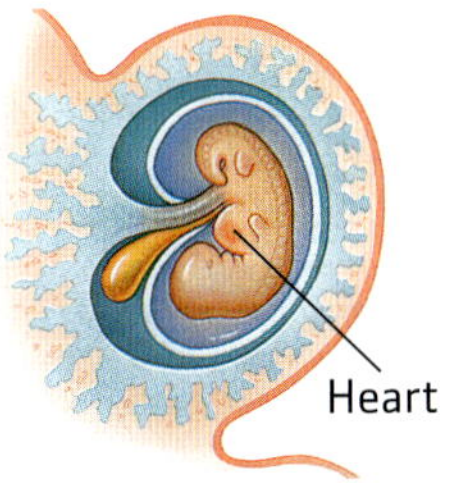

Day 28 The heart begins to beat.

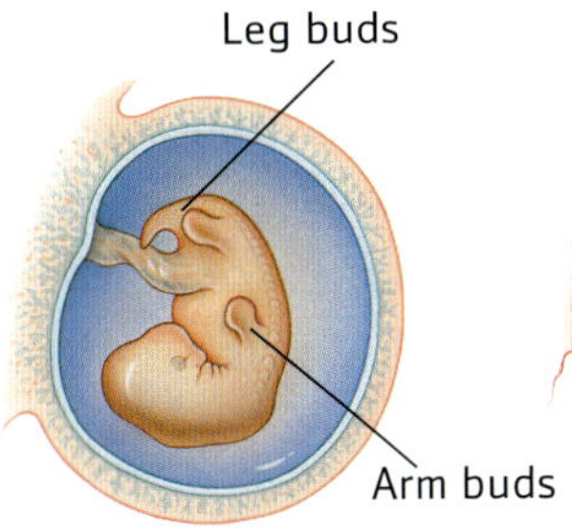

Day 35 Arms, legs, and organs are growing.

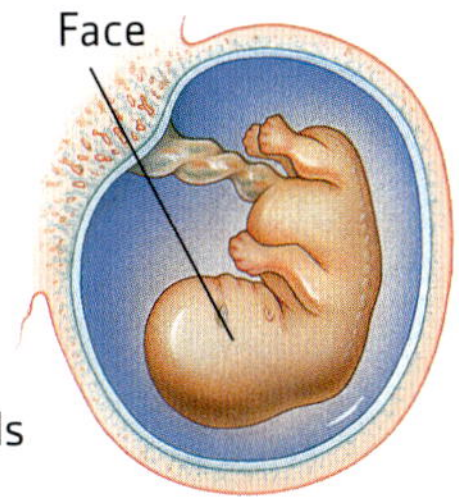

Day 49 The face starts to form.

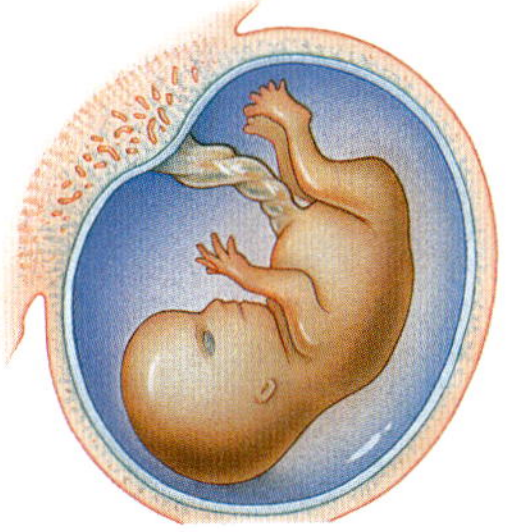

Day 56 All the main organs have formed. So have the fingers and toes.

Respiration

Respiration *(REHS puh RAY shuhn)* is how people and other living things get and use the oxygen they need to live. Oxygen is a gas in the air. Oxygen is also mixed into the waters of lakes, the ocean, and other bodies of water.

When you breathe in, muscles in your chest make your lungs *expand* (get larger). The expansion causes air to move into your lungs through your nose and mouth. Some of the oxygen enters tiny tubes in your lungs. Blood flows through these tubes. The blood in these tubes carries oxygen from the lungs to every other part of your body. Every cell that makes up your body uses oxygen to make energy for you to live.

When your cells use energy, they also make a gas called *carbon dioxide*. Carbon dioxide is a waste product of respiration. Your body does not need carbon dioxide, so it leaves the cells and goes into the blood. The blood then carries the carbon dioxide to the lungs. When you breathe out, the muscles in your chest make your lungs *contract* (get smaller). The contraction causes the lungs to push carbon dioxide out of the body.

Some animals conduct respiration without lungs. For example, fish and shellfish breathe with body structures called *gills*. Their gills *extract* (pull) oxygen out of water. Insects breathe through tiny tubes that bring air into their bodies. In many plants, respiration takes place through small openings in leaves called *stomata (STOH muh tuh)*.

Other articles to read include: **Asthma; Carbon dioxide; Carbon monoxide; Cough; Diaphragm; Emphysema; Lung; Mouth; Nose; Pneumonia; SARS; Sneezing.**

People and many other animals have lungs for breathing gases in and out. The body takes in oxygen from the atmosphere and releases carbon dioxide into the atmosphere. Breathing is controlled by a part of the brain called the *respiratory center.*

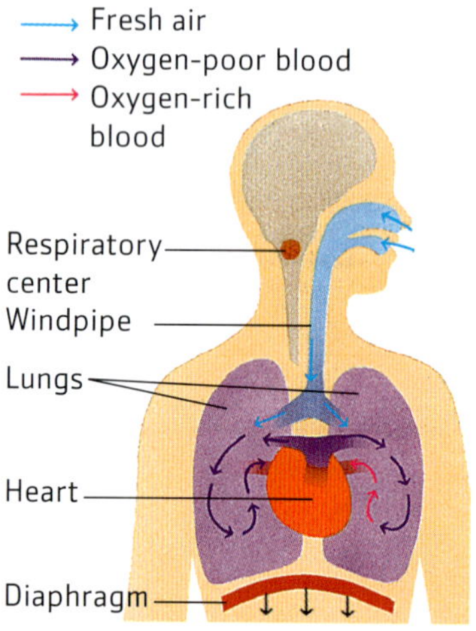

Inhalation—the act of drawing air into the lungs—occurs when certain muscles *contract* (get smaller). The *diaphragm,* a large muscle between the chest and abdomen, contracts, making the chest *expand* (grow larger). The lungs expand, drawing in air from the atmosphere.

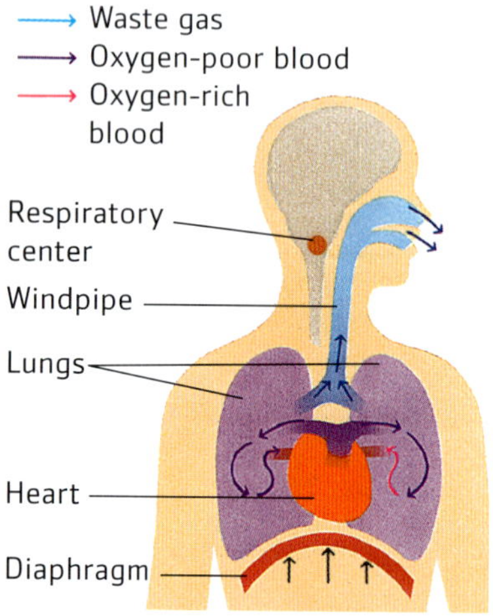

Exhalation—the act of letting gas out of the lungs—takes place when the same muscles relax. The relaxation removes the force expanding the lungs, which thus contract. The contraction forces gas out of the lungs and into the atmosphere.

Rheumatology

Rheumatology *(ROO muh TOL uh jee)* is the study of diseases that affect the body's joints. These diseases are called *rheumatic diseases*. Doctors who specialize in the treatment of rheumatic diseases are called *rheumatologists*.

Rheumatologists mainly treat patients who have various forms of joint disease called *arthritis*. Rheumatologists also care for patients with general back pain and aching muscles, bones, and joints. Rheumatologists do not perform surgery. But they often work closely with surgeons and other doctors to treat injured people.

Other articles to read include: **Arthritis; Bone; Cartilage; Disease; Joint; Medicine.**

Rib

Ribs are long, slender bones in the chest. Human beings and many other animals have ribs. Ribs protect the heart and lungs. They also help move air in and out of the lungs.

Human beings have 24 ribs, 12 ribs on each side of the body. A small joint connects each rib to the backbone.

Some ribs also connect in the front of the body. The upper seven ribs on each side connect directly to the breastbone. They are connected by a tough, elastic material called *cartilage (KAHR tuh lihj)*. These ribs are called the *true ribs*.

The five lower ribs on each side are called *false ribs*. They are not joined directly to the breastbone. The top three false ribs are connected to each other by cartilage. The lowest two ribs are connected only to the backbone. They are known as *floating ribs*. The spaces between the ribs contain arteries, veins, muscles, and nerves.

Other articles to read include: **Bone; Cartilage; Heart; Lung; Skeleton; Spine.**

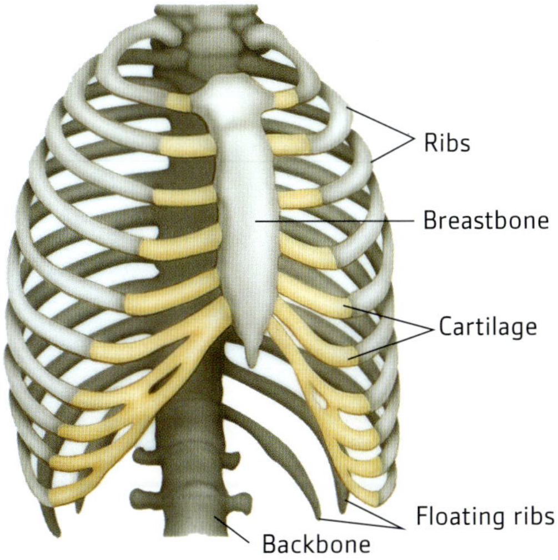

The ribs are connected to the backbone, from which they curve downward and forward to form a protective cage around the heart and lungs. The human body has 24 ribs, 12 on each side.

Ribosome

A ribosome *(RY buh sohm)* is a structure in a living cell. Ribosomes build *proteins*. Proteins make up a large part of every cell. Thus, ribosomes are a vital part of cells. All kinds of living things have ribosomes in their cells. One cell can have from thousands to millions of ribosomes.

Plant and animal cells have a structure called the *nucleus*. The nucleus contains chemical "instructions" for building each protein. The nucleus copies these instructions into a chemical called *messenger RNA*. *RNA* stands for *ribonucleic acid*.

Proteins are made of long chains of *amino acids*. The amino acids must be arranged in a specific order. Messenger RNA provides the proper order of amino acids for building a particular protein. Messenger RNA passes out of the nucleus. It passes into a ribosome. The ribosome uses the messenger RNA like a blueprint to build the protein.

Other articles to read include: **Amino acid; Cell; Nucleus; Protein; RNA.**

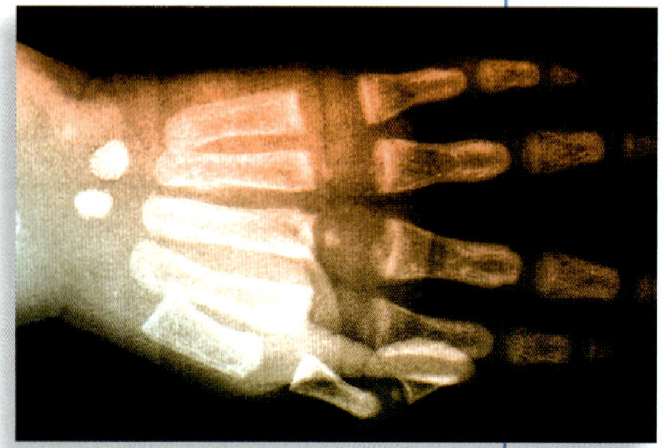

This X-ray image shows thickened, softened bones in the wrist and hand of a young child with rickets.

Rickets

Rickets is a bone disease. It occurs mostly in children. Children with rickets have very soft bones. The bones bend instead of growing straight. The bones may also grow bumps.

Children may get rickets from a lack of certain *nutrients (NOO tree uhnts)*, mainly calcium and vitamin D. Nutrients are substances that the body needs to grow. People get calcium from milk and green vegetables. They get vitamin D from milk, sunlight, and fish.

Children developing rickets usually feel weakness, pain in the bones, and sometimes pain all over the body. Doctors treat such children with vitamin D and calcium.

Other articles to read include: **Bone; Child; Disease; Nutrient; Vitamin.**

Ringworm

Ringworm is the name of several different diseases of the skin. All of these diseases are caused by tiny living things called *fungi (FUHN jy).*

One of the most common kinds of ringworm occurs mostly in children. It begins with a small red spot. The spot grows larger and may get as big as a silver dollar. Then the inside of the spot clears up, leaving a red ring. Sometimes the spots and rings itch.

Children and adults can get a different kind of ringworm called *athlete's foot.* Athlete's foot affects the skin between the toes. People can also get ringworm of the scalp.

Ringworm may spread very quickly from one person to another. Doctors can give people medicine that kills the ringworm.

Other articles to read include: **Athlete's foot; Disease; Skin.**

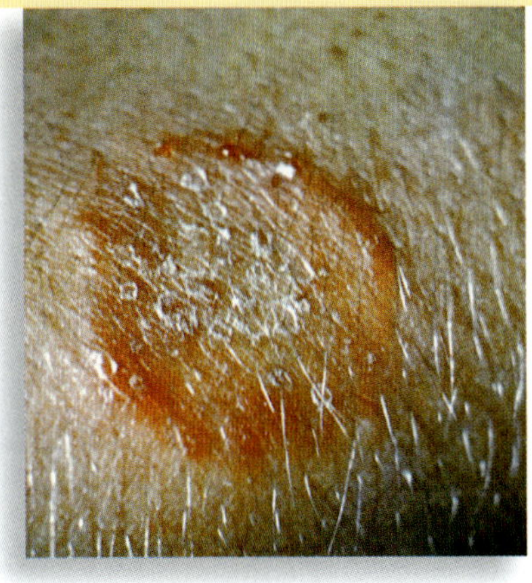

Ringworm may begin with a small red spot on the skin. As the spot grows, its center clears up, leaving a red ring.

RNA

RNA is a complex *molecule* found in living things. Molecules are units of matter made up of atoms. The letters *RNA* stand for *r*ibo*n*ucleic *(RY boh noo KLEE ihk) a*cid. RNA plays a major role in all living cells. It helps produce substances called *proteins.* Living cells use proteins to build themselves and carry out their work.

RNA is similar in structure to *DNA*, another important molecule found in cells. Both molecules contain hundreds of smaller chemical units. The order of these units can act as a code, carrying instructions for making proteins.

Different types of RNA do different jobs in the cell. *Messenger RNA* copies the instructions from DNA for making proteins. Other kinds of RNA speed *chemical reactions* inside the cell. A chemical reaction is when one or more chemicals changes into one or more other chemicals.

Other articles to read include: **Cell; DNA; Protein.**

Rubella

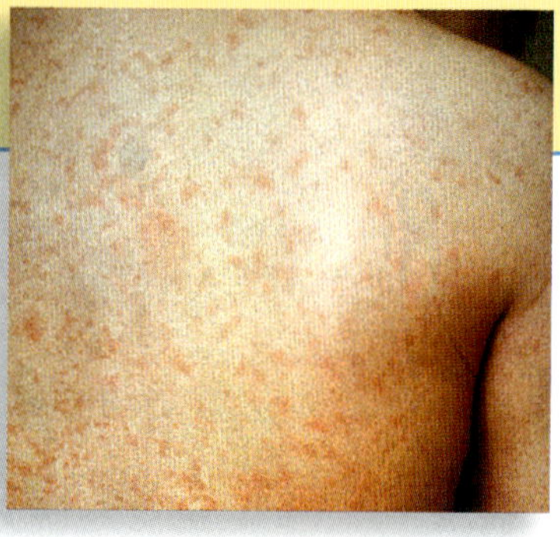

A rash caused by the rubella virus covers the back of a child. The virus can be spread to other people from about seven days before the rash develops to about five days after it disappears.

Rubella *(roo BEHL uh)* is a disease caused by a tiny living thing called a *virus*. It is spread when someone who has rubella coughs or sneezes. The illness is also known as *German measles*.

People who get rubella usually get it when they are children or teenagers. These people may have a low fever, sore throat, and runny nose. Swelling may occur in the neck and behind the ears. A large red rash may also develop.

Young people who have rubella usually do not get very sick. They can go back to school about a week after the rash goes away. But rubella can be dangerous for a woman who is expecting a baby. The baby may be born with such problems as bad eyesight or a bad heart.

In 1969, scientists developed a *vaccine (VAK seen)* (special shot) to prevent rubella. Most children get the shot at about 15 months old and then again at 4 years old or older.

Other articles to read include: **Cough; Disease; Immunization; Measles; Skin; Sneezing; Virus.**

Saliva is made by three pairs of glands inside the mouth and cheeks. One pair is in front of the ears. Another pair is under the jaw, and a third pair is under the tongue.

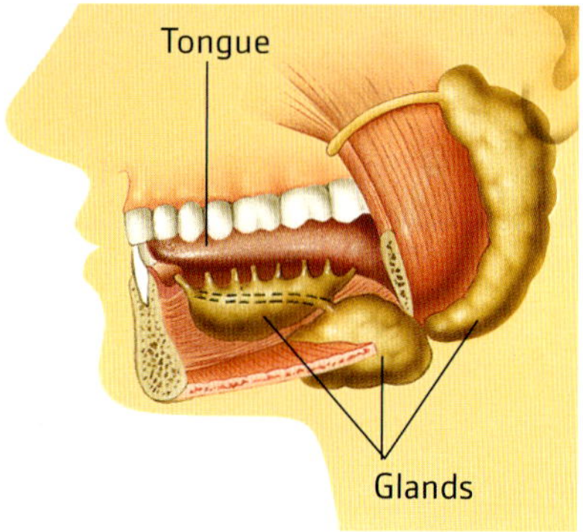

Saliva

Saliva is a sticky liquid made in the mouth. It helps *digest,* or break down, food. Saliva looks clear and watery, but it contains a slimy liquid called *mucus (MYOO kuhs)*. Saliva helps protect the body from the acids that are in some foods and drinks. It also contains a material that breaks down starch in foods.

Saliva moistens and softens the food people eat. It helps people chew and swallow. It also keeps the mouth from getting dry.

Three pairs of body parts called *glands* inside the mouth and cheeks make saliva. One pair is in front of the ears. Another pair is under the jaw, and a third pair is under the tongue. There are several other small glands in the mucous membrane of the mouth that also help make saliva.

Other articles to read include: **Digestive system; Gland; Food; Mucus; Teeth; Tongue.**

Salk, Jonas Edward

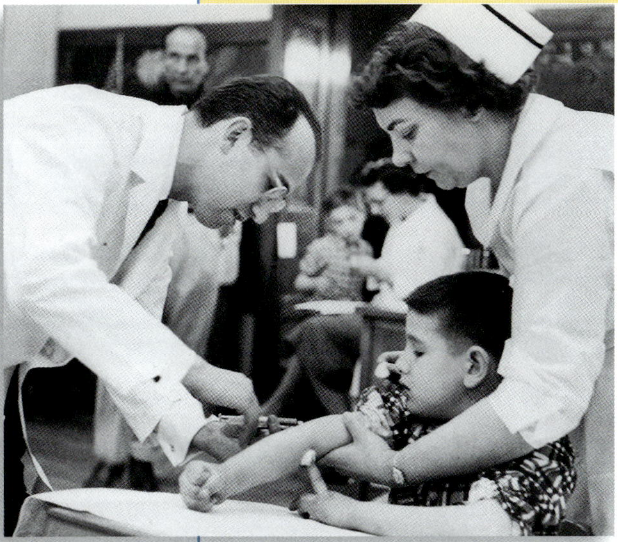

Jonas E. Salk gives a young boy an injection of his polio vaccine during its testing in 1954. Salk's vaccine was the first to successfully prevent the feared disease.

Jonas Edward Salk (1914–1995) was an American scientist. He developed the first *vaccine* that prevented a crippling disease called *polio.* A vaccine is a substance that keeps people from getting sick from a certain disease.

Salk was born in New York City. He graduated from the New York University School of Medicine in 1939. Then he began to study germs called *viruses* that caused flu and polio. When he began his work, outbreaks of polio were common. The disease was greatly feared because it left many patients paralyzed for life.

Many scientists had studied what makes people *immune (ih MYOON),* or protected, from catching diseases. Salk learned from their work. He used what he learned to make a polio vaccine. He had to weaken the virus that caused polio but not destroy it completely. When Salk injected the weakened virus into a patient, it would not cause the disease. But the weakened virus would cause the person's immune system to protect against polio. The immune systems would then make proteins called *antibodies* to fight the disease.

In 1953, Salk tried out the vaccine on himself, his wife, and his three sons. It was safe and seemed to work. In 1954, the vaccine was tested on nearly 2 million children. It was a success, and Salk received many honors. He would not take any money awards, and he went back to work to improve his vaccine.

Salk spent much of life teaching. In 1963, an institute was started in his name in California, and he continued his work there. He died on June 23, 1995.

Other articles to read include: **Antibody; Immune system; Immunization; Paralysis; Poliomyelitis; Virus.**

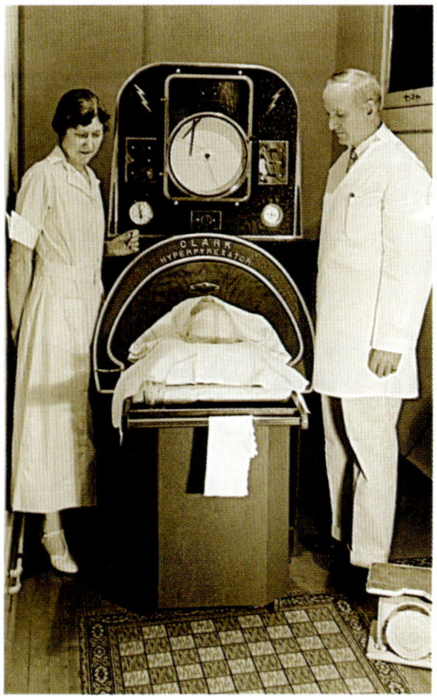

Before Salk developed a vaccine for the disease, polio left many people paralyzed. The disease could paralyze the breathing muscles, confining the patient to an artificial breathing device called an *iron lung* (right).

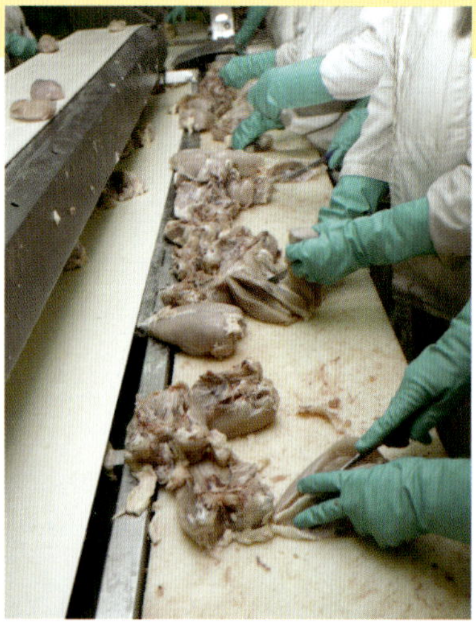

People can get salmonellosis by taking in food or water contaminated with *Salmonella* bacteria. Chicken and other poultry may become contaminated in food processing facilities.

Salmonellosis

Salmonellosis *(SAL muh nuh LOH sihs)* is a common type of food poisoning. It is often called *salmonella* because it results from infection by certain types of bacteria called *Salmonella.* People get salmonellosis from eating food or drinking water containing these bacteria. Most often, people get salmonella from poultry, milk, eggs, and egg products. Other types of *Salmonella* bacteria can cause other infectious diseases. For example, the *Salmonella typhi* bacterium causes a serious disease called *typhoid fever.*

Salmonellosis is usually confined to the intestines. The bacteria cause symptoms of the disease by releasing a *toxin* (poison). The toxin causes the secretion of fluids in the small intestine, producing diarrhea. Other symptoms of salmonellosis include nausea, abdominal pain, and fever.

Most adults who get salmonellosis recover in two to five days. The disease may last longer and be more severe in infants and elderly people. Severe cases are sometimes treated with antibiotics. People can best prevent salmonellosis by refrigerating prepared foods, thoroughly cooking foods that may carry the bacteria, and carefully washing their hands before meals.

Other articles to read include: **Bacteria; Disease; Food poisoning; Food preservation; Intestine; Toxin; Typhoid fever.**

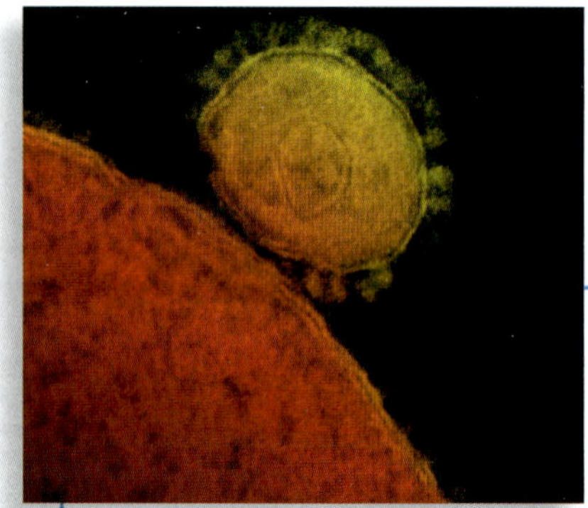

The kind of germ that causes SARS is called a *coronavirus.* Under a microscope, the virus looks like a tiny crown.

SARS

SARS is a *respiratory (REHS puhr uh TAWR ee)* (breathing) disease. It was first recognized in human beings in 2003. *SARS* stands for *s*evere *a*cute *r*espiratory *s*yndrome.

Symptoms (signs) of SARS include a high fever followed by coughing and breathing problems. In some people, SARS leads to *pneumonia (noo MOHN yuh),* a lung disease.

The first SARS outbreak started in China in November 2002. At first, doctors did not recognize SARS as a new illness. They believed it was a *strain* (type) of *influenza (IHN flu EHN zuh),* or flu. Several months later, SARS was discovered to be a new disease. By then, it had spread to several countries. Scientists do not know exactly how or where SARS began. They think the disease may have originated in bats.

Other articles to read include: **Cough; Disease; Fever; Lung; Pneumonia; Respiration; Virus.**

Scarlet fever

Scarlet fever is a disease. It affects mostly children. It can spread from person to person. Its name comes from the bright red skin rash it causes. People get scarlet fever from a type of germ called *bacteria*. The bacteria makes a poison. The poison can affect the skin, the tongue, and the throat.

Scarlet fever was once a serious and widespread disease. Since the 1950's, fewer people have gotten the disease. This is because of the use of *antibiotics* (germ-killing drugs).

Scarlet fever sometimes occurs along with another disease called *strep throat*. People with both diseases have a sore throat, fever, and headache. The tongue may become very red. Most of the time, the disease disappears after two weeks.

Other articles to read include: **Antibiotic; Bacteria; Disease; Skin; Tongue.**

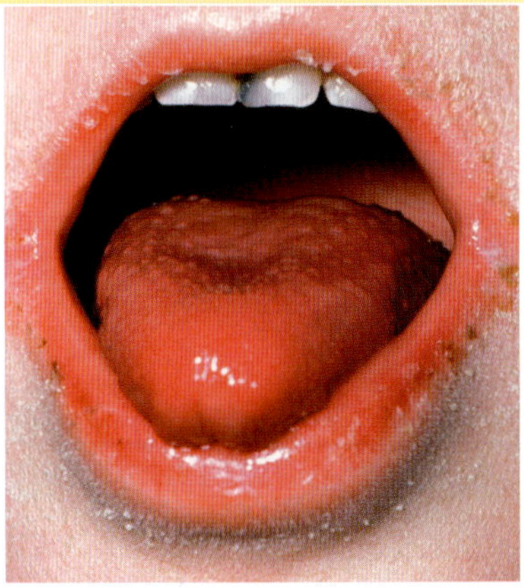

Scarlet fever may cause the tongue to become very red, called ***strawberry tongue***.

Schizophrenia

Schizophrenia *(SKIHT suh FREE nee uh)* is a severe mental disease. People with schizophrenia have unpredictable disturbances in thinking. The word *schizophrenia* means a *splitting of the mind*. It means that the mind is split from reality. It does not mean that a person has more than one personality.

Schizophrenia is one of the most common mental disorders. It starts usually in the late teens to mid-20's. Men get it earlier than women. It is often more severe in men.

Many people with schizophrenia behave as though they live in a fantasy world. They may hear "voices" that others cannot hear. The patients may believe that the "voices" are messages from important people, even from God. Some people with schizophrenia may display odd emotions, such as laughing at sad situations. Some patients withdraw from family and friends.

Doctors do not know what causes schizophrenia. They know that it involves chemicals in the brain. But they think other factors are also involved.

Scientists have developed drugs to reduce the disease's effects. As a result, most patients do not have to be hospitalized.

Other articles to read include: **Emotion; Mental illness; Mind; Psychiatry.**

Astronomy is the scientific study of the universe. Some astronomers use huge telescopes to view faraway objects in space.

Science

Science is the study of why and how things happen. It includes everything people do to learn about the world, especially about nature. People who do this kind of study are called *scientists.* They study many different subjects. For example, scientists try to find out how the universe started and how plants and animals live and grow.

Science is important in our lives today. Most modern *technology (tehk NAHL uh jee)* is based on science. Technology includes all the tools, materials, machines, and sources of power that make our lives easier.

Modern science and technology have changed the world in many ways. Airplanes, cars, computers, plastics, and television are only a few of the inventions that science and technology have brought us. Farmers can grow many more crops because scientists have created better plants and fertilizers. New drugs and medicines help doctors treat many serious diseases.

Science and technology have also created some serious problems, however. Factories and cars cause air and water pollution. Nuclear weapons can kill millions of people.

Science can be divided into four major branches, or groups. These branches are (1) mathematics, (2) the physical sciences, (3) the life sciences, and (4) the social sciences.

Mathematics is a tool needed for all scientific study. Scientists use mathematics to describe their work and their findings. They also use mathematics to figure out what might happen in the future.

The physical sciences are the study of the physical world around us. They include the basic sciences of physics and chemistry. They also include sciences that study a certain part of the physical world. These parts include such things as the outside universe, studied in *astronomy;* the Earth, *geology;* and the oceans, *oceanography.* Scientists also study the forces that make these things behave in certain ways.

The life sciences are the study of living things. The life

Continued on the next page

sciences are also called *biology (by AHL uh jee).* Some biologists study the parts of living things and how they work together. Others study how living things pass their own appearance and behavior on to their young. Some biologists study certain types of living things, such as birds or fish. Other biologists study the living things in a certain environment. For example, a *marine biologist* studies plants and animals that live in the sea.

The social sciences deal with people. They look at human relationships and how people treat one another. Social scientists study many areas of human life. They learn about our physical appearance and functions, how we produce goods and use money, how we make and follow laws, and how our thoughts and feelings affect our behavior.

Scientists use certain steps in their work. These steps are often called the *scientific method.* One of the oldest steps in the scientific method is looking carefully at nature. For example, the ancient Egyptians and other early people watched the movements of the stars and planets. What they saw helped them figure out when the seasons would change.

Doing experiments is another important step in the scientific method. Scientists do experiments to test their ideas and learn about the laws of nature. During the late 1500's, the Italian scientist Galileo did experiments to study how things speed up as they fall. In his experiments, Galileo rolled balls of different weights down slopes to find out how long they took to reach the bottom. His experiments showed that all falling objects speed up at the same rate.

Another step in the scientific method is forming a *hypothesis (hy PAH thuh sihs).* A hypothesis is an opinion about how a scientific experiment will turn out. Scientists form a hypothesis using information they already have. Then they do an experiment to test the hypothesis.

From earliest times, people have wanted to know more about the world around them. Thousands of years ago, people learned

Continued on the next page

Archaeology **is the scientific study of human cultures in the past. This archaeologist is studying paintings from Ancient Egypt.**

A scientist makes a new material by coating a piece of metal with a thin layer of diamond. Modern science often makes use of complex technology.

An *ecologist* takes water samples from a stream. Ecology is a science concerned with the relationships among living things and their environment.

Science *Continued from the previous page*

to count, and they made up stories to explain the rising and setting of the sun. They studied the behavior of animals they hunted. They learned that some plants could be used as medicine, and they collected other simple knowledge about nature. Learning about these things was the beginning of science. Mathematics and medicine were the first sciences. They were followed by the physical sciences, life sciences, and social sciences.

Over the centuries, scientists have learned a great deal about our world. The science of today and tomorrow will tell us more about the universe.

People often disagree about how scientific knowledge should be used, however. In the future, scientists and non-scientists will need to work together to make sure that scientific knowledge is used in the best possible ways.

Other articles to read include: **Aerospace medicine; Animal experimentation; Anthropology; Archaeology; Biology; Biomedical engineering; Classification, Scientific; Genetics; Marine biology; Medicine.**

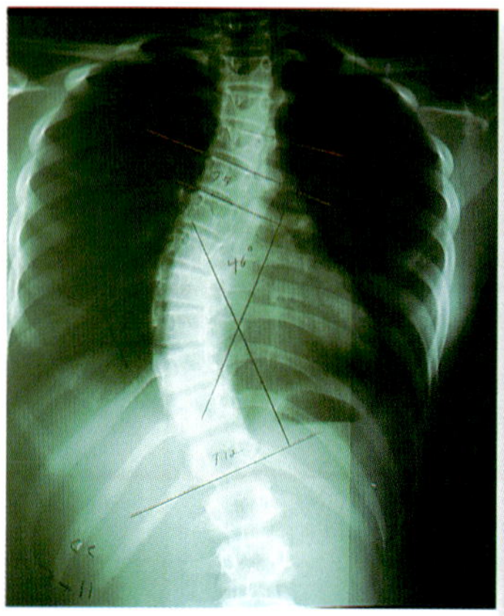

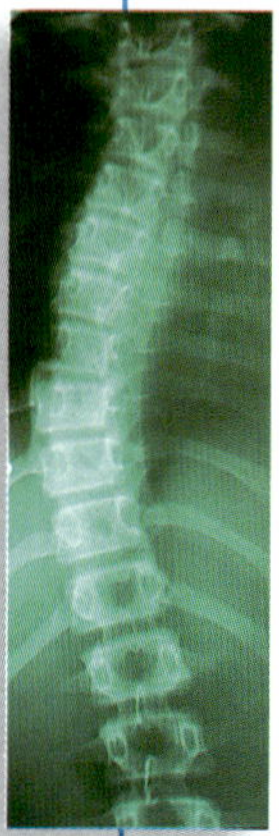

Scoliosis is an abnormal sideways curve of the spine. These X-ray images show a back view (above) and side view (above right) of a person with scoliosis.

Scoliosis

Scoliosis *(SKOH lee OH sihs)* is a sideways curve of the spine. In most cases, doctors notice scoliosis before a person becomes a teenager. It affects more girls than boys. If scoliosis is not corrected, it may affect the heart, lungs, and nervous system. Doctors do not know what causes most cases.

Many people have some form of scoliosis, but only a very few people need to be treated by a doctor. Some cases are simply examined to make sure they do not become worse. Physicians usually have people with scoliosis wear a back brace and do special exercises.

If a doctor finds the scoliosis early enough, there is no need to operate. Many schools test all students between 10 and 15 years old for scoliosis.

Other articles to read include: **Bone; Disease; Spine.**

Scurvy

Scurvy is a disease caused by a lack of vitamin C. Foods rich in vitamin C include citrus fruits, tomatoes, lettuce, celery, onions, carrots, and potatoes. Eating such foods will prevent or cure scurvy. If a person does not get enough vitamin C, wounds will heal poorly, the gums will bleed, and the teeth may become loose. The person will bruise easily and have sore joints. If left untreated, scurvy can cause death.

Scurvy has been known since ancient times. It was once common among sailors. During long voyages, sailors rarely had fresh fruits and vegetables. They lived on salt beef and dry biscuits for weeks at a time. The Portuguese navigator Vasco da Gama once lost about 100 of 170 of his crewmen to scurvy. In 1753, James Lind, a Scottish doctor, showed that eating oranges and lemons would cure scurvy, and that adding lemon juice to the diet would prevent the disease. In 1795, the British Navy followed his advice and began giving its men daily rations of juice. Today, scurvy is rare.

Other articles to read include: **Disease; Food; Fruit; Nutrition; Vitamin.**

Orange juice is a rich source of vitamin C. Including foods with vitamin C in the diet may prevent or cure scurvy.

Senility

Senility *(suh NIHL uh tee)* is a term sometimes used to describe memory loss and decreased mental ability among the elderly. A person with memory loss is sometimes said to be *senile (SEE nyl).* But most experts avoid using the term *senile* to describe people.

People with memory loss and decreased mental ability may forget the time and where they are. They may not recall common facts or recognize people they know. These problems may be signs of another condition. If a person is thought to be senile, the person and family members should seek a doctor's advice. In many cases, the problems can be improved by medical treatment.

Alzheimer's disease is commonly associated with senility. This disease gradually destroys brain cells. Many other conditions can produce senility. These conditions include other illnesses, head injury, medications, depression, and poor nutrition.

Other articles to read include: **Aging; Alzheimer's disease; Brain; Memory.**

Senses

Senses are how we learn what is happening around us. They include the five main senses of (1) hearing, (2) sight, (3) smell, (4) taste, and (5) touch. They also include senses that tell us about the position, movement, and needs of the body, such as balance, hunger, thirst, and pain.

Our senses are divided into two main groups. *External senses* tell us about things that occur far from the body and that come in contact with it. *Internal senses* give us information about changes that occur inside our bodies.

Scientists divide the senses into two groups. These groups are (1) *external senses* and (2) *internal senses.*

Our external senses tell us about things outside the body. Some external senses—including senses of sight, hearing, and heat—can tell us about things that happen far from the body. Other external senses—such as taste, touch, and smell—involve things that make contact with the body.

Our internal senses tell us about changes that take place inside the body. They send messages about such changes to the

Continued on the next page

The external senses of hearing and sight tell us about things that happen far from the body. The external senses of taste, touch, and smell tell us about things that come in contact with the body. This drawing shows where the some of the *receptors* of these senses are concentrated.

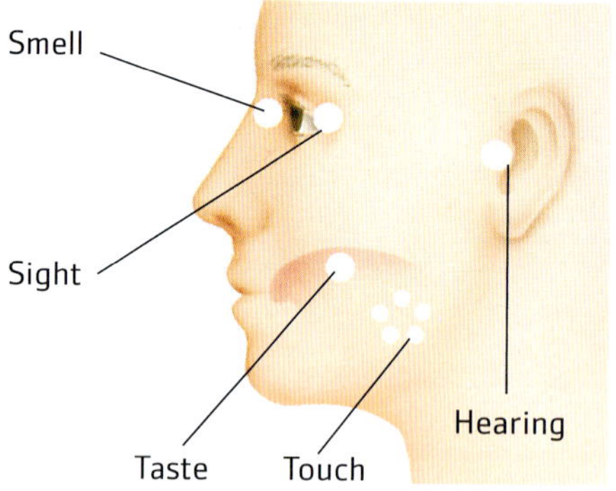

External senses and their receptors

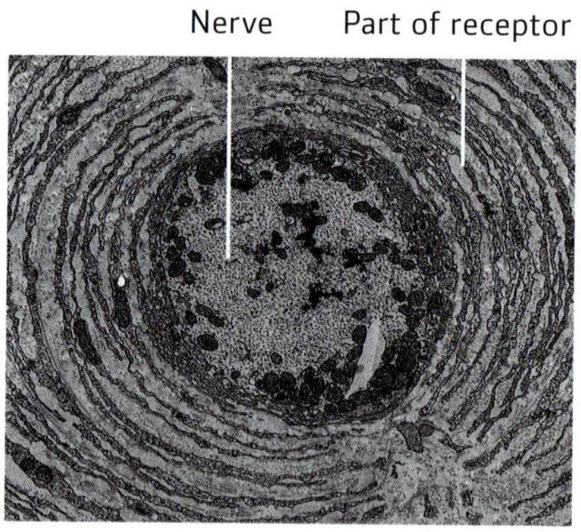

The end of a nerve is magnified 2,000 times in this image. The nerve leads from a touch receptor.

The internal senses send messages to the brain about changes inside the body. These senses control such feelings as fatigue, hunger, pain, and thirst. They also respond to tension in the muscles. This drawing shows the receptors that sense tension in muscle fibers.

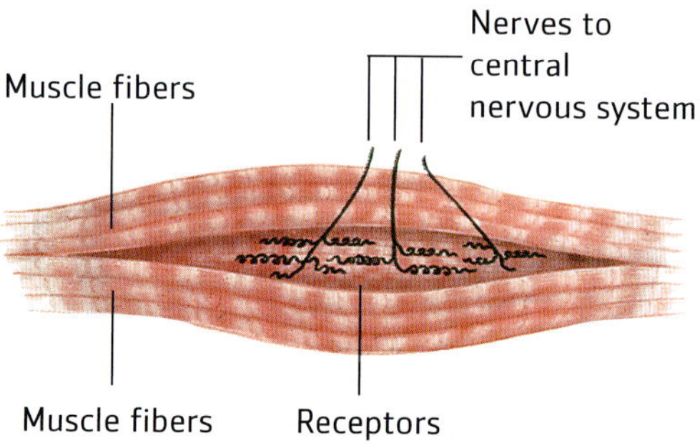

Receptors of the internal sense of muscular tension

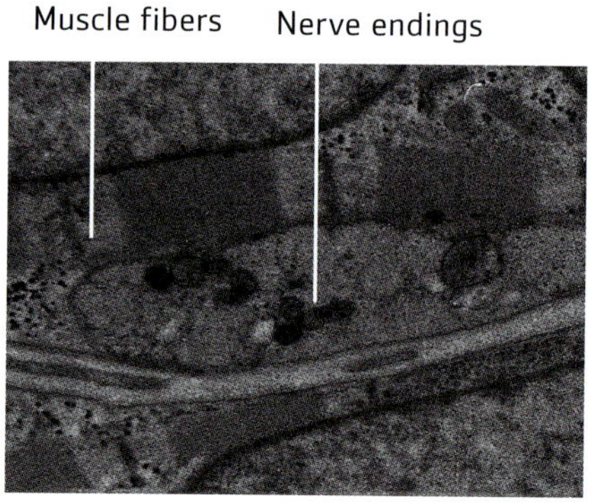

Nerves of a muscle tension receptor, magnified 6,000 times in this image, connect to muscle fibers.

brain. For example, these senses tell us when we are hungry, thirsty, tired, or in pain. Our internal senses also react to changes in our muscles. When we move our head, arms, or legs, our internal senses keep track of what is happening inside the body.

Some animals react to things that people do not even notice. These animals have senses that are more easily affected than the senses of people. For example, some animals can hear sounds that are too high or too low for people to hear. Other animals can see types of light that we cannot see. Still others can sense electric currents or magnetic forces that we cannot sense.

Other articles to read include: **Blindness; Deafness; Ear; Eye; Hearing; Nervous system; Nose; Optical illusion; Pain; Smell; Taste; Tongue; Touch; Vision.**

People experience the world around them through the senses.

Serum

Serum *(SIHR uhm)* is a part of the blood left after a clot forms. Serum is a clear liquid. It is similar to *plasma*, the clear liquid part of the blood. But unlike plasma, serum does not contain substances that cause blood to clot. Doctors sometimes take samples of serum from a person. They can check the samples for certain diseases and other medical problems.

Serum contains salt, proteins, sugars, fats, and other substances. It also contains *antibodies*. Antibodies are proteins that the body makes to fight diseases and poisons.

Doctors sometimes take a serum containing antibodies from a person or animal. They then inject it into a patient. Such a treatment is called an *antiserum*. Antiserums are used to prevent rabies. They are also used to treat poisonous snake and spider bites.

Other articles to read include: **Antibody; Blood; Blood clot; Circulatory system; Plasma.**

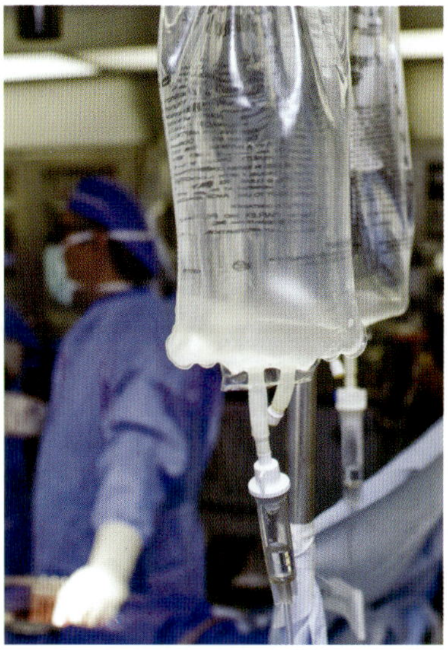

When blood serum is lost through injury, patients in a hospital may receive special liquids to replace it.

Adolescence is a time when most people establish their inner sense of being male or female, a strong component of sexuality.

Sexuality

Sexuality is everything that distinguishes a person as either male or female. Human beings are typically born male or female. Physical differences of the sexes play an important role in determining our sexuality. But sexuality also involves our inner sense of being a male or female, as well as ways of behaving.

Sexuality influences how we view our roles in life, especially in family relationships, at school, in the workplace, and in our community. Sexuality helps define our attitudes about love and sexual relationships. It partially determines who we are sexually attracted to and how we express ourselves within a relationship.

Biological factors are an obvious influence on sexuality. The physical features of males differ from those of females. Personal beliefs, emotions, and feelings also influence our sexuality. As young children, we develop a concept of ourselves as either male or female. We also learn how a person of our sex is expected to act in society. Attitudes about sexuality vary widely from culture to culture. Sometimes a person's concept of their own sexuality is not the same as their biological sex.

Other articles to read include: **Adolescent; Behavior; Homosexuality; Menstruation; Pregnancy; Reproduction, Human; Sexually transmitted disease.**

Sexually transmitted disease

A sexually transmitted disease is an illness that spreads through close sexual contact. It is often abbreviated STD. STD's are caused by bacteria, viruses, and other kinds of germs.

STD's are a major health problem around the world. *HIV,* the virus that causes AIDS, is a deadly sexually transmitted disease. Other common STD's include *chlamydia (kluh MIHD ee uh), gonorrhea (gon uh REE uh),* genital herpes, and syphilis.

People who think they may have an STD should see a doctor immediately. They should also stop all sexual activity. They should not resume until a doctor tells them there is no risk of infecting others.

Continued on the next page

The most effective way to avoid STD's is to not have sex. A person can also limit sexual contact to one person with no other sexual partners. People can reduce the risk of infection by using *condoms.* A condom is a protective sheath worn over the penis during sex. People can also reduce their risk by avoiding illegal drug use and *prostitutes.* Prostitutes are people who perform sex acts for money.

A person with an STD may have few or no *symptoms* (signs of illness). The person may need to get an STD test from a doctor.

Doctors use drugs called *antibiotics* to treat many STD's. Chlamydia, gonorrhea, and syphilis can be cured if the drugs are given soon enough. If a person does not receive treatment, they can get serious, even life-threatening problems.

STD's caused by viruses are incurable. These STD's include herpes and HIV. Patients may carry and spread these diseases for many years without developing symptoms.

Other articles to read include: **AIDS; Antibiotic; Disease; Sexuality.**

Shaken baby syndrome

Shaken baby syndrome is a pattern of severe injuries seen in infants. These injuries occur when an adult or older child shakes an infant violently. The most common injuries are bleeding into the brain and the eyeball. The injuries can kill a baby or cause permanent brain damage.

Shaken baby syndrome is difficult for doctors to detect. A shaken baby may seem less alert than usual. Shaken babies may also *vomit* (throw up) or have seizures. An eye examination may reveal blood in the eyeball. X rays and other tests may show bleeding in the brain. Shaken babies may also have bruises, bumps, or other signs of head injury. They may have broken bones, burns, or other signs of child abuse. Doctors suspect shaken baby syndrome if an examination fails to reveal another likely cause of these problems. They may also be suspicious if a caregiver cannot or will not explain how the baby got hurt.

Doctors report suspected cases of shaken baby syndrome to the police or other authorities. These authorities take steps to protect the baby from further abuse.

Other articles to read include: **Baby; Brain.**

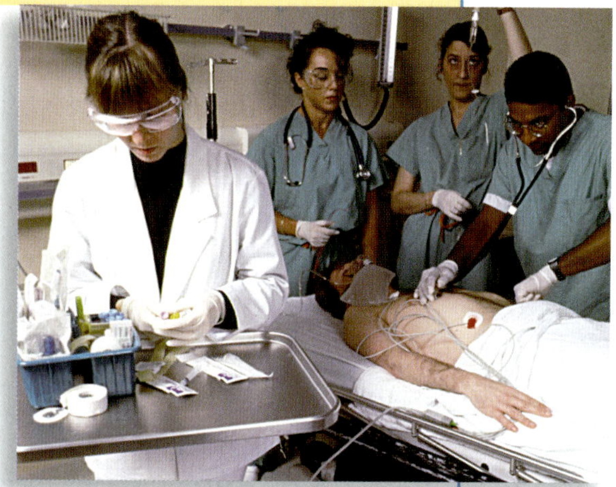

Doctors and nurses treat a patient with shock in a hospital's emergency room.

Shock

Shock happens when blood fails to flow through the body properly. Shock can occur with any serious illness or injury. It can also be caused by emotional strain. If shock lasts long enough, it can affect the important functions of the body. Shock that goes untreated can kill a person.

A person sweats heavily after going into shock. Also, the person may feel restless, sick, or anxious. In most cases, the heart beats faster and breathing becomes fast and uneven. Then, the brain does not receive enough blood, causing the person to fall unconscious.

It is important to keep a shock victim's body temperature normal. The victim should be warmed with blankets in cool conditions or shaded and cooled if it is hot.

Other articles to read include: **Blood; Consciousness; Emotion.**

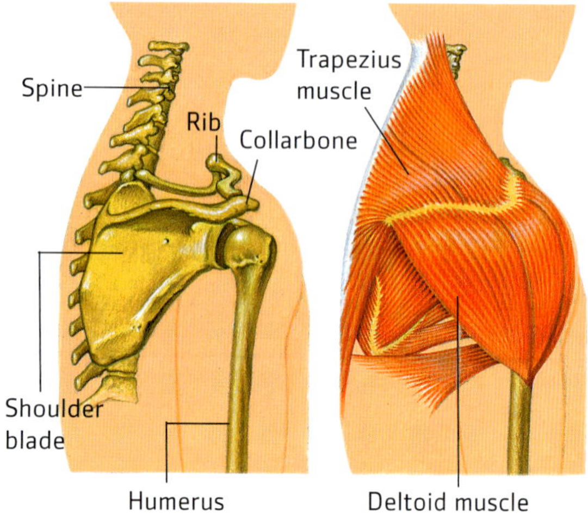

Parts of the shoulder include the *collarbone,* the *shoulder blade,* and the *humerus,* or upper arm bone (above left). The humerus forms a ball-and-socket joint with the shoulder blade. The *deltoid muscle,* one of the largest shoulder muscles, helps move the upper arm (above right). The *trapezius muscle* helps rotate the shoulder blade.

Shoulder

The shoulder is a part of a person's body between the neck and the arm. The bones and muscles that connect the arm to the body are part of the shoulder.

The shoulder is made up of three parts. They are (1) the shoulder blade, (2) the collarbone, and (3) the *humerus (HYOO muhr uhs)* (upper arm bone). The shoulder has two main muscles. They are the *deltoid (DEHL toyd) muscle* and the *trapezius (truh PEE zee uhs) muscle.* Both muscles help the shoulder move. They also help move the arm.

The shoulder is more flexible than any other part of the human body. The shoulder can also be easily hurt if a person falls or is pushed too hard from behind.

Other articles to read include: **Arm; Bone; Collarbone; Joint; Muscle.**

Sickle cell anemia

Sickle cell anemia *(uh NEE mee uh)* is also called *sickle cell disease*. It is a disease that a parent can pass on to a child. In the United States, it occurs mainly among African Americans. The disease causes pain and fever, problems related to blood flow, and *anemia*. Anemia is a condition in which the number of healthy red blood cells is low.

Sickle cell patients do not have the normal type of *hemoglobin (HEE muh GLOH buhn)*. Hemoglobin is the oxygen-carrying protein that gives red blood cells their color. The abnormal hemoglobin causes the red blood cells to change into twisted forms. These forms resemble sickles.

The best way to fight the disease is to find it early in life. Doctors can give people drugs to help them. Some young children with sickle cell anemia get *bone marrow* from another person in a transplant operation. Bone marrow is where blood cells come from.

Other articles to read include: **Anemia; Blood; Disease; Hemoglobin; Red blood cell.**

Sickle cell anemia is a disease that affects the red blood cells. It causes the cells to be shaped like sickles.

Sinus

A sinus *(SY nuhs)* is a space in the body of human beings and other animals. Sinuses are filled with air. The word *sinus* usually refers to hollow spaces in the front of the skull. There are four groups of sinuses in the human skull. They are found near the forehead, on the sides of the nose, and above the nasal cavity. The presence of sinuses helps to make the skull lighter. This makes it easier to hold the head up.

The sinuses are lined with *mucous (MYOO kuhs) membranes*, like those in the nose. Infections of the nose can spread to the sinuses. This can make the head and face hurt. It can also cause dizziness and runny nose. Rest and medicine cure most sinus infections.

Other articles to read include: **Headache; Mucus; Nose; Skull.**

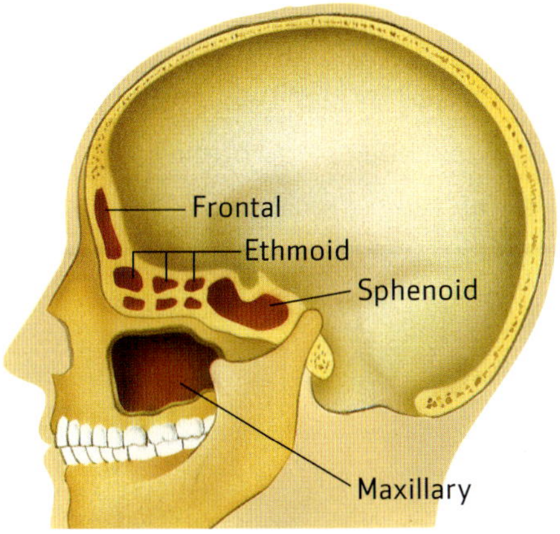

Humans have four groups of sinuses: the *frontal sinuses,* in the forehead; the *maxillary sinuses,* in the cheekbones; the *ethmoid sinuses,* above the nasal cavity; and the *sphenoid sinuses* behind them.

Skeleton

The skeleton is the framework of the body. In *vertebrates (VUR tuh brihts)* (animals with backbones), the skeleton is made up of all the bones inside the body. Human beings are a type of vertebrate.

The skeleton has several functions. It gives the body its shape. It protects the organs, such as the heart and the lungs. It works with the muscles to make the body move. The bones of the skeleton contain *bone marrow*, the tissue in which blood cells are made. The bones also store materials that the body needs to work. These materials include such chemical elements as calcium and phosphorus.

The human skeleton has about 206 bones. These bones fit together and are held in place by strong bands of tissue called *ligaments (LIHG uh muhnts)*.

Continued on the next page

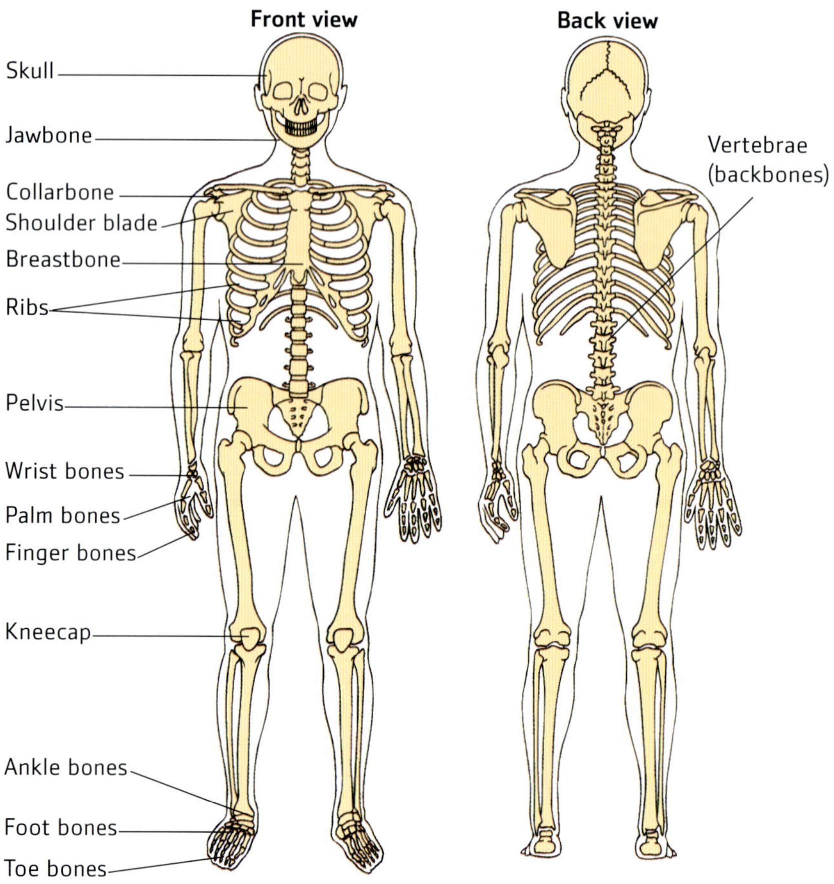

The *skeleton* is a strong, flexible framework that supports the body and protects the internal organs. It also provides a system of levers, operated by the muscles, that enables the body to move. The human skeleton consists of about 206 bones, some of which are *fused* (joined) in adults.

The bones are joined to other bones by joints. Some of the joints move and others do not move. The joints in the arms and legs can move, for example. But the joints of the skull—except for the jaws—cannot.

The skeletons of different kinds of vertebrates have a lot in common. For example, a giraffe's neck has the same number of bones as a mouse's neck. However, the giraffe's neck bones are longer and larger.

Many *invertebrates (ihn VUR tuh brihts)* (animals without backbones) have a type of skeleton called an *exoskeleton (EHK soh SKEHL uh tuhn)*. An exoskeleton is a hard, outside covering that supports and protects the soft parts inside the body. Invertebrates include such animals as insects, spiders, and lobsters.

Other articles to read include: **Ankle; Arm; Bone; Cartilage; Collarbone; Finger; Foot; Hand; Human body; Knee; Leg; Ligament; Muscle; Pelvis; Rib; Shoulder; Skull; Spine; Tendon; Wrist.**

Skin

Skin is the covering on the bodies of human beings and many other animals. Skin protects the body in many different ways.

Skin keeps important fluids inside the body. These fluids help keep the different parts of the body healthy. Skin also keeps certain harmful things, such as germs, out of the body.

Skin helps keep the body's temperature normal. It makes sweat when a person becomes hot. The sweat cools the body. Skin also helps keep heat inside the body when it is cold outside.

The color of skin comes from a substance called *melanin*. Skin has special cells that make melanin. The skin cells of dark-skinned people make more melanin than those of light-skinned people.

Other articles to read include: **Acne; Dermis; Epidermis; Freckle; Melanin; Mole; Perspiration; Plastic surgery; Skin cancer; Skin grafting; Sunburn; Touch; Wart.**

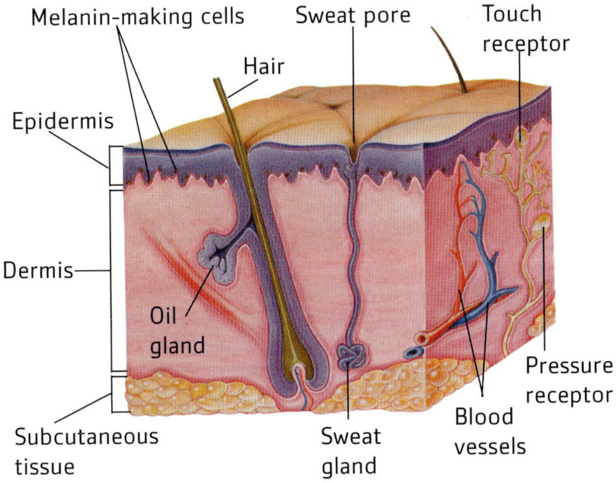

Skin consists of three layers: (1) the epidermis, (2) the dermis, and (3) subcutaneous *(suhb kyoo TAY nee uhs)* tissue. Skin also holds hair, sweat and oil glands, blood vessels, and many nerve endings, including receptors for touch and pressure.

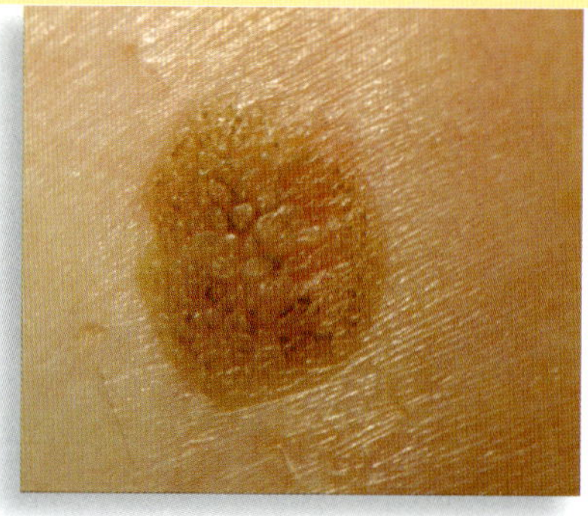

A skin cancer called *melanoma* arises among the cells that make the pigment that gives skin its natural color.

Overexposure to the sun's rays can lead to skin cancer. Doctors recommend that people protect exposed skin with a sunscreen when outdoors.

Skin cancer

Skin cancer is the uncontrolled multiplication of cells in the skin. Skin cancer is the most common form of cancer in the world.

Skin cells constantly multiply, making new cells to replace worn ones. But some things can damage skin, particularly the sun's rays. Sometimes, damaged skin cells multiply wildly, rather than in a normal, orderly manner. This uncontrolled multiplication is skin cancer.

Doctors recognize two types of skin cancer: *melanoma (*MEHL *uh NOH muh)* and *nonmelanoma*. Melanoma is the most serious type. It is a dangerous cancer that can spread to other parts of the body. If melanoma is found early, it can usually be cured by removing skin from the affected area. Nonmelanoma skin cancer seldom spreads. It is much easier to treat.

The best way to prevent skin cancer is to protect the skin from too much sun. Doctors recommend using sunscreen regularly and wearing protective clothing. They also recommend learning the warning signs of melanoma and examining the skin regularly. People should ask a doctor about any change in the skin that lasts longer than about three weeks.

Other articles to read include: **Cancer; Cell; Disease; Skin; Sunburn.**

Skin grafting

Skin grafting is an operation that uses replacement skin to cover wounds on the body. The skin used to cover the wound is called a *graft*. Skin grafts are especially useful in treating severe burns.

Most skin grafts use healthy skin from one part of the body to cover a wound on another part. The final result does not feel or appear exactly like normal, uninjured skin. But after a few years, the differences are usually slight.

Other articles to read include: **Burn; Skin; Surgery.**

Skinner, B. F.

B. F. Skinner (1904–1990) was an American scientist who studied the mind. He was best known for his ideas about how people learn.

Skinner was a leading supporter of *behaviorism*. Behaviorism is the idea that people's minds should be studied through their actions. Skinner studied animal behavior using a special cage called a *Skinner box*. He put animals in the box and gave them food or other rewards for performing certain actions.

Skinner also became famous for his belief in a *planned society*. In a planned society, people give up some freedoms to gain a better quality of life. Skinner described his ideas for a planned society in a popular book *Walden Two* (1948). He argued that individual freedoms should be limited for the good of society in another book, *Beyond Freedom and Dignity* (1971).

Skinner was born on March 20, 1904, in Susquehanna, Pennsylvania. His full name was Burrhus Frederic Skinner. He attended Hamilton College and Harvard University. He died on Aug. 18, 1990.

Other articles to read include: **Behavior; Learning; Mind; Psychology.**

B. F. Skinner, an American scientist, was best known for his research on how people learn.

The human skull has 22 bones. They make up the face and form a protective case surrounding the brain.

Skull

The skull is a group of connected bones that form the framework of the head. Skulls are found in all animals with backbones. The skull protects the brain from bumps and bruises.

When a baby is first born, its skull bones are soft. After a few years, the bones grow hard. They fit tightly together. The skull protects the brain from bumps and bruises.

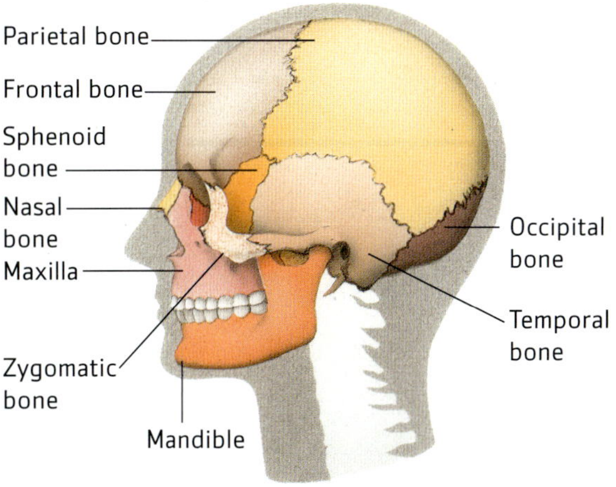

The human skull has 22 bones. Eight bones make up the *cranium (KRAY nee uhm),* which surrounds the brain. The other 14 bones make up the face and jaw. They are called *facial bones.*

Animal skulls are shaped to suit each animal's way of life. For example, wolves have long jaws. This helps them hold and tear their *prey* (animals hunted for food).

Other articles to read include: **Bone; Brain; Mandible; Nose.**

People typically sleep lying down with eyes closed. A sleeping person may change position and awaken briefly several times a night.

Sleep

Sleep is a state of rest. A person who is sleeping is no longer aware of his or her surroundings. All human beings and many kinds of animals need a certain amount of sleep each day.

When a person falls asleep, the body's actions slow down. The muscles relax and the heartbeat slows. The person's breathing slows, too.

Sometimes during sleep, the brain works very fast. The sleeper's eyes move very quickly under the closed eyelids, as if they were watching a dream.

Most human adults sleep 7 to 8 ½ hours every night. But everyone needs a different amount of sleep. Children need more sleep than do adults.

Different kinds of animals have different sleep patterns. Animals that are active at night sleep during the day.

Other articles to read include: **Consciousness; Dream; Insomnia.**

Sleeping sickness

Sleeping sickness is a disease that attacks the nervous system. In severe cases, it causes a person to sleep for long periods. The disease is often deadly if untreated. Sleeping sickness occurs only in Africa. There, it is a serious health problem for both people and animals. It can affect horses and cattle, making farming impossible in some areas.

Sleeping sickness is caused by single-celled *parasites,* tiny living things that can infect the body. The parasites are spread by the *tsetse (TSEHT see) fly.* The fly becomes infected with parasites by feeding on the blood of an infected person or animal. A person becomes infected when bitten by an infected fly.

Most cases of sleeping sickness begin with fever, headache, and chills. These signs are followed by swelling in parts of the body, skin rash, and weakness. In severe cases, the parasites infect the brain. This causes deep sleep, coma, and death.

Other articles to read include: **Disease; Fever; Headache; Nervous system; Sleep.**

Smallpox

Smallpox was one of the most feared diseases in history. In the 1900's alone, smallpox killed more than 300 million people. It scarred and blinded millions more. Smallpox was also the first disease to be wiped out in nature by human beings.

Smallpox was caused by a virus that infects only human beings. It spread from person to person through the air. The disease was marked by aches, fever, and a rash of small, painful pimples called *pox*.

In 1796, the British doctor Edward Jenner developed a vaccine to prevent smallpox, the world's first vaccine. The vaccine's use quickly spread to other parts of the world. But smallpox continued to exist almost everywhere until the 1960's. International health organizations then began a program to wipe out smallpox. By 1980, the disease had been eliminated worldwide.

Other articles to read include: **Disease; Immunization; Jenner, Edward; Virus.**

Edward Jenner (above) developed a vaccine to prevent smallpox in 1796. By 1980, the disease had been eliminated worldwide.

Smell

Smell is an important sense in human beings and other animals. Human beings use smell for many things. For example, our sense of smell helps us taste food. When our noses are stuffed up, it is harder to taste food. Some animals use their sense of smell to identify their home and to recognize other animals. They also use smell to find food.

People and other animals notice smells by breathing or sniffing air that carries odors. Odors come from tiny *particles* (bits) that have been let out into the air from many different things. These particles cause special cells in the nose to send messages to the brain. When the brain gets these messages, it senses the smell.

Other articles to read include: **Brain; Nose; Senses; Taste.**

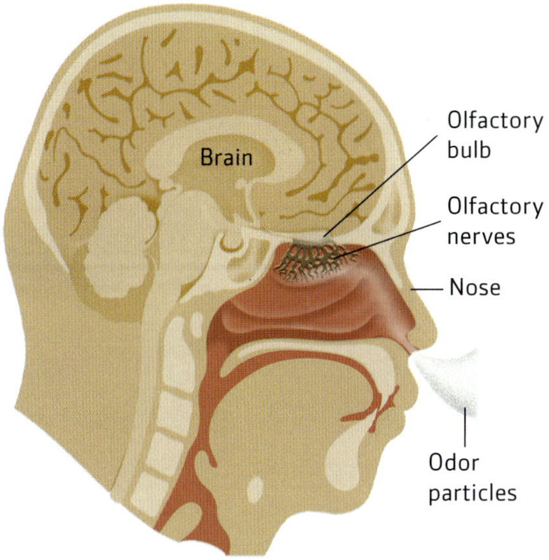

Odor particles travel through the nose and stimulate *olfactory nerves.* The nerves send impulses to the *olfactory bulb,* which relays the message to the brain.

EXPERIMENT

Test your sense of smell

1. Prepare a number of different "smell" jars by placing a small bit of each food or spice in each jar. Don't let the players see them.

2. Have each player put on a blindfold. Open a jar and allow each player to smell it.

3. After every player has smelled the jar, ask each one to name the smell.

4. Repeat with the different smell jars. Take turns being the tester.

After the players have smelled all the jars, ask them which smells were easiest to identify.

What you need:

- a blindfold for each player
- 10 small jars with lids
- 10 different foods or spices that have strong odors, such as vanilla, peanut butter, onion, sage, cinnamon, and peppermint

http://bit.ly/12M4huS

Sneezing

Sneezing is a sudden rush of air out of the nose and mouth. A person cannot control sneezing. The body sneezes to get rid of tiny, bothersome objects in the nose. Special cells in the nose react to such objects by causing the sneeze.

A condition called *hay fever* also makes people sneeze. Hay fever happens when pollen—a powder from flowers—gets inside the nose and causes sneezing.

Sneezing helps the body. However, it can be harmful to other people. For example, the sneezer's nose may be full of germs. Sneezing helps clear the nose. But unless the sneezer covers the mouth and nose, the germs go out into the air. Then they may make others sick.

Other articles to read include: **Allergy; Cold, Common; Cough; Disease; Germ; Nose.**

A sneeze sends a cloud of droplets into the air, potentially spreading germs. Covering sneezes and coughs can help prevent the spread of colds and other diseases.

Sociobiology

Sociobiology is a branch of science that uses ideas from biology to explain social behavior. Scientists who specialize in sociobiology are called *sociobiologists.* They may study animal behavior to understand why people behave in certain ways.

Sociobiologists try to understand social behavior by studying the influence of *genes.* Genes determine how each living thing will develop. All living things pass on genes to their offspring. Understanding the influence of genes can help to explain behaviors that might otherwise be puzzling.

For example, a sociobiologist might ask why worker bees sting to defend their hives. When the bee stings an attacker, it dies. Animals usually do not sacrifice themselves to save others. But in this case, the sacrifice helps protect the queen bee, who is the mother of all the workers. The queen and the workers share many genes. Thus, even though they die, the workers help make sure their genes are passed on. Human beings also sacrifice themselves to protect other people. People are likelier to make such sacrifices for their close relatives. Sociobiologists argue that such behavior shows the influence of genes.

Other articles to read include: **Behavior; Biology; Gene.**

Species

A species is a particular kind of living thing. It is the most basic unit of *scientific classification*. Scientific classification is the way scientists arrange living things into groups. All the living things placed in a particular group are alike in certain ways because they share a common ancestor.

Members of a species are similar in many ways. For example, human beings make up a species. Human beings have much more in common with one another than they do with members of other species. For example, chimpanzees are another species. They rank among the closest living relatives of human beings. Still, chimpanzees and humans have many differences. They are easy to tell apart.

In general, only members of a species can reproduce with one another. For example, human parents produce human children. But a chimpanzee could never give birth to a human child.

Scientists identify each species with a scientific name made up of two words. Each word is usually in the language of Latin or Greek. The scientific name for human beings is *Homo sapiens.* These are Latin words that mean *wise human being.*

Other articles to read include: **Classification, Scientific; Darwin, Charles Robert; Human being.**

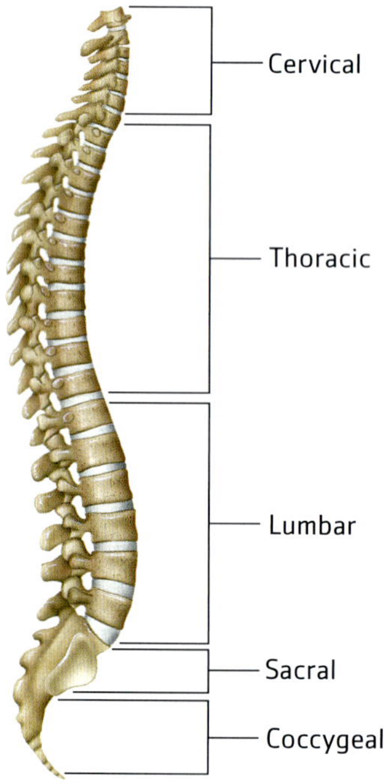

The human spine is made up of 33 small bones called *vertebrae.* The different kinds of vertebrae are named for their position along the spine.

Spine

The spine is the part of the skeleton that runs down the center of the back in human beings and many other animals. The human spine helps the body to stay *erect* (straight up) and to move. It also protects the *spinal cord*, a bundle of nerves that runs from the neck down the back. The spinal cord carries information between various parts of the body and the brain.

In human beings, the spine is made up of 33 *vertebrae (VUR tuh bree).* Vertebrae are small bones shaped somewhat like cylinders. They fit together in a way that allows the head to swivel and the body to twist and turn. The vertebrae are separated by thin disks of a jellylike material that keeps the bones from rubbing together.

Other articles to read include: **Bone; Nervous system; Scoliosis; Skeleton.**

Spleen

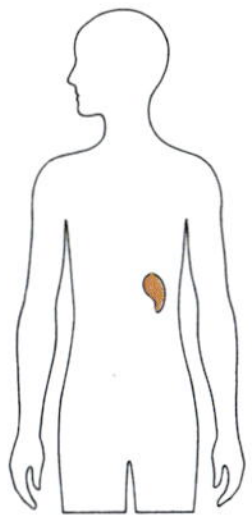

The spleen is a spongy, purplish organ found behind and to the left of the stomach in human beings. In other *vertebrates* (animals with backbones), the spleen is near the stomach or intestine.

A person's spleen is about the size of his or her fist. It helps *filter* (remove) useless substances from the blood. Blood passes through the spleen, where special cells destroy old or damaged blood cells.

The spleen also helps the body fight infection. White blood cells in the spleen release substances called *antibodies* that weaken or kill germs that can cause infection.

Other articles to read include: **Antibody; Blood; Red blood cell; White blood cell.**

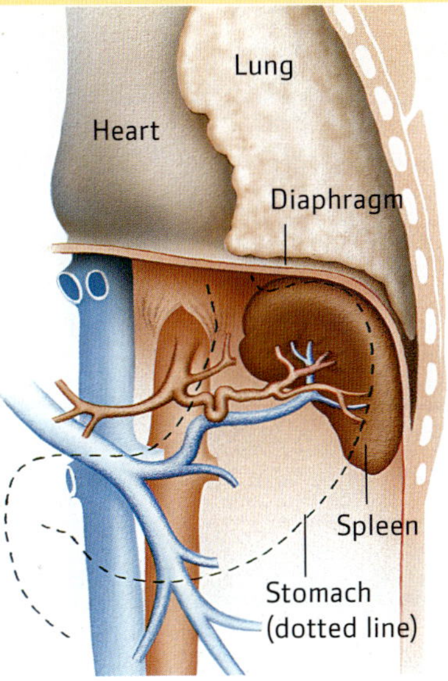

The *spleen* is a spongy organ that filters foreign substances and damaged cells from the blood. It also stores red blood cells to be released into the bloodstream when needed.

Spock, Benjamin McLane

Benjamin McLane Spock (1903–1998) was an American *pediatrician*. A pediatrician is a doctor who works with children. Spock became famous for his books on child care. These books had a great influence on parents during the 1950's and 1960's.

Spock's best-known book was called the *Common Sense Book of Baby and Child Care* (1946). It was translated into more than 25 languages. Spock's other books include *Feeding Your Baby and Child* (1955), *Baby's First Year* (1955), *Dr. Spock Talks with Mothers* (1961), *Problems of Parents* (1962), and *Caring for Your Disabled Child* (1965).

Spock was born on May 2, 1903, in New Haven, Connecticut. He graduated from Yale University and received his medical degree from Columbia University. In the 1960's, Spock became an outspoken opponent of the Vietnam War (1957–1975). He died on March 15, 1998.

Other articles to read include: **Baby; Child; Pediatrics.**

Benjamin Spock, an American doctor, became famous worldwide for his books on child care.

Athletic trainers use knowledge from sports medicine to help people exercise and maintain physical fitness without injury.

Sports medicine

Sports medicine is a field that provides health care for physically active people. Its main purpose is to limit the risk of injury and to treat injuries that do occur. Sports medicine draws on the knowledge of many specialists, including physicians, athletic trainers, and physical educators.

Experts in sports medicine aid in determining the kind of training needed to help athletes perform to their highest level without injury. They also examine coaching methods, the enforcement of regulations, and the design and use of athletic equipment and sports fields and gyms. Sports medicine has led to improved research in finding the reason for, and treatment of, common problems, including knee and muscle injuries, that affect the general public as well as athletes.

Other articles to read include: **Exercise; Fitness; Medicine.**

Starvation

Starvation occurs when a living thing suffers from a severe lack of any food substance necessary for life. Essential food substances are called *nutrients*. There are six groups of nutrients: (1) carbohydrates, (2) fats, (3) minerals, (4) proteins, (5) vitamins, and (6) water. Nutrients provide energy for body processes and help build and maintain body tissues. Plants get energy from sunlight. Human beings and other animals get energy from *carbohydrates* (starches and sugars), fats, and proteins in food. Plants, human beings, and animals need minerals and water. Human beings and animals also need vitamins.

In humans, the most important nutrient is water. Death occurs when a person loses 20 percent of his or her total body water. Most people can live only about a week without water. How long a person can survive without food depends on the person's supply of body fat. Fat is the body's most important form of stored energy. Most people can live 60 to 70 days without food.

Other articles to read include: **Dehydration; Famine; Fat; Food; Malnutrition; Mineral; Nutrient; Protein; Vitamin.**

Stem cell

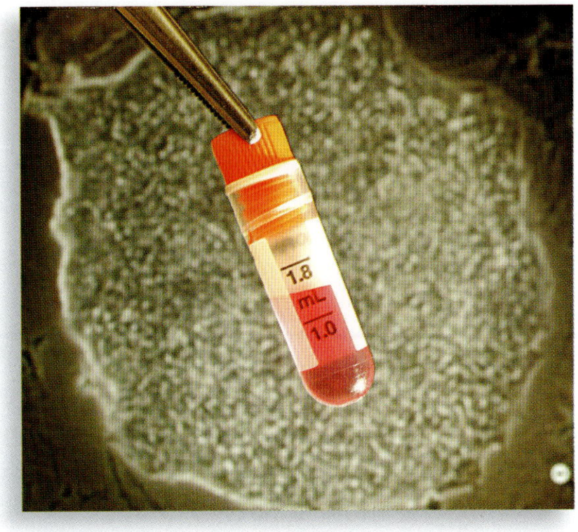

Stem cells are stored in this tiny container. A photograph of a greatly magnified stem cell from a human embryo is shown in the background.

A stem cell is a cell that can develop into any of the different cell types that make up the tissues and organs of the body. The original cells from which an organism develops are stem cells. Stem cells are also found in many adult organs.

Stem cells can divide forever, producing more stem cells or other types of cells. Many scientists think that it might be possible to use stem cells to replace damaged tissues and treat patients with certain diseases. This idea has led people to question if it is right to destroy human *embryos (EHM bree ohz)* to get stem cells for medical research. An embryo is a human or other animal in an early stage of its development.

Stem cells are found in many places in the body of adults. They are found in the skin, liver, and muscles. Scientists are working to develop ways of using such adult stem cells. If successful, they will not have to use stem cells from embryos to develop treatments.

Other articles to read include: **Cell; Cloning; Embryo.**

Steroid

Steroids *(STEHR oyds)* are a group of chemicals that play a key role in living things. Both plants and animals produce steroids naturally. Scientists can also make steroids in the laboratory. All steroids are alike in basic structure. But each steroid has different effects on living things. Many steroids are used as medicines.

Many substances in the body are steroids. One example is *cholesterol*, a fatty substance found in animals. Many *hormones*, including sex hormones, are also steroids. Hormones are "chemical messengers" that regulate body processes.

Some athletes take *anabolic (AN uh BOL ihk)* steroids to increase their strength and body weight. But in sports, this use of steroids is considered cheating. It can also cause health problems and aggressive behavior.

Other articles to read include: **Cholesterol; Drug; Drug testing; Hormone; Sports medicine.**

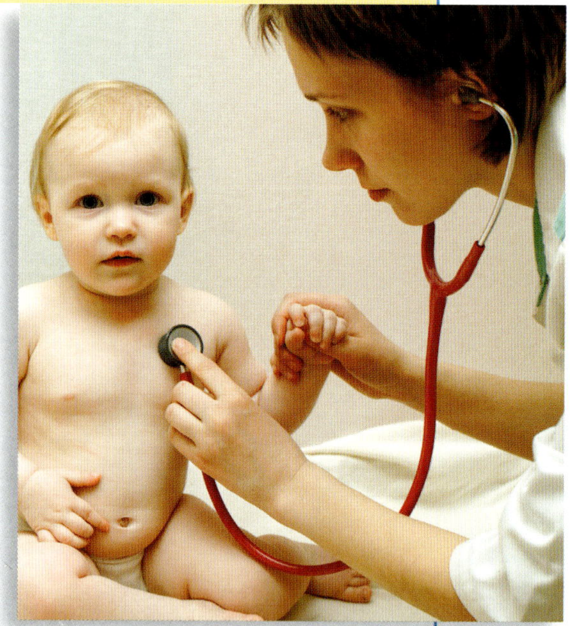

A doctor uses a stethoscope to listen to a child's heart. A medical examination often includes listening to body sounds.

Stethoscope

The stethoscope *(STEHTH uh skohp)* is a tool that doctors use to hear sounds produced inside the body. A stethoscope can pick up sounds made by the heart, lungs, intestines, veins, and arteries.

A stethoscope is made up of several pieces. One piece, which may be shaped like a small disc, is placed against the skin. The shape helps pick up high-pitched sounds made by the body. Hollow rubber tubes are connected to this piece. At the ends of the tubes are earpieces. They help a doctor hear the sounds.

The first stethoscope was made in 1816 from a hollow wooden tube. Before the invention of the stethoscope, doctors had to place an ear next to a person's body to hear the sounds inside.

Other articles to read include: **Heart; Medicine; Physician.**

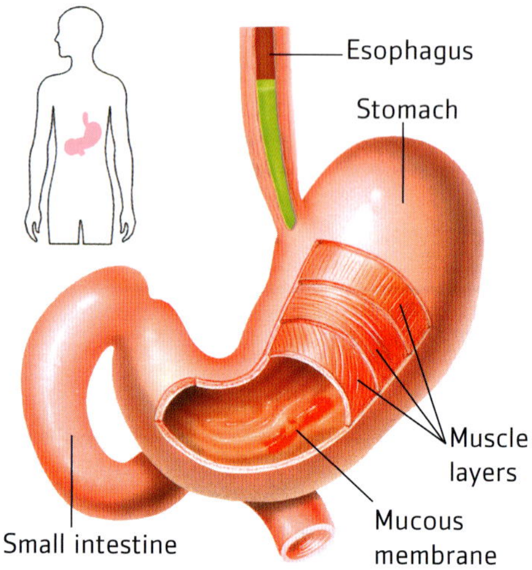

The human *stomach* is a saclike organ in the abdomen. *Mucous membrane* lines the stomach, and three muscle layers make up the stomach wall.

Stomach

The stomach is an organ that holds and breaks down food. A person's stomach is shaped like the letter *J.* A tube called the *esophagus (ee SAHF uh guhs)* runs from the mouth to the upper end of the stomach. The lower end of the stomach is connected to the small intestine.

When food reaches the stomach, slimy *mucus (MYOO kuhs)* in the stomach keeps it moist. Parts of the stomach called glands make a juice that helps *digest,* or break down, the food.

Muscles in the stomach mix the food and move it toward the intestines. When the food is almost liquid, it passes into the small intestine.

Other articles to read include: **Digestive system; Esophagus; Food; Intestine; Mucus.**

Stone Age

The Stone Age was a time when people used stone tools, rather than metal tools. It began about 2 ½ million years ago. At that time, people first made stone into such chopping tools as axes and cleavers. The Stone Age ended at different times in different parts of the world.

In southwestern Asia, the Stone Age ended about 5,000 years ago. Around that time, people there began making tools from a metal called *bronze*. This new technique marked the beginning of the Bronze Age.

Even after that time, however, many farmers in parts of Asia, Europe, Africa, and elsewhere continued to use Stone Age-type tools. They would not begin using metals for hundreds or thousands of years. When Europeans began exploring new lands during the 1400's, they discovered that many people in Australia, southern Africa, Pacific islands, and the Americas were still using stone tools. Today, a few groups of people in New Guinea and Australia continue to live with Stone Age technology.

Scientists have divided the Stone Age into different *periods* (parts). They call the earliest part of the Stone Age the *Paleolithic Period*. This period ended about 10,000 years ago. People during this time used their stone tools to hunt wild game and gather wild vegetables. Then people started to farm in southwestern Asia. *Mesolithic* and *Neolithic* are terms sometimes used to refer to later periods of the Stone Age.

Other articles to read include: **Farm and farming; Prehistoric people.**

During the Stone Age, people used stone sickles and hoes for farming (below) and stone axes and spears for hunting (bottom).

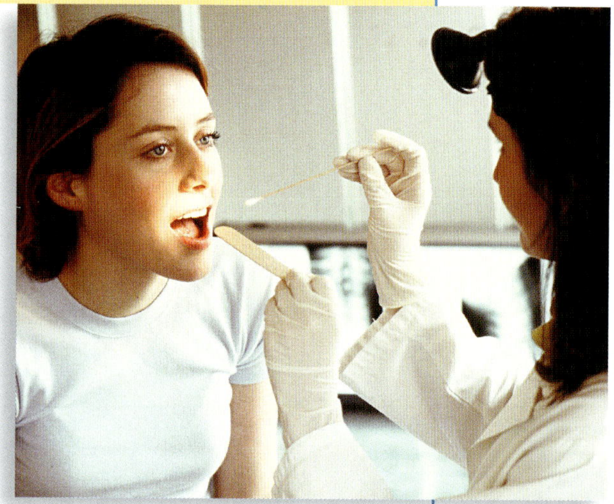

A doctor performs a test called a *throat swab* by collecting material from a patient's throat. The material is analyzed to see if strep throat bacteria are present.

Strep throat

Strep throat is a disease that affects the throat and the tonsils at the back of the throat. It often strikes children from 5 to 12 years of age.

Strep throat is caused by tiny living things called *bacteria*. Strep stands for *streptococcus,* a type of bacteria that cause the disease. The bacteria spread from person to person in drops of moisture from the nose and mouth. A medical test can tell if a person has strep bacteria in the throat.

A person with strep throat has a sore throat, headache, and fever. The person may also throw up and have a stomachache and swollen tonsils. Strep throat is usually treated with a drug called *penicillin (PEHN uh SIHL uhn).* If left untreated, the bacteria may cause problems in other parts of the body, including the lungs and heart.

Other articles to read include: **Bacteria; Disease; Penicillin; Tonsil.**

Test taking is a common source of stress.

Stress

Stress is the body's way of dealing with real or imagined danger. A stress reaction prepares the body for a burst of action to fight or run away from a threat. The heart races, hands get cold and sweaty, and muscles become tense. Stress that lasts a long time can make you very tired and cause you to become worried.

Stress is not always a useful response to events. A little bit of stress can provide a sense of excitement and help people perform better. However, a large amount of stress can affect your health.

Anything from being sick to taking tests can cause stress. Even watching the news on television and reading newspapers can upset some people greatly. People can deal with stress by exercising, eating healthful foods, and relaxing.

Other articles to read include: **Anxiety disorder; Emotion; Suicide.**

Stress test

A stress test measures how well the heart works during exercise. Doctors use stress tests to find heart problems, especially *coronary artery disease*. This disease involves a narrowing of certain blood vessels. These vessels supply oxygen to the heart. Coronary artery disease is the most common form of heart disease. Doctors can treat it better if it is found early.

In a stress test, a person exercises on a treadmill or an exercise bike. The speed of the treadmill or bike is gradually increased so that the exercise becomes more difficult. A machine measures electrical activity in the heart. Doctors can study this information to find heart problems.

Other articles to read include: **Arteriosclerosis: Heart; Heart attack.**

Stroke

A stroke is a sudden loss of activity in the brain. It is a medical emergency. A stroke may result in *paralysis,* or not being able to move a part of the body. It may cause serious brain damage or even death. Most strokes happen when a thick mass of blood, called a *clot,* blocks the flow of blood to the brain. When this happens, the brain is no longer getting the oxygen and nutrients it needs to work. If the blockage lasts more than a few minutes, the damage cannot be healed. Strokes also may happen when one of the vessels that carries blood to the brain breaks open. The bleeding that results causes pressure on the brain. This pressure damages the brain. Stroke is a major health problem throughout the world today.

Other articles to read include: **Bleeding; Blood clot; Blood vessel; Brain; Paralysis.**

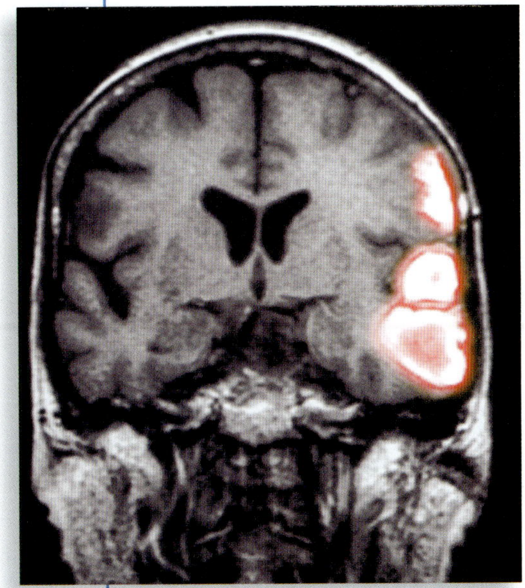

This medical image shows the brain of a stroke patient. Light pink areas indicate where blood vessels have broken open.

Common types of sugar include white table sugar, sold in cubes and powdered form, and brown sugar. Honey is a sugar-rich syrup made by bees.

Sugar

Sugar is a food used to make other foods sweet. For example, people sprinkle sugar on such foods as grapefruit and cereal to make them taste better. Some people add it to coffee, tea, and other drinks. In addition, food companies add sugar to many foods. Candy, canned fruit, jams, jellies, and soft drinks all contain a large amount of sugar. Sugar is also added to many bakery goods, such as cookies and cakes.

All green plants make sugar. But most of the sugar that people use comes from sugar cane or sugar beets. The sugar made by these plants is called *sucrose (SOO krohs).* This sugar is the kind people keep in a sugar bowl. Sugar beets store sucrose in their roots. Sugar cane is a tall grass that stores sucrose in its stalks. Other sources of sugar include cornstarch, milk, maple syrup, and honey. Cornstarch is an especially important source of sugar-rich syrups in the United States.

Sugar belongs to the group of foods called *carbohydrates (KAHR boh HY drayts).* Carbohydrates give energy to plants and animals.

Sugar can lead to tooth decay. It can also cause a person to gain too much weight. To avoid these problems, some people use *artificial (AHR tuh FIHSH uhl)* sweeteners instead of sugar. These sweeteners are much sweeter than natural sugar, so smaller amounts are needed.

Other articles to read include: **Carbohydrate; Food; Glucose.**

Suicide

Suicide *(SOO uh syd)* is the act of killing oneself. It is one of the leading causes of death worldwide.

Some people are more likely than others to commit suicide. Such people include those who have attempted suicide in the past, have a family history of suicide, or know someone who committed suicide. People with certain mental disorders are more likely to commit suicide, as are people suffering a physical illness.

Continued on the next page

Some people commit suicide because of a stressful experience or situation. Such experiences may include child abuse, family conflict, relationship problems, or the loss of a loved one. The use of alcohol or drugs may make some people more likely to commit suicide. Other things that may lead people to end their lives include feelings of hopelessness, low *self-esteem* (respect for oneself), and lack of involvement in school or work.

Health professionals can work with people who are suicidal to help them cope with their feelings and get the support they need. Doctors may prescribe certain drugs to help people who suffer from mental or emotional problems.

Other articles to read include: **Death; Depression; Emotion; Mental illness; Stress.**

Sunburn

Sunburn is a painful swelling and redness of the skin. It happens when the skin is left in the rays of the sun for too long. Sunburn may be slight, with mild redness. Or sunburn can be serious, with blistering, bright red skin that peels. A bad sunburn can cause chills, dizziness, fever, and weakness.

The seriousness of a sunburn depends on the strength of the sunlight and the length of time spent in the sun. The sun's burning rays are strongest during the summer. They are also strongest in the late morning and early afternoon.

Sunburn can easily be avoided. People need to cover their skin or use a lotion that helps block the sun.

Other articles to read include: **Burn; Skin cancer.**

UV index value	Sunlight intensity	Time to sunburn with unprotected exposure
0–2	Minimal	30 minutes for those who never tan/always burn; 120 minutes for those who always tan/rarely burn
3–4	Low	15–20 minutes for "always burn" 75–90 minutes for "rarely burn"
5–6	Moderate	10–12 minutes for "always burn" 50–60 minutes for "rarely burn"
7–9	High	7–8 minutes for "always burn" 33–40 minutes for "rarely burn"
10–15	Very high	4–6 minutes for "always burn" 20–30 minutes for "rarely burn"

Source: United States National Weather Service

The time it takes for ultraviolet (UV) rays from the sun to cause sunburn depends on sunlight intensity, sometimes measured by *UV index,* and individual skin type.

Surgery

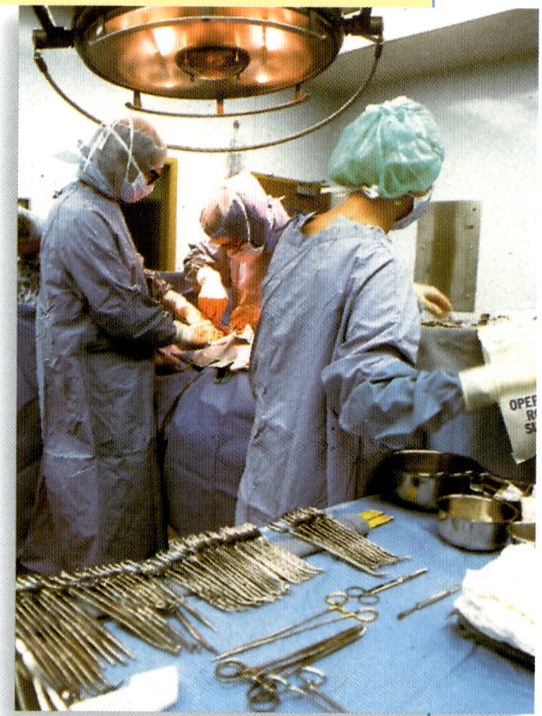

Surgeons use a variety of tools to perform operations. Such tools include *scalpels* (knives) to make cuts and *clamps* to hold body parts.

Surgery *(SUHR juhr ee)* is the treatment of diseases and injuries by performing an operation on a person, called a *patient*. The doctor who performs the operation is called a *surgeon*.

In a surgical operation, many medicines, tools, and surgical methods must be used together to make sure that the patient stays safe and comfortable. Each operation also requires a special team of people. This team is usually made up of the chief surgeon, at least one assistant surgeon, a doctor known as an *anesthesiologist (AN uhs THEE zee OL uh jihst)*, and one or more nurses. The anesthesiologist gives medicine to keep the patient from feeling pain during the operation.

A surgeon uses a wide variety of tools to perform an operation. These tools include scissors, knives known as *scalpels*, and *retractors*, which hold back flaps of skin. Other tools are used to look inside—or remove bits of tissue from—body parts. *Lasers* may be used to make very precise cuts. A laser is a tool that makes light travel in a thin, powerful beam. *Sutures (SOO chuhrz)* are threads used to sew up surgical openings after the operation. All the tools a surgeon uses must be cleaned in a special way. Such cleaning keeps germs from entering the patient's body during the operation.

Surgeons sometimes use robots to assist them in an operation. Robots can make very precise moves in small spaces inside a patient's body. In some cases, a surgeon in one city can control a robot doing the operation in another city. This form of surgery is called *remote surgery*.

Other articles to read include: **Anesthesia; Anesthesiology; Medicine; Organ donation; Physician; Plastic surgery; Skin grafting; Transplant.**

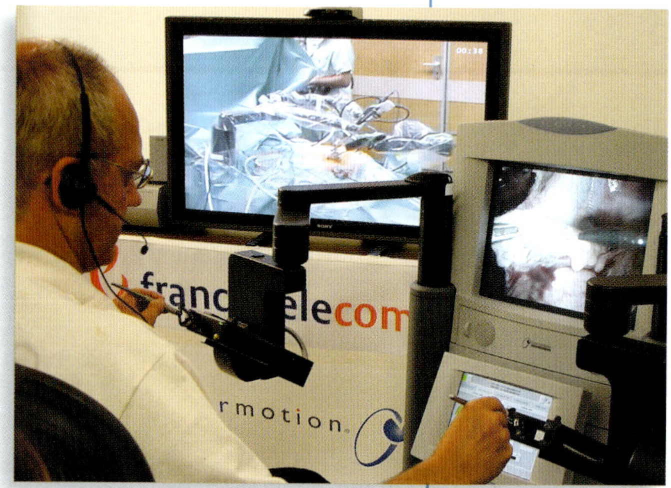

A surgeon in New York City operates on a patient in France via a remote controlled robot. The screen displays the operation safely taking place over 4,000 miles (6,400 kilometers) away.

Taste

Taste is an important *sense* in people and many other animals. A sense helps us know what is happening around us. Our sense of taste helps us decide which foods to eat.

We taste food when it touches groups of cells called *taste buds* on our tongues. Taste buds on different areas of the tongue are sensitive to different tastes, such as sweet or sour. Some of the tastes in food are most easily picked up by taste buds on the front of the tongue. Other tastes are picked up more easily by taste buds on the back or sides of the tongue.

When food touches the taste buds, they send information about the food to cells called *nerves*. The nerves send this information to the brain. We then notice the taste of the food.

Other articles to read include: **Food; Nervous system; Senses; Smell; Tongue.**

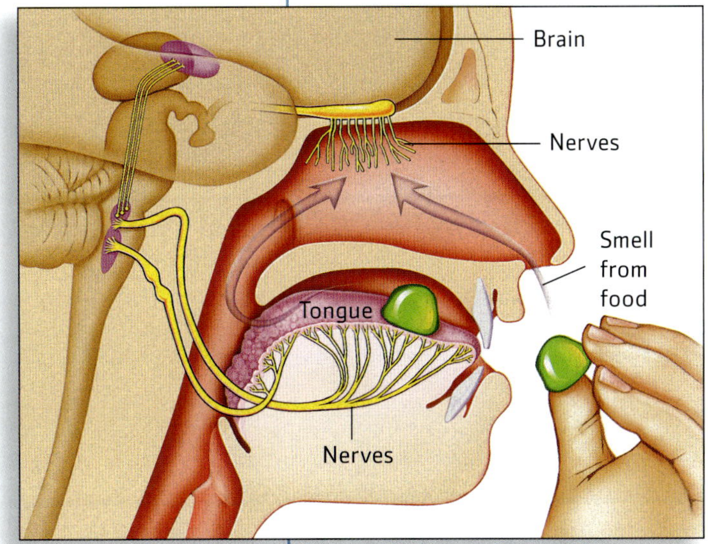

The tastes in food are picked up by ***taste buds*** on the tongue. Information about the taste then travels through nerves to the brain. This information is combined with information about the smell of the food.

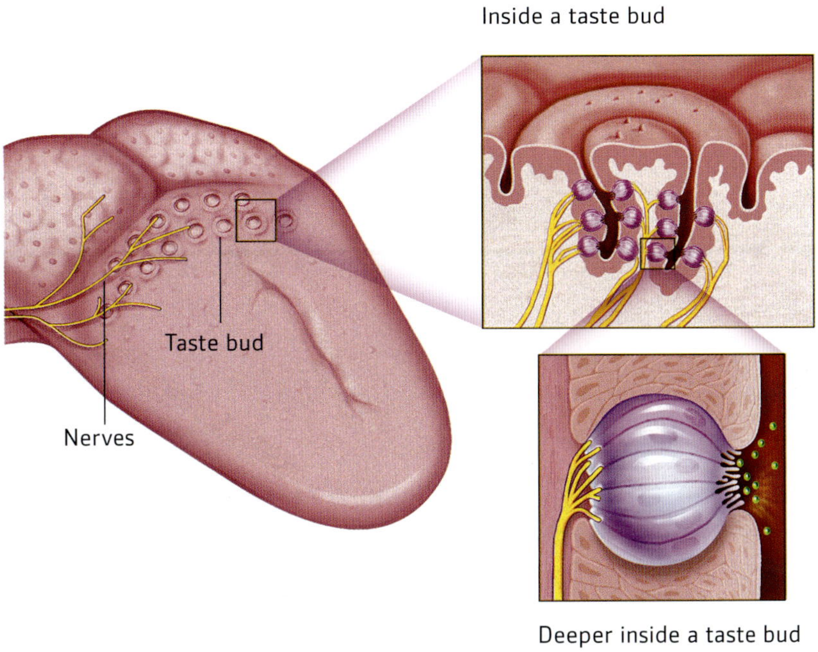

The tongue has many taste buds on its surface. Inside each taste bud are clusters of special skin cells. These cells touch tiny bits of food and then send information about the taste to nerves.

EXPERIMENT

Taste Test

1. Prepare a number of testers by placing different foods in bowls or plates. Do not let the players see them.

2. Have each player put on a blindfold. Ask the players to pinch their noses and take a small taste of a food.

3. After every player has tasted the food, ask each one to name the taste. If no one can name it, let the players try it without pinching their noses.

4. Repeat with the different foods. Take turns being the tester.

Which foods were easiest to name? Which ones were more difficult?

What you need:

- a blindfold for each person
- spoons or forks for each person
- foods with different flavors, such as a lemon, salty crackers, butter, vinegar, raw apple, raw potato, onion, jelly, honey, and pudding

http://bit.ly/YNEnUi

Tay-Sachs disease

Tay-Sachs disease is a disorder of the nervous system. It is passed down from a person's parents. The disease occurs chiefly among Jewish children with ancestors from eastern Europe. Tay-Sachs disease causes brain damage, *convulsions* (strong shaking), blindness, deafness, lack of energy, and eventually death. Children with Tay-Sachs disease begin to have symptoms when they are about 6 months old. There is no treatment for Tay-Sachs disease. Most victims live for only three or four years.

Tay-Sachs disease occurs in children who have too little of an *enzyme* called hexosaminidase A. Enzymes are protein substances that affect the body's chemical reactions. Tay-Sachs symptoms were first reported during the 1880's by two physicians: Waren Tay of the United Kingdom and Bernard Sachs of the United States.

Other articles to read include: **Brain; Disease; Enzyme; Nervous system.**

Tear

A tear is a drop of salty liquid from the eye. Tears keep the *cornea (KAWR nee uh)* moist. The cornea is the clear outer layer of the eyeball. Tears also help prevent infection. They help keep the eye free of germs and dirt. Tears keep the eye from drying out, which could lead to blindness.

Tears are made by tiny body parts called the *lacrimal (LAK ruh muhl) glands.* There is one lacrimal gland above each eyeball. Tiny *ducts* (tubes) in the eyelid carry tears from the lacrimal gland to the cornea. With each blink, the ducts brings some liquid from the gland to the eye. Tears flow out of the eye through two ducts at the eye's inner corner.

When a person feels sad or angry, the muscles around the lacrimal glands may tighten. This squeezes out tears. Laughing too hard can also squeeze out tears.

Other articles to read include: **Cornea; Eye; Gland.**

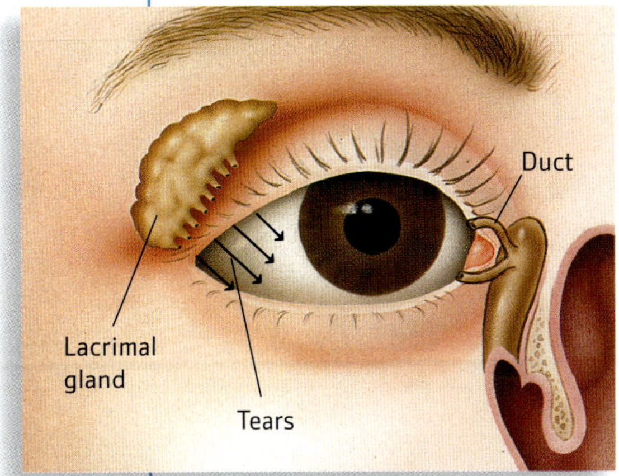

Tears are made by a *lacrimal gland* above each eyeball. The tears wash across the eye and empty into ducts. The ducts drain through a passage into the nose.

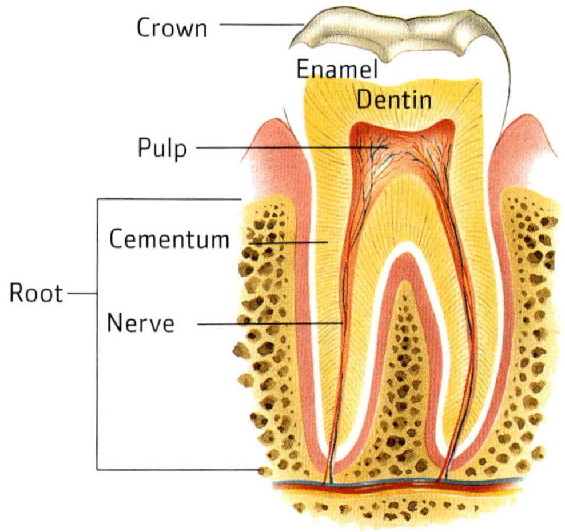

Teeth

Teeth are the hard, bonelike parts in the upper and lower jaws. They are the hardest parts of the body. People use their teeth mostly to chew food. Teeth are also important for speaking. The teeth and tongue are used together to form certain sounds, such as the *th* sound, that make up words.

People grow two sets of teeth: first the *deciduous (dih SIHJ u uhs) teeth*—also known as the *milk teeth* or *baby teeth*—and then the *permanent teeth*. People have 32 permanent teeth—16 in the lower jaw and 16 in the upper jaw. They include four *incisors* and two *canines* in each jaw. These sharp teeth are used to bite into food. The four *premolars* in each jaw crush and grind food. The six *molars* in each jaw are also used for grinding food. They are bigger than the premolars.

The part of the tooth above the gum is called the *crown*. The root of the tooth goes below the gum into the bone of the jaw.

A tooth is made up of four kinds of materials. They are *pulp, dentin, enamel*, and *cementum*.

The pulp is deep inside the tooth. The blood that flows through the pulp keeps the tooth strong and healthy. Dentin is a hard, yellow material that surrounds the pulp. Enamel covers the dentin in the crown of the tooth. Enamel is the hard whitish material that keeps a tooth from wearing down. Cementum covers the dentin in the root of the tooth.

Other articles to read include: **Dentistry; Mouth; Orthodontics.**

The main parts of a tooth include the *crown,* which can be seen inside the mouth, and the *root,* which lies inside the jawbone.

The 20 *deciduous teeth* (baby teeth) are gradually replaced by the 32 permanent teeth, which form in the jaws near the roots of the deciduous teeth. The last permanent teeth come in between the ages of 17 and 21.

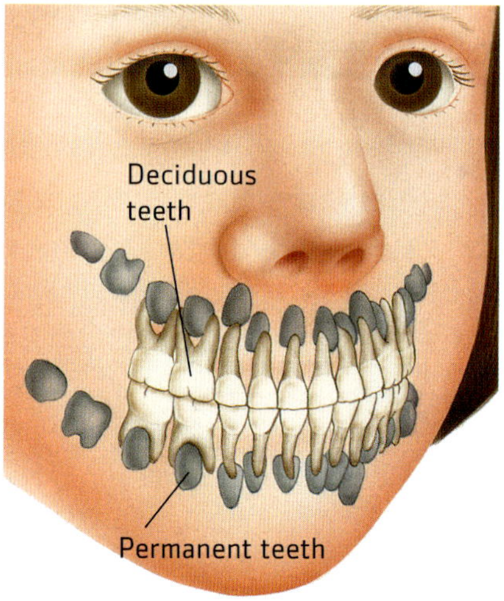

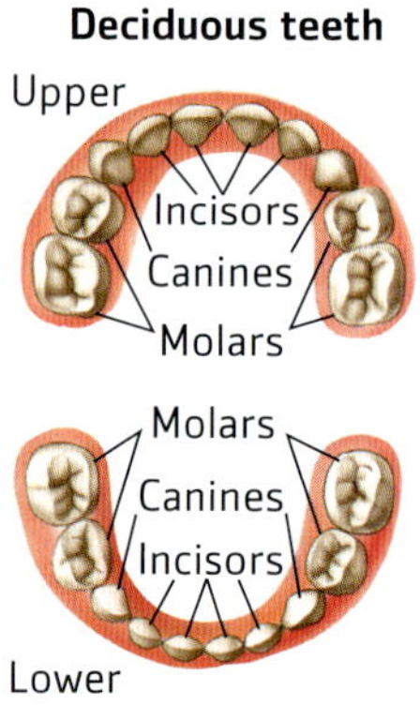

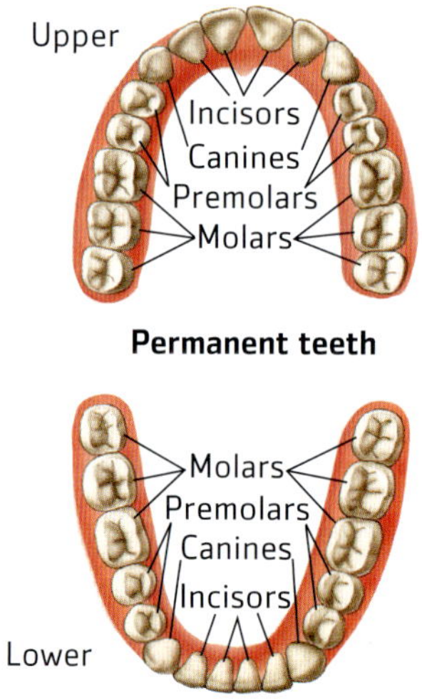

Tendon

A tendon is a strong white tissue that attaches muscles to bones. Tendons are also called *sinew (SIHN yoo).*

Muscles move bones by pulling on tendons. A tendon is a bundle of many tough strands. Some tendons are round, while others are flat. One end of a tendon arises from the end of a muscle. The other end is woven into the material of a bone.

The tendon may slide up and down inside a covering of tissue, just as an arm moves in a coat sleeve. The tendon and this tissue are held in place by strong, *flexible* (able to bend) bands called *ligaments (LIHG uh muhnts).*

A cut tendon can be sewed back together. It may take six weeks or more for the tendon to heal.

Other articles to read include: **Achilles tendon; Bone; Ligament; Tissue.**

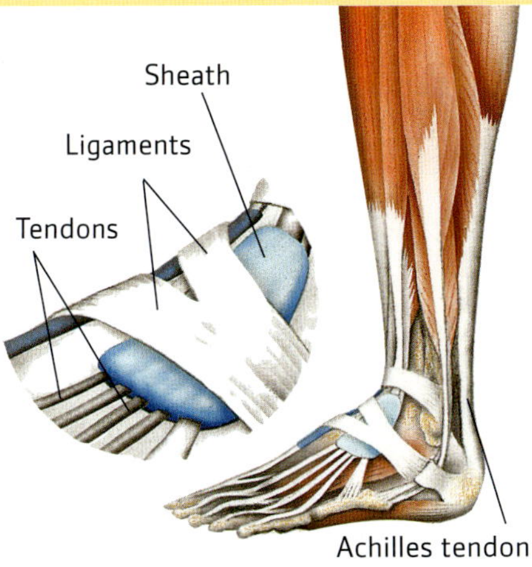

Tendons in the foot are covered by protective tissue called *sheaths.* The tendons and sheaths are held in place by *ligaments.* One of the main tendons in the leg is the *Achilles tendon,* which connects leg muscles to the heel bone.

Testicle

The testicles *(TEHS tuh kuhls)* are a pair of glands in the male reproductive system. They are small and oval in shape. They hang behind the penis in a sack called the *scrotum.* The testicles are also called *testes.* They produce *sperm* (male sex cells) and *hormones.* Hormones are chemicals that help regulate the body.

Each testicle is covered in tough, stringy material. The material also divides the testicle into about 250 sections. Each section contains up to four twisting tubes. Sperm are made in these tubes.

The testicles produce the hormone *testosterone (tehs TOS tuh rohn).* It is made in the tissue between the tubes. Testosterone controls the development of characteristics found in adult males. These include a beard, enlarged muscles, a deep voice, and larger sex organs.

Other articles to read include: **Gland; Hormone; Reproduction, Human; Sexuality; Testosterone.**

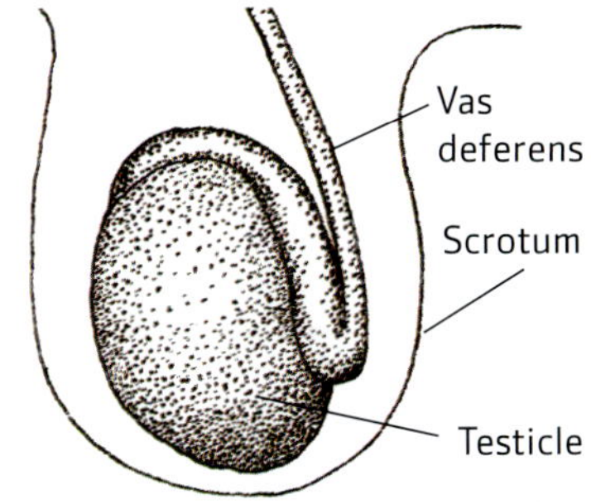

Each *testicle* is small and oval in shape. The paired testicles are located in a pouch called the *scrotum.* A tube called the *vas deferens* carries sperm away from each testicle.

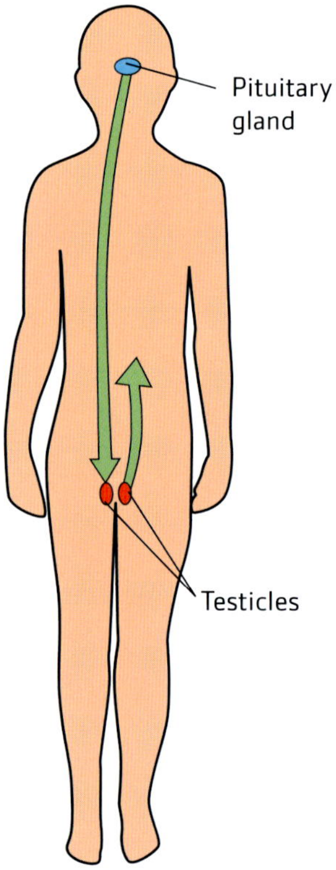

Testosterone

Testosterone *(tehs TOS tuh rohn)* is a chemical in the body. It causes male traits in human beings and other animals. It is a type of *hormone (HAWR mohn)*. A hormone is a substance made in one part of the body that causes changes in other parts of the body.

Testosterone is made mostly in the *testicles (TEHS tuh kuhlz)*. The testicles are two glands on a male's body. They are involved in reproduction. The bodies of females also produce small amounts of testosterone.

Testosterone causes changes to the male body during *puberty (PYOO buhr tee)*. Puberty is when a child's body slowly changes into the body of an adult. Testosterone causes hair to grow on the face and elsewhere. Muscles also begin to grow larger. The voice begins to sound deeper. In addition, testosterone helps the body produce *sperm*, the male sex cells.

Other articles to read include: **Gland; Hormone; Pituitary gland; Puberty; Reproduction; Human; Sexuality; Testicle.**

In the male body at puberty, a gland connected to the brain called the *pituitary gland* increases its production of certain hormones. These hormones travel to the *testicles,* where they boost the production of testosterone.

Tetanus

Tetanus *(TEHT uh nuhs)* is a serious disease that affects muscles. It is also called *lockjaw* because it causes *spasms* (violent contractions) of the jaw muscles. These spasms make it hard to open the mouth. Tetanus results from *toxins* (poisons) produced by a bacterium called *Clostridium tetani*. These germs thrive in dust and dirt. They enter the body through breaks in the skin. Any dirt in a wound may contain tetanus germs.

Tetanus symptoms usually start within several weeks after infection. The victim has headaches and soon has trouble opening the mouth or swallowing. After a while, all of the body muscles tighten, and spasms may interfere with breathing. If untreated, the victim may die from exhaustion.

To prevent tetanus, all wounds should be cleaned thoroughly. People may also be immunized through a *tetanus shot*. If tetanus develops, doctors treat it with antitoxin. People with severe tetanus may need a surgeon to make an opening in the *trachea* (windpipe) to help the patient breathe.

Other articles to read include: **Bacteria; Disease; Immunization; Muscle; Toxin.**

Thymus

The thymus *(THY muhs)* is a gland in the upper chest. It plays an important role in the body's *immune system.* The immune system defends against disease. The thymus lies behind the *sternum* (breastbone).

The thymus helps the body produce *lymphocytes (LIHM fuh syts).* Lymphocytes are white blood cells. They fight disease. Lymphocytes are made in the *bone marrow,* a tissue in the centers of long bones. Certain lymphocytes called *T cells* enter the bloodstream from the marrow. They move to the thymus, where they finish developing. The fully developed T cells can attack such harmful things as bacteria, cancer cells, and viruses.

Other articles to read include: **Gland; Immune system; Lymphatic system; White blood cell.**

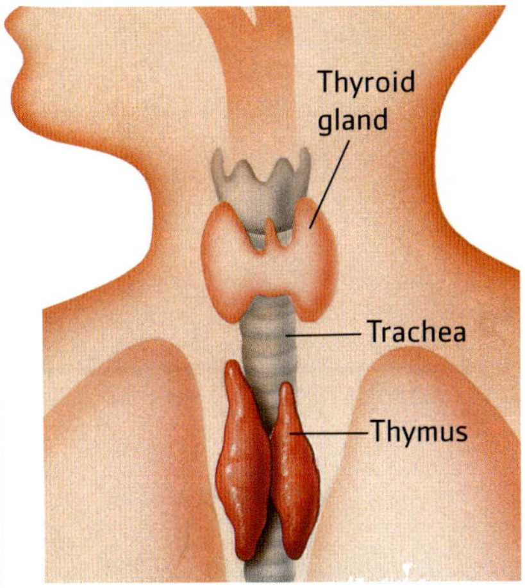

The thymus lies in the upper chest, in front of the *trachea* (windpipe) and below the thyroid gland.

Thyroid gland

The thyroid gland is in the front of the neck. It has two parts. One part is on each either side of the *trachea* (windpipe).

The thyroid gland makes a *hormone (HAWR mohn).* Hormones are chemicals made in certain parts of the body. They cause changes in other parts of the body. Thyroid hormone controls the rate of growth in people. It also controls *cell metabolism.* Cell metabolism is how cells convert food into energy and living tissue.

The thyroid gland sometimes may make too much or too little hormone. This can cause metabolism to be too fast or too slow. Medicines can usually correct these problems. In some cases, a surgeon must remove all or part of the thyroid.

Other articles to read include: **Cell; Gland; Hormone; Metabolism; Trachea.**

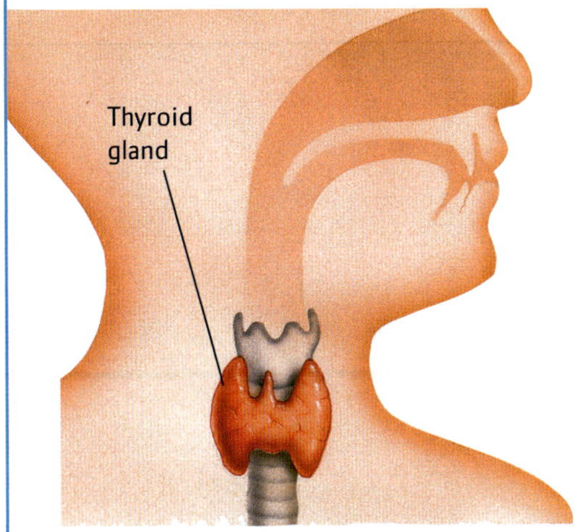

The thyroid gland sits on either side of the *trachea* (windpipe).

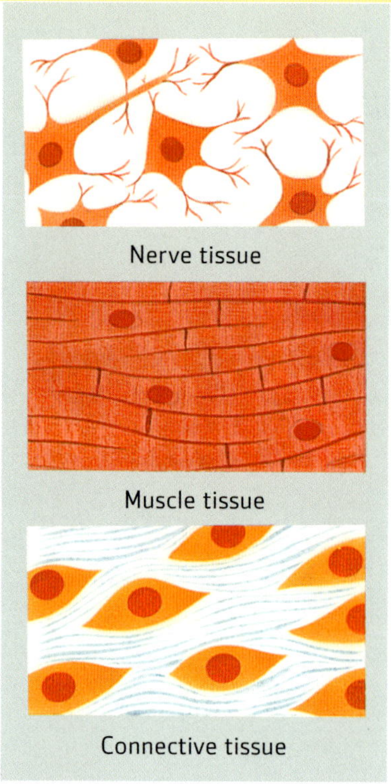

Tissues form organs in plants and animals. These drawings shows the main types of cells and tissues that make up the human heart.

Tissue

A tissue is a group of cells that work together to perform a specific body function. Similar cells performing a similar task form tissues. Groups of different tissues form organs.

There are four main kinds of animal tissues. *Connective tissue* surrounds and joins other tissues and organs. *Epithelial (EHP uh THEE lee uhl) tissue* forms *membranes*—such as the outer layer of skin—and glands. *Muscle tissue* is made up of cells that *contract* (draw together) to make body movements. *Nerve tissue* sends information throughout the body in the form of electrical and chemical impulses.

Plants also have tissues. *Meristematic (MEHR uh stuh MAT ihk) tissue* is formed by cells that constantly divide, such as at the growing tips of roots. *Permanent tissue* is made up of cells that perform such tasks as carrying water throughout the plant.

Other articles to read include: **Cell; Gland; Muscle; Nervous system; Skin.**

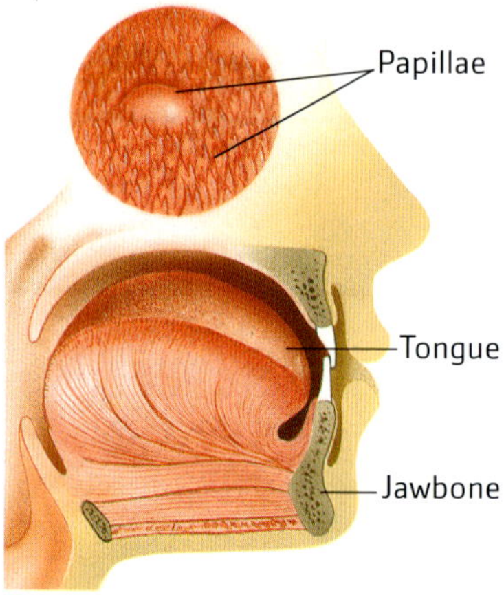

The tongue consists of bundles of muscle. The upper surface of the tongue has tiny bumps called *papillae*.

Tongue

The tongue is a part of the body that helps you taste, chew, swallow, and speak. It is made up of muscles. These muscles let you move your tongue in different ways. You use your tongue to move food around the mouth and to clean the mouth. When you speak, the tongue helps you form the sounds of words.

The top of the tongue has bumps called *papillae (puh PIHL ee)*. They make the tongue's upper surface rough. *Taste buds* in the papillae help you tell the difference between sweet, sour, salty, and bitter tastes.

The tip of the tongue has many clusters of nerve cells called *touch organs*. Because of this, the tongue's tip can feel things better than can any other part of the body.

Other articles to read include: **Digestive system; Food; Mouth; Taste; Touch.**

Tonsil

Tonsils are small parts of the body that are located at the back of the throat. The word *tonsils* usually means the deep pink areas on each side of the back of the throat. People have tonsils at the back of the tongue, too. Other tonsils, also called *adenoids (AD uhn oydz),* are near the passage that leads to the nose. Together, these three kinds of tonsils form a ring around the back of the throat.

Many medical scientists believe that the tonsils help prevent infections that may enter the body through the mouth. Sometimes the adenoids and the tonsils at the back of the throat become badly swollen and must be removed by an operation.

Other articles to read include: **Adenoids; Mouth; Tonsillitis.**

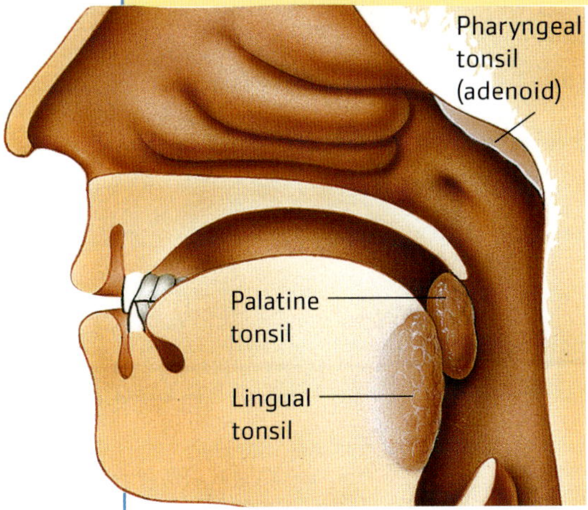

Three kinds of tonsils are found in the throat. As children grow older, their tonsils usually become smaller.

Tonsillitis

Tonsillitis *(TON sihl LY tihs)* is a painful disease caused by swollen tonsils. It is caused by germs called bacteria or viruses. Most attacks of tonsillitis happen in people between the ages of 10 and 40. An attack begins with swelling and pain in the throat. It also becomes hard to swallow. People with a serious case of tonsillitis may also get a fever, headache, backache, or stiff neck. They may get sick to the stomach, too.

Doctors tell people with tonsillitis to stay in bed, take aspirin, and gargle with salt water. Some people get cases of tonsillitis that last for a long time. Or they get it again and again. These people often have their tonsils taken out. The operation to take out the tonsils is called a *tonsillectomy (TON sihl EK tuh mee).*

Other articles to read include: **Bacteria; Disease; Germ; Tonsil; Virus.**

The tonsils of a child with tonsillitis can be seen as swollen reddish structures flecked with white patches. The white patches are infected with germs.

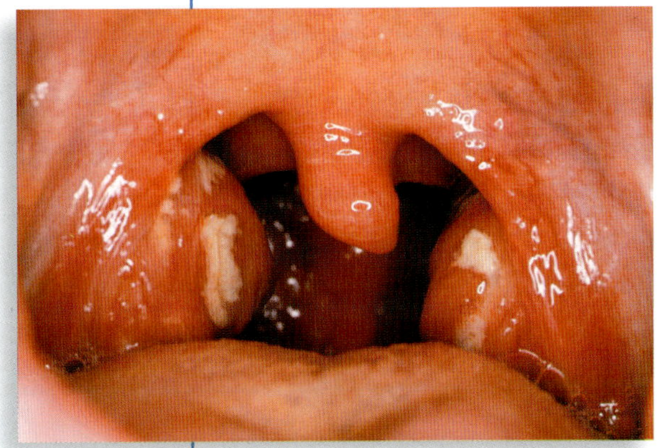

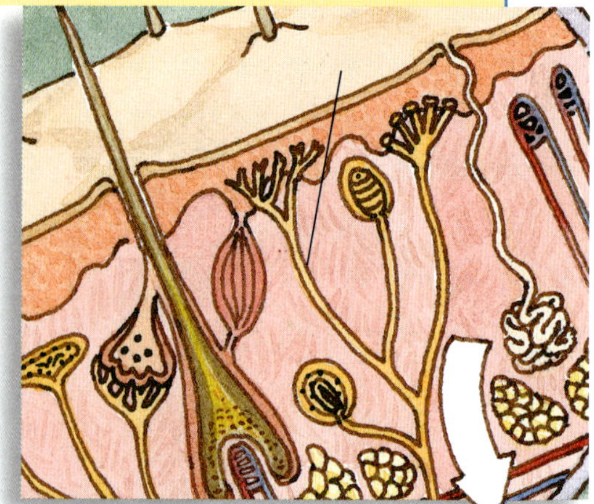

Touch is the body's ability to feel objects. Nerves in the skin send touch sensations to the brain.

Touch

Touch is the *sense* that lets us know we have come in contact with an object. A sense helps people and animals learn about the world around us. By touching an object, we can learn about its shape and hardness and whether it is hot or cold. If the object is too hot or sharp, we feel pain.

Certain parts of the body can feel things better than other parts can. The tip of the tongue, the tips of the fingers, and the end of the nose can feel even the lightest touch. These body parts have many clusters of nerve cells called *touch receptors*. When an object makes contact with these parts, the touch receptors get pressed out of shape. Then, nerve cells in the touch receptors send messages about the feel of the object to the brain.

Other articles to read include: **Finger; Nervous system; Nose; Pain; Senses; Skin; Tongue.**

Snake venom is a toxin often delivered by a bite. A person bitten by a venomous snake must receive immediate medical treatment.

Toxin

A toxin *(TOK suhn)* is a kind of poison. It is made by a plant, animal, or other living thing. Toxins can make a person seriously ill. Toxins can even be deadly.

Some animals make toxins. For example, certain insects, snakes, spiders, and scorpions make toxins. This kind of toxin is called *venom.* These animals use toxins to catch food. Some deliver their toxins by biting. Others use a stinger.

Microbes inside the body may release toxins. These toxins can cause illnesses, such as scarlet fever and tetanus.

Certain microbes release toxins into food. People who eat the food may become ill. Also, some tropical fish contain toxins. A person who eats the fish may become ill.

Other articles to read include: **Food poisoning; Poison; Scarlet fever; Tetanus.**

Trachea

The trachea *(TRAY kee uh)* is a tube in the body. It carries air into the lungs. It is also called the *windpipe*. When a person inhales air, it goes from the nose and mouth into the trachea. Two tubes carry it into the lungs.

An adult human trachea is about 5 inches (13 centimeters) long. It is about 1 inch (2.5 centimeters) wide. About half of its length is inside the chest. The rest is in the neck.

The trachea is held open by 16 to 20 C-shaped rings. The rings are made of *cartilage (KAHR tuh lihj)*. Cartilage is a rubbery tissue inside the body. The rings make up the hard ridges in the neck just below a small bump in the neck called the *Adam's apple*. The Adam's apple is formed by the *larynx (LAR ihngks)* (voice box).

Other articles to read include: **Cartilage; Larynx; Lung; Respiration.**

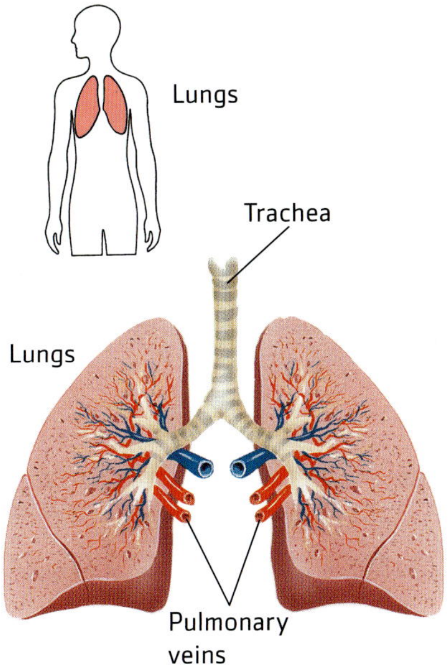

The trachea splits into two branches that carry air to each lung.

Tranquilizer

A tranquilizer *(TRANG kwuh* LY *zuhr)* is a drug that calms a person. It works by acting on the nervous system. There are two main types of tranquilizers. They are (1) *antipsychotic (*AN *tee sy KOT ihk)* drugs and (2) *antianxiety (*AN *tee ang ZY uh tee)* drugs.

Antipsychotic drugs are used to treat people with severe mental illness. They help reduce confusion and excitement.

Antianxiety drugs are used to treat emotional problems, particularly *anxiety* (worry). They relax the muscles and reduce tension and stress.

Some tranquilizers have side effects. They may cause weakness in the muscles and general tiredness. They may also make a person sleepy. For this reason, a person should not drive for several hours after taking a tranquilizer. Sleepiness is more likely if the person drinks alcohol before or after taking the drug.

Some people become *addicted* to tranquilizers. This means they cannot stop or control their use of the drug. For this reasons, tranquilizers are usually given only by a doctor's orders.

Other articles to read include: **Anxiety disorder; Drug; Mental illness; Narcotic; Nervous system; Sleep.**

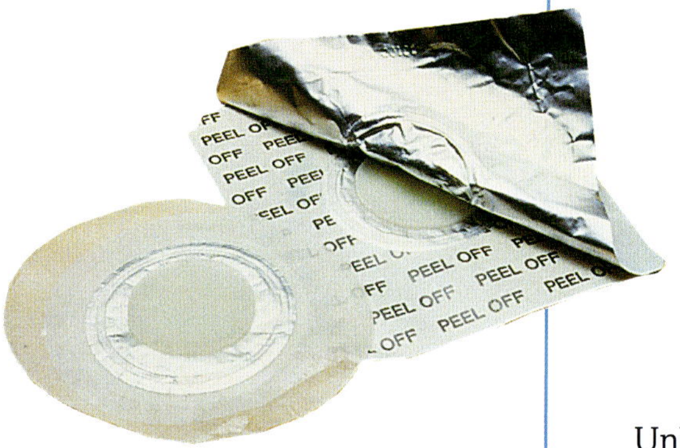

This transdermal patch, shown beside its packaging, sticks to the skin like an adhesive bandage. It holds medicine that spreads through the skin and into the bloodstream.

Transdermal patch

A transdermal patch is a sticky pad filled with medicine. It is placed on the skin. An *adhesive* (sticky substance) helps the pad stick to the skin. In most transdermal patches, the medicine is mixed with the adhesive. The medicine spreads through the skin and into the bloodstream.

Unlike an injection, a transdermal patch provides a slow, steady dose of medicine. Transdermal patches are often used to treat pain or high blood pressure. They are also a popular way to give a steady dose of *nicotine*. Nicotine is the *addictive* (habit-forming) ingredient in cigarette smoke. Nicotine patches can help people quit smoking.

Other articles to read include: **Drug; Hypertension; Pain.**

Transplant

A transplant, in medicine, is an operation that moves any type of tissue or organ from one person to another. A *tissue* is a group of similar cells that work together. *Organs* are made up of at least two kinds of tissue and do a certain job for the body. Organs commonly transplanted from one person to another include the heart, kidney, liver, and lung.

Transplanted tissues and organs replace diseased, damaged, or destroyed body parts. They can help save a person's life or make a seriously ill person healthy again.

Some organs cannot survive outside the body for long. Doctors must transplant these organs quickly. Some tissues can be stored in refrigerators or freezers at special places called *tissue banks*.

The body's immune system, which fights diseases, responds to transplanted tissues and organs in different ways. It recognizes that many transplanted organs

Continued on the next page

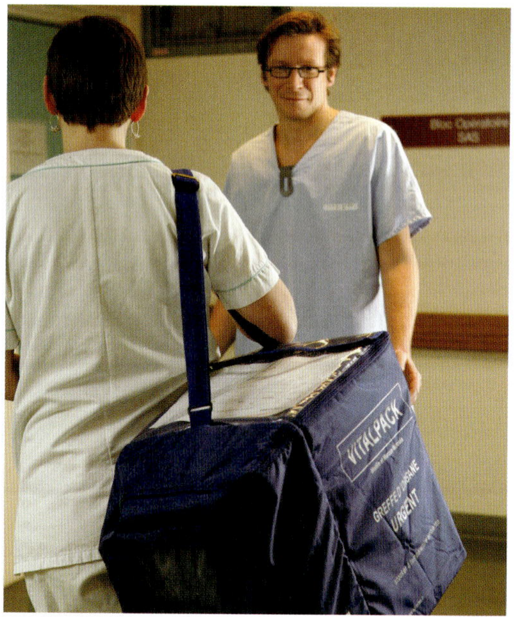

A medical worker delivers an organ to a transplant surgeon. Organs sometimes must be transported long distances. They are stored in special insulated containers that keep organs cold so they can survive longer outside the body.

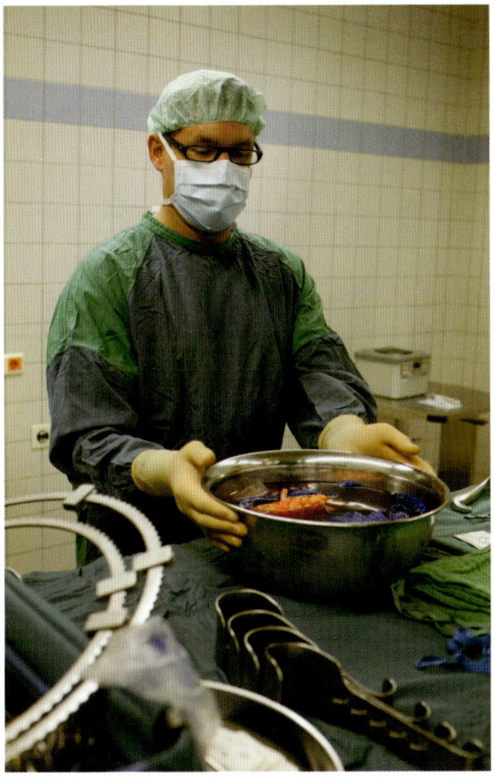

come from outside the body and so attacks them. Doctors use special medications to protect transplanted organs. The immune system responds less strongly to most transplanted tissues.

Doctor obtain organs for transplant from *donors.* Most organs used in transplant operations come from otherwise healthy patients who suffer *brain death* (a permanent end of brain function), often following a fatal head injury. In many countries, people can use a donor card or mark a space on their driver's license to give permission to donate their organs after death.

Other articles to read include: **Immune system; Organ donation; Skin grafting; Surgery; Tissue.**

A surgeon prepares a kidney obtained from an organ donor for transplant into a patient.

Tuberculosis

Tuberculosis *(too* BUR *kyuh LOH sihs)* is a disease that mainly affects the lungs. It can also affect other organs. Tuberculosis is caused by a type of bacterium that can spread from person to person, for example through coughing or sneezing.

Tuberculosis is often called *TB.* In the past, it was called *consumption (kuhn SUHMP shuhn)* and was one of the most common causes of death in the world. Today, improved ways of preventing, finding, and treating tuberculosis have cut down on the number of people who get the disease and the number of people who die from it. However, tuberculosis is still a major problem in some regions.

Tuberculosis strikes people of all ages and races. Those most likely to get the disease are homeless people or people who are weak from other diseases, such as cancer or AIDS.

Other articles to read include: **Bacteria; Cough; Disease; Lung; Respiration; Sneezing.**

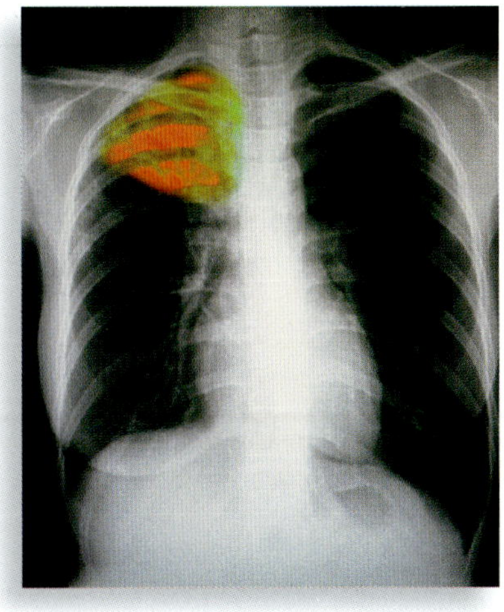

A patient with tuberculosis has hard lumps of infected tissue in one of her lungs, seen in this colored X-ray image.

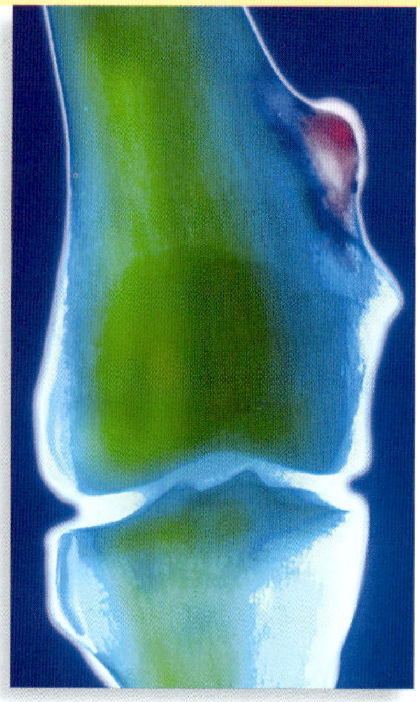

A small tumor growing on a leg bone appears as a reddish bump in this X-ray image.

Tumor

A tumor *(TOO muhr)* is an abnormal growth of tissue in the body. Some tumors are harmless, but others can hurt or kill people and other animals. Tumors are also called *neoplasms (NEE oh plaz uhmz)*.

Some tumors are *benign (bih NYN)*. Benign tumors do not spread elsewhere in the body. Once benign tumors are removed, they usually do not grow again.

Malignant (muh LIHG nuhnt) tumors are also called *cancers*. Those cancers that are not completely removed can spread throughout the body, often destroying other tissues in the body.

Tumors can grow from any kind of tissue in the body. They may develop in the skin or in muscles, nerves, blood vessels, or bones. They may also develop in any of the body's organs, such as the liver, stomach, or lungs.

Other articles to read include: **Biopsy; Cancer; Mole; Wart.**

Typhoid fever

Typhoid is spread through contaminated food and water. The washing of food can help prevent the disease where it is common.

Typhoid *(TY foyd)* fever is a disease that causes fever, weakness, and sometimes death. It was once common in cities. But it became less common as sanitation and *hygiene* (cleanliness) improved. Today, typhoid fever is rare in areas with modern sanitation.

Typhoid fever is caused by tiny living things called *bacteria*. People with typhoid fever spread the bacteria through their *feces* (solid body waste) and *urine* (liquid body waste). Without proper sanitation, the bacteria can get into food or drinking water. Healthy people called *carriers* can also spread typhoid fever. Carriers do not have the disease. But they release the bacteria in their feces and urine.

People swallow the bacteria in unclean food or water. Signs of typhoid fever usually begin one to three weeks later. Most cases last about four weeks.

The best way to prevent typhoid fever is good hygiene and public sanitation. A vaccine can provide some protection. It is usually given to people who live in or travel to countries with widespread typhoid fever. Doctors use drugs called *antibiotics* to treat typhoid fever.

Other articles to read include: **Antibiotic; Bacteria; Disease; Fever; Public health.**

Ulcer

An ulcer *(UHL suhr)* is an open sore in the skin or in *mucous membranes (MYOO kuhs MEHM braynz)*. Mucous membranes are linings inside the body.

Peptic ulcers form in the *digestive system*. The digestive system includes the parts of the body that break down food. One type of peptic ulcer is called a *duodenal (DOO uh DEE nuhl)* ulcer. It forms in the small intestine. Another type of peptic ulcer is called a *gastric ulcer*. It forms in the stomach. Peptic ulcers develop when digestive juices eat through the lining of the stomach or small intestine. Certain bacteria can cause peptic ulcers.

Ulcers that form in the skin include leg ulcers and bedsores. These can be caused by poor blood circulation or lying in bed too long. People recovering from a serious illness and confined to bed may develop bedsores.

Other articles to read include: **Bacteria; Circulatory system; Digestive system; Intestine; Stomach.**

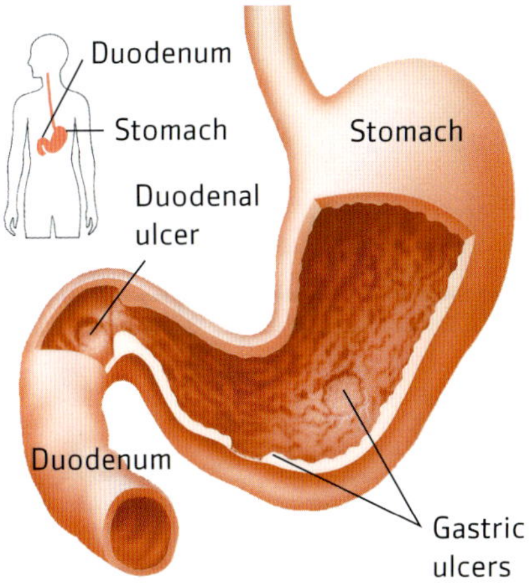

Peptic ulcers may form in the stomach or in the *duodenum* (upper part of small intestine).

Ultrasound

Ultrasound is sound that is too high for human beings to hear. However, many animals can hear ultrasound.

Bats, dolphins, and certain other animals use ultrasound to find objects—including food—in the dark. In a process called *echolocation (EHK oh loh KAY shuhn)*, these animals send out short bursts of ultrasound. The sound waves that make up the ultrasound bounce off objects, producing echoes. These echoes tell the distance and direction to the objects.

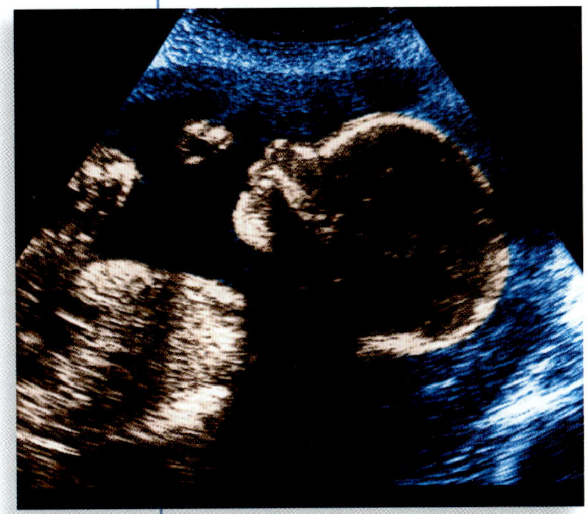

This ultrasound image shows the head and arms of an unborn baby.

People have invented machines that can use ultrasound to make pictures of the inside of a person's body. For example, an ultrasound image can show a baby that is still in the mother's womb. Other devices that use ultrasound include burglar alarms, automatic door openers, and instruments that study the ocean floor.

Other articles to read include: **Pregnancy; Radiology.**

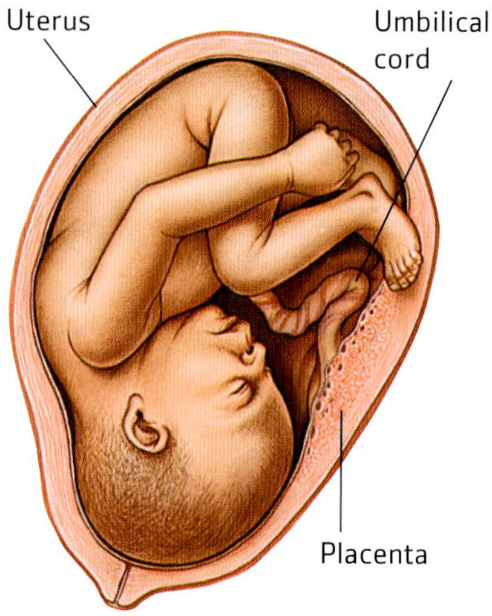

The *umbilical cord* supplies an unborn baby in the *uterus* (womb) with food and oxygen from the placenta.

Umbilical cord

The umbilical *(uhm BIHL uh kuhl)* cord is a tube in the body of a pregnant mother. The umbilical cord carries food and oxygen to the *fetus* (unborn baby). It connects the fetus to the *placenta (pluh SEHN tuh)*. The placenta is an organ in the mother. It provides the fetus with food and oxygen and carries away its wastes.

The umbilical cord has two *arteries* and one *vein*. The arteries carry blood and waste products from the fetus to the placenta. The vein brings oxygen-rich blood and food to the fetus from the placenta.

When a baby is born, a doctor cuts the umbilical cord. The *navel* (belly button) marks the spot where the umbilical cord was attached.

Other articles to read include: **Artery; Baby; Fetus; Placenta; Pregnancy; Uterus; Vein.**

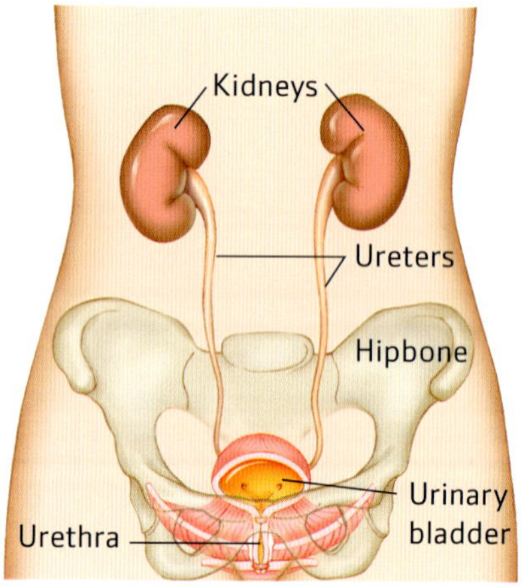

Waste substances filtered from the blood by the *kidneys* pass through the *ureters* into the *urinary bladder.* The waste is stored in the urinary bladder until it leaves the body through the *urethra.*

Urinary system

The urinary *(YUR uh NEHR ee)* system flushes wastes from the body. It is a system of tissues and organs. Without the urinary system, various poisons would stay in the body. This would cause illness.

The main organs of the urinary system are the two *kidneys*. Each kidney has many filtering units known as *nephrons (NEHF ronz)*. Blood passes through a nephron. There, tiny blood vessels and other tubes filter out water and various chemicals. Water and substances important to the body are taken in by special cells. These substances stay in the body.

Waste substances go into two tubes called *ureters (yu REE tuhrz)*. These wastes include ammonia, uric acid, and excess water. They form a yellowish liquid called *urine (YUR uhn)*. The urine moves from the kidneys to the *urinary bladder*. There it is stored until it leaves the body. Urine is squeezed out of the bladder through movements of muscles. It leaves the body through a tube known as the *urethra (yu REE thruh)*.

Other articles to read include: **Bladder; Kidney; Poison; Urine.**

Urine

Urine *(YUR uhn)* is a liquid waste made by the body. A healthy person's urine is usually golden-colored. An adult produces about 1 ½ quarts (1.4 liters) of urine a day. But the amount may vary.

Urine is mostly water. The water holds dissolved wastes. The kidneys remove the water and wastes from the blood. Urine passes from the kidneys to the bladder through two small tubes. Urine is stored in the bladder. It is then is pushed out of the body through another tube, the urethra *(yu REE thruh).*

The condition of urine can be a sign of the person's health. Sugar in the urine is a sign of diabetes. Blood in the urine may mean that the kidneys have been damaged. It may also mean an infection of the bladder or kidneys.

Other articles to read include: **Bladder; Kidney; Urinary system.**

Uterus

The uterus *(YOO tuhr uhs)* is a hollow, muscular organ in a woman's body in which an unborn baby develops. The uterus is near the bottom of the stomach. In a woman who is not pregnant, the uterus looks like an upside-down pear about as big as a fist. The uterus is also called the *womb (woom).*

The bottom part of the uterus is called the *cervix (SUR vihks).* The cervix contains an opening that looks like a neck that leads into the *vagina (vuh JY nuh).* At birth, a baby passes down through the cervix and through the vagina. It then comes out of the woman's body.

The uterus expands a lot when a woman is expecting a baby. It can expand to about 24 times its normal size. During childbirth, the muscles of the uterus force the baby out of the mother's body. Each month during a woman's childbearing years, blood vessels, glands, and cells build up in the lining of the uterus. But if the woman does not become pregnant during a month, the built-up lining is discharged from the body. The discharge process is called *menstruation (mehn stru AY shuhn).*

Other articles to read include: **Childbirth; Menstruation; Pregnancy; Reproduction, Human; Vagina.**

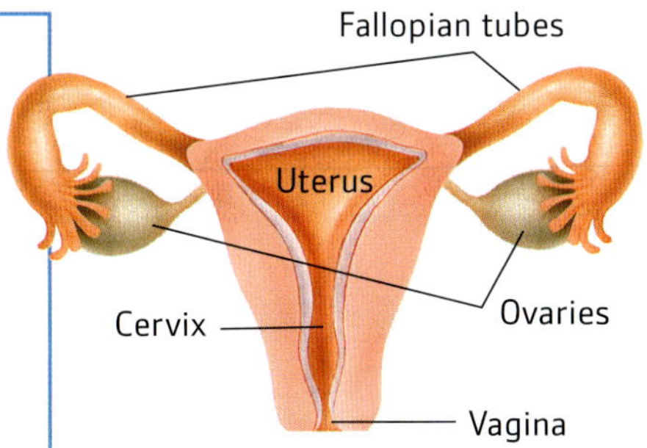

In the female reproductive system, eggs pass from the *ovaries* through the *fallopian tubes* and into the *uterus.* During childbirth, the baby passes down through the *cervix* and out through the *vagina.*

Vv

The *vagina* is a canal that leads from the *uterus* (womb) to the outside of a woman's body. The vagina lies behind the bladder and the *urethra* (urinary canal). The vagina extends from the *cervix* (lower part of the uterus) to an opening between the legs.

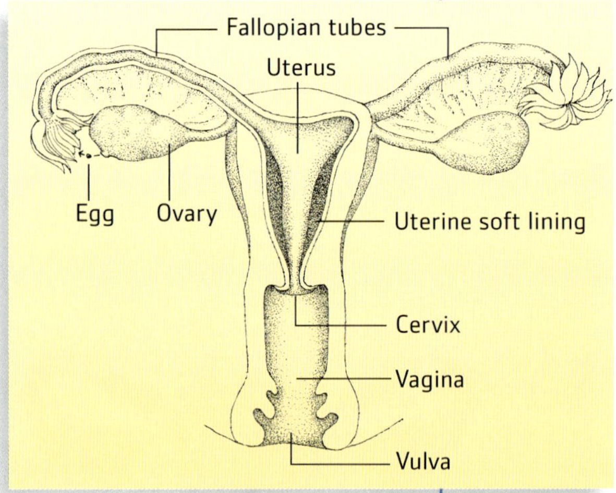

Vagina

The vagina *(vuh JY nuh)* is a female reproductive organ. It is a tube-shaped passage. It lies behind the bladder and the *urethra* (urinary canal) and in front of the *rectum* (end of the intestines). The vagina reaches from an opening between the legs to the *cervix*. The cervix is the lower part of the *uterus* (womb).

During sexual intercourse, the male inserts his penis into the vagina of the female. The vagina is also the passage through which a baby is born. The vagina regularly carries blood and cells from the uterus out of the body. This release is called *menstruation*.

The vagina has muscular walls. During childbirth, the walls stretch enormously to let the baby pass.

The vagina's lining has many sensitive nerve endings. Glands in the cervix moisten and lubricate the lining. In females who have not had sexual intercourse, the vagina's opening may be partially covered by a thin piece of flesh. This piece of flesh is called the *hymen*.

Other articles to read include: **Menstruation; Penis; Pregnancy; Reproduction, Human; Sexuality; Uterus.**

Vegetarianism

Vegetarianism *(VEHJ uh TAIR ee uh NIHZ uhm)* is the practice of avoiding meat in the diet. Some vegetarians do not eat meat, milk, eggs, or any other foods that come from animals. Other vegetarians sometimes drink milk and eat milk products, such as butter and cheese.

A healthy vegetarian diet includes a wide variety of fruits, grains, and vegetables. Vegetarians must make sure to eat foods that contain *proteins*, substances that are used to build and repair the body. Most people get proteins from meat. However, milk, eggs, beans, and peas also contain proteins.

Different people are vegetarians for different reasons. Some vegetarians do not eat meat because they believe it is wrong to kill animals for food. Other vegetarians believe that eating meat is unhealthy.

Other articles to read include: **Diet; Food; Fruit; Malnutrition; Nutrition; Protein.**

A healthy vegetarian meal includes various kinds of fruits, grains, beans, and vegetables.

Vein

A vein *(vayn)* is a tube that carries blood through the body. It is part of a system of tubes called *blood vessels*. The heart pumps blood through the blood vessels.

Veins are the blood vessels that return blood to the heart after it has been used by different parts of the body. Veins are similar to *arteries*, which are the blood vessels that carry fresh blood out of the heart. The walls of veins are thinner and not quite as strong as the walls of arteries.

The blood in veins travels through the right side of the heart to the lungs. There, it leaves behind a waste gas called *carbon dioxide*, which the lungs get rid of when we breathe out. As we breathe in, we take in oxygen through the lungs. The blood picks up the oxygen. The heart pumps the oxygen-carrying blood back into the body through the arteries.

Other articles to read include: **Artery; Blood; Blood vessel; Capillary; Carbon dioxide; Circulatory system; Heart; Respiration; Vein.**

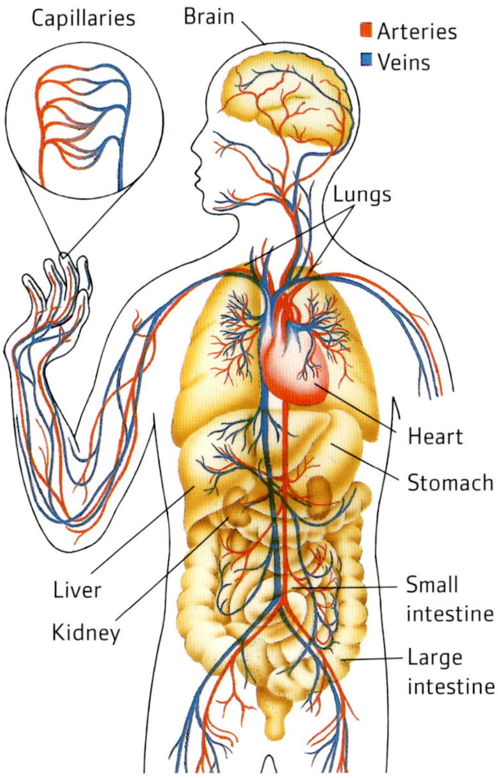

▲ *Veins* are the blood vessels that return blood to the heart after it has been used by the body. *Arteries* carry blood out of the heart. *Capillaries* connect veins to arteries.

Vesalius, Andreas

Andreas Vesalius *(ahn DREH ahs vih SAY lee uhs)* (1514–1564) was a Flemish physician. He is known as the father of *anatomy (uh NAT uh mee),* the study of body structures. In 1543, Vesalius published *On the Structure of the Human Body*, also known as *Fabrica* from its title in Latin. It was the first book about human anatomy that featured detailed drawings and descriptions.

Vesalius first learned about anatomy from the writings of Galen. Galen was a doctor who practiced in the Roman Empire in the A.D. 100's. However, as Vesalius performed *dissections* (cutting something open to examine its internal structure) on human bodies, he discovered that many of Galen's ideas had been incorrect. Vesalius wrote *Fabrica* to correct many errors in Galen's writings. In addition, *Fabrica* contained descriptions of many body structures that had previously been unknown.

Other articles to read include: **Anatomy; Galen; Medicine.**

Andreas Vesalius

Virus

A virus is a tiny thing that attacks the *cells* of plants, animals, and bacteria. A cell is a tiny building block of life. A virus lives inside of a cell, where it can make copies of itself. A virus is so tiny that you could only see it if you used a powerful microscope.

Some viruses can make people and other animals sick by infecting their cells. Viruses cause the common cold, flu, and measles in people. The rabies virus may cause death in people, dogs, and many other mammals.

A virus can get into the human body through a cut on the skin. You can also breathe in some viruses. A person may even eat or drink something that contains a virus.

Other articles to read include: **Cell; Disease; Germ; West Nile virus.**

Some viruses, such as tobacco viruses, look like rods. Other viruses, such as polio viruses, are more round. A third kind, the *bacteriophage*, looks like it has a tail when viewed under a microscope. Bacteriophages infect tiny living things called *bacteria.*

Tobacco virus

Polio virus

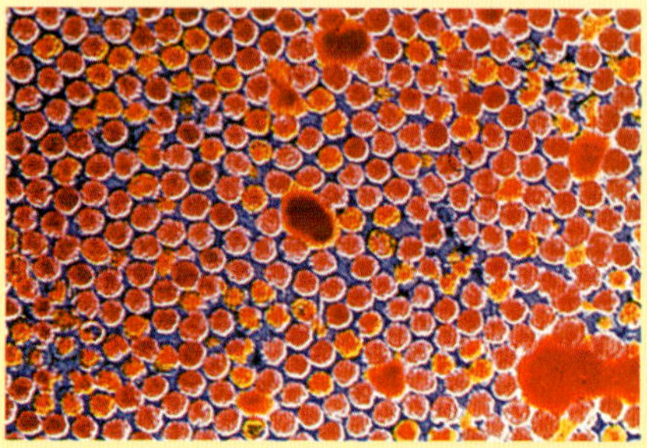

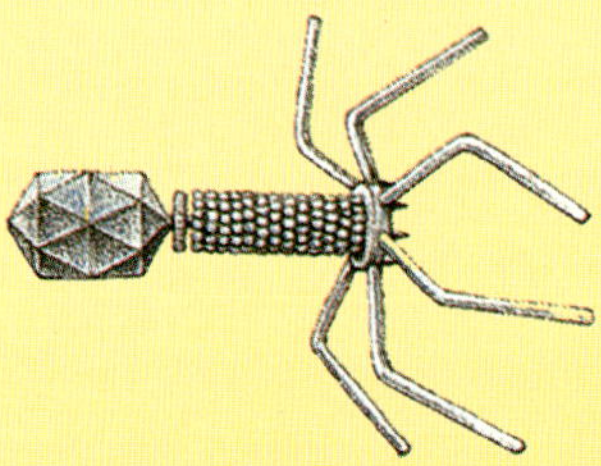

Bacteriophage

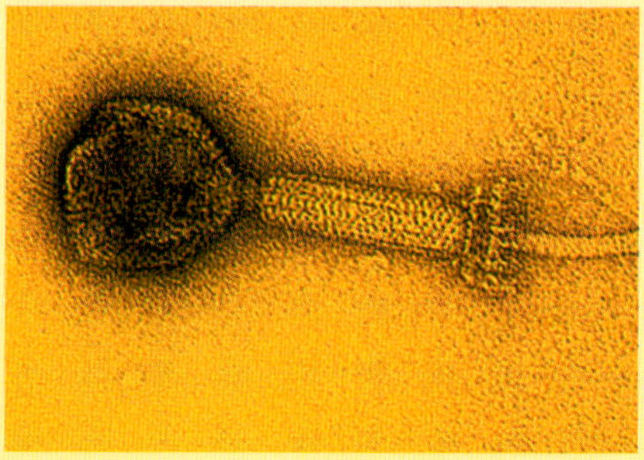

Vision

Vision, or *sight,* is the ability to sense light with the eyes. It is one of the five senses. The other senses are smell, hearing, taste, and touch.

Rays of light enter the human eye through the *cornea (KAWR nee uh).* The cornea is the clear outer layer of the eyeball. Light then travels through a fluid called the *aqueous (AY kwee uhs) humor.* From there, the light travels through a round opening called the *pupil* and through the lens, which bends the light.

Light then reaches the large central chamber of the eye. This chamber contains a jellylike fluid called the *vitreous (VIHT ree uhs) humor.* The light passes through this fluid. It reaches the *retina (REHT uh nuh)* at the back of the eyeball. Nerves in the retina change the light into electrical impulses. These signals are carried to the brain by the *optic nerve.* The brain interprets the signals, allowing us to see.

Other articles to read include: **Blindness; Contact lens; Cornea; Eye; Farsightedness; Glasses; Nearsightedness; Ophthalmology; Optical illusion; Optometry; Senses.**

How the eye focuses

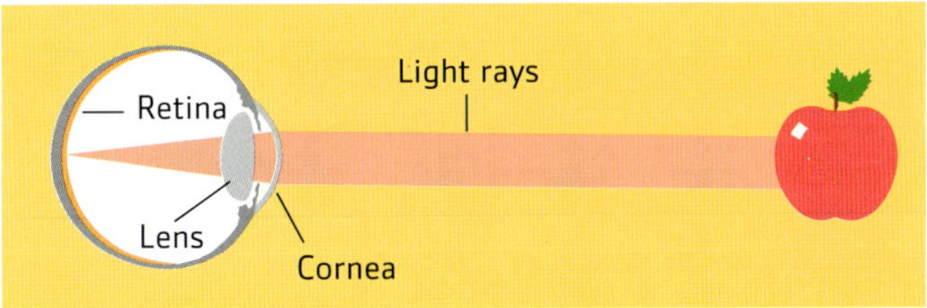

Distance vision
Distant objects reflect light rays that are nearly parallel as they enter the eye. The cornea and the lens bend the rays toward one another, making them come together on the retina to form a clear visual image.

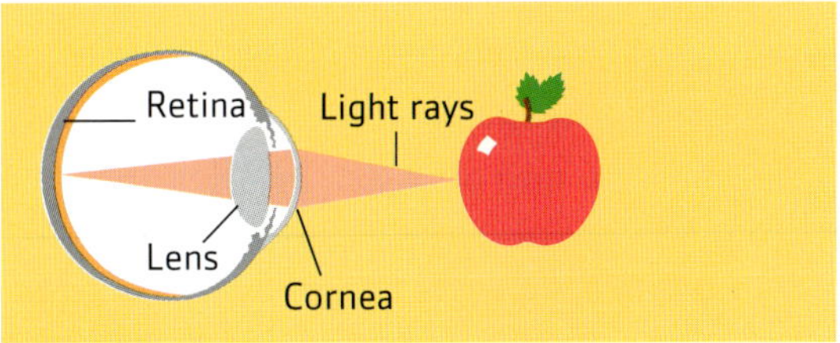

Near vision
Nearby objects reflect light rays that are spreading as they enter the eye. Greater bending power is thus needed to bring these rays together. The lens provides this power by becoming rounder and thicker.

How we see depth

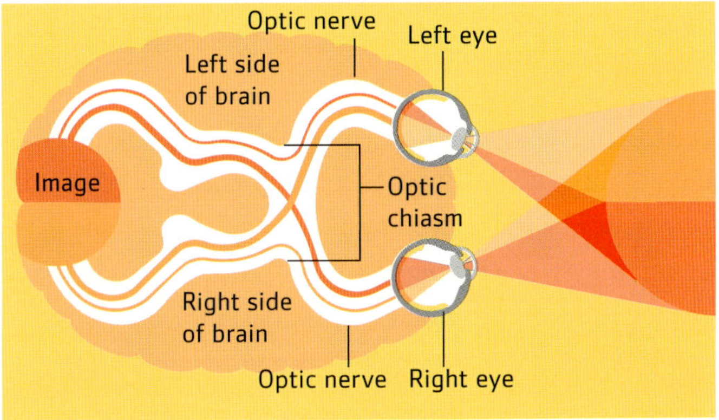

Depth perception is the ability to judge distance and to tell the thickness of objects. Because the eyes are set slightly apart, each one sees objects from a slightly different angle. As a result, each eye sends a slightly different message to the brain. Some of the nerve fibers from each eye cross over at the *optic chiasm (KY az uhm).* Each side of the brain thus receives visual messages from both eyes. The brain puts the images together to provide depth perception.

Vitamin

Vitamins are substances found in foods that help the body grow and stay healthy. There are 13 vitamins. They are vitamins A, C, D, E, K, and a group of 8 B vitamins. Each vitamin does things for the body that no other vitamin can do. For example, vitamin A is necessary for healthy skin and bones. It is found in liver, eggs, and milk. Vitamin C is needed for the ligaments, which hold the bones together, as well as for healing cuts. It is found in fruits and potatoes. Vitamin D prevents *rickets,* a disease that harms bones. It is often added to milk. Vitamin E helps the body's cells stay healthy. It is found in vegetable oils and whole-grain cereals. Vitamin K helps make blood thicken near a cut, so that the cut stops bleeding. Cauliflower and green leafy vegetables, such as kale and spinach, are rich in vitamin K.

The best way for a healthy person to get vitamins is by eating a balanced diet. A balanced diet includes grains, fruits, vegetables, milk or cheeses, and meats, beans, or nuts. Some people take vitamin pills every day to make sure they get enough vitamins. But too much of certain vitamins can also make a person sick.

Over time, a person who does not get enough of a certain vitamin can become ill. Scientists discovered vitamins while searching for the causes of certain illnesses.

Other articles to read include: **Diet; Food; Health; Nutrition; Rickets; Scurvy.**

Some important vitamins needed for good health

Vitamin	Some benefits	Some places found
A	Helps keep skin, eyes, bones, teeth, and various body systems healthy	Carrots, dark green leafy vegetables, deep yellow fruits and vegetables, sweet potatoes, eggs, liver, and milk
B_1	Helps the heart and nervous system work properly	Legumes, nuts, certain meats, pork, whole grains, yeast, enriched breads, and most vegetables
B_2	Helps keep skin healthy	Cheese, fish, green vegetables, liver, milk, poultry
Niacin	Helps keep skin healthy	Fish, liver, enriched breads, lean meat, whole grains
B_6	Helps the body digest fat, protein, and carbohydrates	Eggs, fish, nuts, certain meats, poultry, whole grains
B_{12}	Helps the nervous system work properly	Eggs, fish, meat, milk, poultry
C	Needed for strong bones and teeth	Cantaloupe, citrus fruits, potatoes, raw cabbage, strawberries, tomatoes
D	Helps the body digest calcium and phosphorous	Eggs, salmon, tuna, fortified milk, body makes from sunlight
E	Helps prevent needed fatty acids in the body from burning up	Almost all foods, but especially in margarine, olives, and vegetable oils

Each vitamin helps the body in different ways. This table shows some important vitamins the body needs, how each vitamin helps the body, and where each can be obtained.

Vocal cord

The vocal cords are the body parts in people that produce the sounds of the voice. They are two small folds of tissue that stretch across the *larynx (LAR ihngks)* (voice box), in the throat. One fold stretches on each side of an opening in the *trachea (TRAY kee uh)* (windpipe). The sounds of the voice are produced when air passes over the vocal cords.

Continued on the next page

Muscles in the larynx stretch and relax the vocal cords. When we breathe, the vocal cords are relaxed so that they form a *V*-shaped opening that lets air through. When we speak, the muscles pull the vocal cords, narrowing the opening. Then, as we drive air from the lungs through the larynx, the air vibrates the tightened vocal cords and sound results.

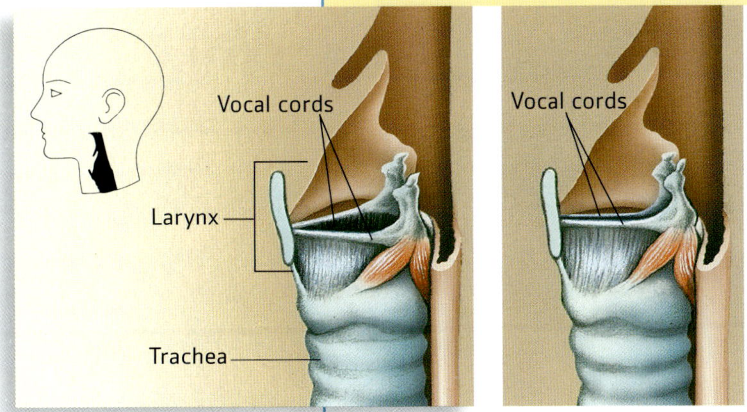

In humans, the sounds of the voice are made chiefly by the *vocal cords,* small bands of tissue that stretch across the *larynx* (voice box) (above left). Muscles in the larynx stretch and relax the vocal cords. When we speak, the larynx muscles pull on the cords, narrowing the opening between them (above). Air forced from the lungs vibrates the tensed cords, producing sound.

The more tightly the vocal cords are stretched, the higher the sounds will be. The more relaxed the vocal cords, the lower the sounds will be.

The length of the vocal cords also affects the sounds of the voice. Women's voices are usually higher than men's voices, because their vocal cords are shorter.

Straining the voice affects the vocal cords and the resulting sound of the voice. The vocal cords and voice can also be affected by muscular tension caused by nervousness.

Other articles to read include: **Larynx; Respiration; Trachea.**

Vomiting

Vomiting *(VOM uh tihng)* is the throwing up of stomach contents through the mouth. Vomiting has many causes, including stress, worry, illness, irritation of the stomach, pregnancy, unusual motion, or severe pain.

When a person vomits, muscles at the bottom of the ribs push on the stomach contents. This pushing is called *retching*. Retching squeezes food and liquids in the stomach upward. A person vomits when retching forces stomach contents through the *esophagus*. The esophagus is a tube connecting the stomach and throat.

Repeated vomiting for many hours can cause *dehydration*, a loss of water from the body. This condition can cause death if it becomes severe. Vomiting after a head injury may be a sign of damage to the brain. A person who vomits after a head injury should go to a hospital right away.

Other articles to read include: **Dehydration; Nausea; Stomach.**

Ww

Wart

A wart is a hard, rough growth on the skin. Warts come in many shapes and sizes. They can grow in many places, including the lips or tongue. Warts on the bottom of the foot grow into thick masses. These warts can make walking painful.

Warts result from certain *viruses*. A virus is a tiny living thing. Wart viruses live inside cells in the top layer of skin.

Many warts go away without treatment. Doctors may remove warts by heating them with an electric needle or with a laser. Freezing warts may also make them go away.

Other articles to read include: **Skin; Virus.**

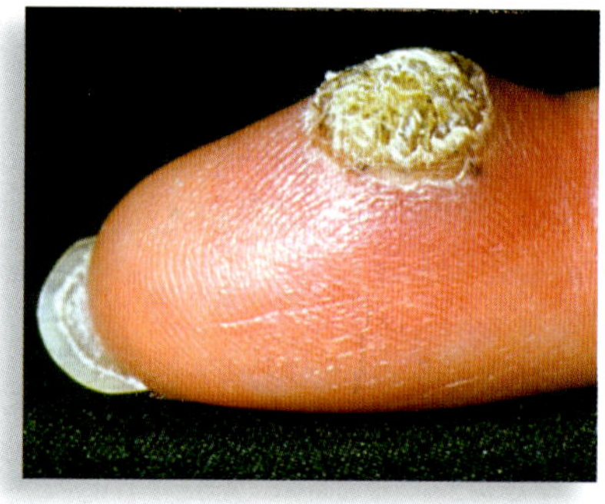

A wart on the tip of a finger can make it painful to touch or hold things.

Watson, James Dewey

James Dewey Watson

James Dewey Watson (1928–) is an American *biologist*. Biologists are scientists who study living things.

In the 1950's, Watson worked with a British biologist named Francis H. C. Crick. They studied *DNA*, which is short for *deoxyribonucleic acid*. DNA is the material inside cells that carries *genes*. Genes are chemical instructions that tell living things how to grow. Genes are passed from parents to their children.

Watson and Crick discovered the shape of DNA. They found that it looks like a twisted ladder. DNA is made up of two long strands. The strands are twisted around each other. The two strands are also connected together with many short pieces. In 1962, Watson and Crick won a Nobel Prize for their discovery.

From 1989 to 1992, Watson served as director of the National Center for Human Genome Research (now the National Human

Continued on the next page

Genome Research Institute) at the National Institutes of Health in Bethesda, Maryland. In that position, he helped launch a project to identify the chemical makeup of the entire *human genome (JEE nohm)*. The human genome includes the full set of genes found in a human being. This project, named the Human Genome Project, was completed in 2003. It provided scientists with a vast amount of information that could be used in fields ranging from medicine to anthropology to criminal investigations.

Other articles to read include: **Crick, Francis H. C.; DNA; Gene; Human Genome Project.**

Weight control

Physical activity can help maintain a healthy body weight. Health experts recommend that children have 60 minutes of physical activity each day. Physical activity causes the body to use additional energy.

Weight control involves maintaining a healthy body weight. In people, this usually means controlling body fat. When people gain too much weight, most of the extra weight is fat. When people lose weight, most of the loss comes from fat.

Two things help determine body fat. The first one is the energy taken in from food. The second thing is the energy the body uses. Energy from food is measured in units called *calories*. If the body takes in more energy than it uses, body fat will increase.

Too much body fat can contribute to many health problems. The condition of having too much fat is called *obesity (oh BEE suh tee)*. Obese people have a higher risk of diabetes, high blood pressure, and heart disease. Many people who are not obese still weigh more than they would like.

There are several ways to lose extra weight. People can eat fewer calories. They can exercise to use more energy. In some cases, doctors treat obesity using drugs and even surgery.

Many obese people are able to lose weight. But it is often difficult to keep from gaining the weight back.

Other articles to read include: **Calorie; Diet; Exercise; Fat; Food; Health; Obesity.**

Astronauts train for the weightless conditions they will endure in space by flying on a special airplane. The plane makes steep dives to create condition called *free fall.*

Weightlessness

Weightlessness is the feeling of being free of *gravity (GRAV uh tee).* Gravity is the force that pulls objects toward one another. Earth's gravity, for example, holds people onto Earth's surface.

All objects have gravity. But only large objects have enough gravity for a person to feel. These objects include planets and moons. A person far from any planet or moon would feel weightless.

Astronauts in orbit around Earth also experience weightlessness. But they still have weight under Earth's gravity. The sense of weightlessness comes from being in *free fall.* A spacecraft in orbit is constantly being pulled down by Earth as it moves around the planet. The craft does not fall back to Earth because it is also moving at a great speed "sideways" to Earth. The sideways speed and the force of gravity cause the craft to "fall" in a circle as it orbits Earth. The constant state of falling is called *free fall.* The astronauts, their spacecraft, and all their equipment fall at the same speed. So from their perspective, the astronauts do not seem to be falling at all. This provides a sensation of weightlessness.

Astronauts train for weightlessness by flying in a large airplane. The plane makes steep climbs and dives. For about 30 seconds during a dive, the astronauts float free inside the plane. This is because the plane and astronauts fall at the same speed. Floating in can also provides a feeling of weightlessness.

Weightlessness can cause several health problems. These include motion sickness, loss of bone and muscle, and poor blood circulation. Exercise, drugs, and special diets can reduce these problems.

Other articles to read include: **Aerospace medicine; Motion sickness.**

West Nile virus

West Nile virus is a disease caused by a virus that affects horses, birds, and human beings. The virus is named for a region in Africa where it was discovered in 1937. The virus has caused many cases of disease in Africa, Europe, Asia, and the Middle East. In the 1990's, the virus spread to the United States and Canada.

The West Nile virus spreads from birds to human beings through the bites of mosquitoes. In most cases, the virus causes mild symptoms, such as fever and headache. But the virus can cause serious illness or death in the elderly or people with weakened immune systems. There is no cure or vaccine for West Nile virus. People can reduce their risk of West Nile virus by avoiding mosquito bites. For example, they can wear protective clothing and use insect repellents.

Other articles to read include: **Disease; Fever; Headache; Virus.**

White blood cell

Both white blood cells and red blood cells can be seen in this picture of the inside of a blood vessel. The picture was taken using a powerful microscope.

A white blood cell is a small structure in the blood that helps protect the body from germs. White blood cells work to destroy the germs and keep the body healthy. White blood cells are also called *leukocytes (LOO kuh syts).*

There are different kinds of white blood cells. Most are round and colorless. Some kinds of white blood cells kill tiny germs called *bacteria* by surrounding the germs and breaking them down. Other kinds of white blood cells produce substances called *antibodies*. Antibodies destroy bacteria, germs called *viruses*, and other harmful things that enter the body.

The blood has two other kinds of cells besides white blood cells. These are called *red blood cells* and *platelets (PLAYT lihtz).*

Other articles to read include: **Antibody; Bacteria; Blood; Germ; Immune system; Red blood cell; Virus.**

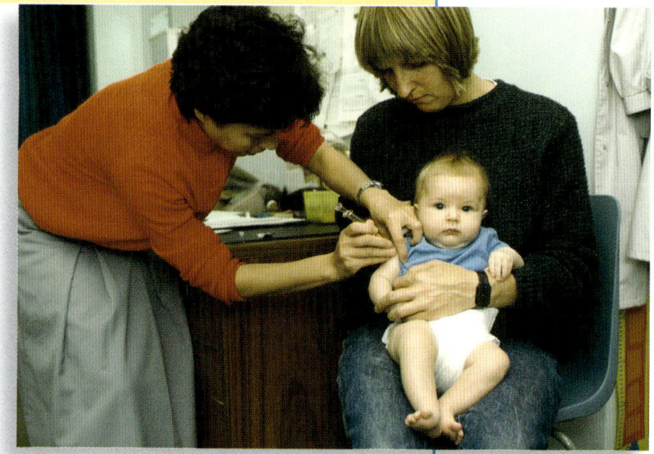

A doctor gives a shot of pertussis vaccine to a young child to protect against whooping cough. The disease is especially dangerous among babies and young children.

Whooping cough

Whooping *(HOO pihng)* cough is an illness that occurs mainly among babies and young children. Whooping cough is also called *pertussis (puhr TUHS ihs).*

Whooping cough begins with a stuffy nose, a cough, and a fever. After about two weeks, the illness becomes more serious. People with whooping cough often wake up at night with such a bad cough that they find it hard to catch their breath. They cough up globs of a sticky substance called *mucus (MYOO kuhs).* Some people, especially babies, can die from whooping cough.

Most children in the United States get a *vaccine* (shot) to keep them from getting whooping cough. However, whooping cough has become more common in the 2000's. Doctors can also give medicine to people with whooping cough at the start of the illness so that it does not become too serious.

Other articles to read include: **Baby; Child; Cough; Disease; Fever; Mucus.**

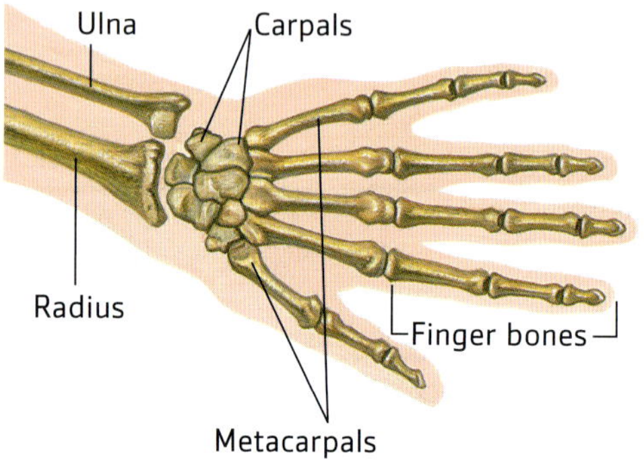

The wrist includes eight small, irregularly shaped bones called *carpals.* The carpals are located between the *metacarpals* (the bones of the palm) and the *ulna* and *radius* (the bones of the forearm).

Wrist

The wrist is the part of the body between the hand and the *forearm.* The forearm is the part of the arm between the wrist and the elbow. A person uses the wrist to move the hand up, down, and sideways.

The word *wrist* can also refer to an area of the upper part of the hand. This area includes eight small bones called *carpals (KAHR puhlz).*

Tissues called *tendons (TEHN duhnz)* extend through the carpal area. These tendons connect the finger bones with muscles in the arm. When the arm muscles pull in, they pull the tendons and make the fingers move. The tendons on the palm side of the carpals bend the fingers. The tendons on the back of the hand straighten the fingers.

Other articles to read include: **Arm; Bone; Finger; Hand; Muscle; Tendon.**

Writing

Writing is a way of using letters, words, numbers, symbols, or signs to show ideas. Today, most people use some sort of alphabet to write words. Certain languages, such as Chinese, instead use symbols called *characters* to write words.

The first step in the development of writing came when early people learned to draw pictures to stand for ideas. Such pictures are called *ideographs (IHD ee uh grafs).* For example, a picture of a smiling face stands for the idea of being happy. People understand the idea of such a picture, no matter what language they speak.

The next step, and the first real writing, came about 5,000 to 5,500 years ago. People learned to show ideas by using signs or symbols to stand for the words of their own language. Such signs are called *logographs (LAWG uh grafs),* and this kind of writing is called *logography (loh GAHG ruh fee).*

The first people to use logography were the Sumerians. They lived in southern Mesopotamia, a region between the Tigris and Euphrates rivers in what is now the Middle East. They used logography to keep track of who owned certain animals. For example, if a man owned five cows, the Sumerians would write one sign for the number *five*, one sign for the word *cow*, and one sign for the owner's name. Over time, the Sumerians found that they could also use the sign for an object that was easy to draw to stand for a word that sounded the same but was hard to make a picture of.

The Egyptians developed a similar system, called *hieroglyphic (HY uhr uh GLIHF ihk)* writing, about 5,000 years ago. About 3,500 years ago, the Chinese began an advanced word writing system.

About 3,500 to 3,000 years ago, the Phoenicians worked out the earliest alphabets, based on the Egyptian system. The alphabet letters stood for certain sounds. The ancient Greeks borrowed the Phoenician symbols and added vowel signs. The ancient Romans learned the Greek alphabet and made their own letters. Those letters looked much the same as the letters used today in English and some other languages.

Other articles to read include: **Communication.**

Children practice writing in school. Learning to write is a basic part of childhood education throughout the world.

Cuneiform (kyoo NEE uh fawrm) was an early system of writing developed by the Sumerians. Most cuneiform writings were inscribed on wet clay tablets using a wedge-shaped tool called a *stylus.* The tablets were then dried in the sun. This tablet is a letter from merchants asking for overdue money from customers.

Yy

Yalow, Rosalyn Sussman

Rosalyn Sussman Yalow

Rosalyn Sussman Yalow (1921–2011) was an American *medical physicist (FIHZ uh sihst)*. Physicists study matter and energy. Medical physicists use this knowledge to help sick people.

Yalow shared the 1977 Nobel Prize in physiology or medicine. She and two other scientists developed a way to "tag" substances in a person's blood. The tag is radioactive. It helps doctors find and measure even the smallest amounts of a substance inside the blood. Yalow first used this tagging method in 1959. She studied a substance called *insulin (IHN suh lihn)* in the blood of patients with the disease diabetes.

Yalow was born in New York City. She studied at Hunter College in New York City and the University of Illinois at Urbana-Champaign. She worked as a scientist and professor at several different schools and hospitals in the United States. She died on May 30, 2011.

Other articles to read include: **Biotechnology; Blood; Insulin.**

Yawning

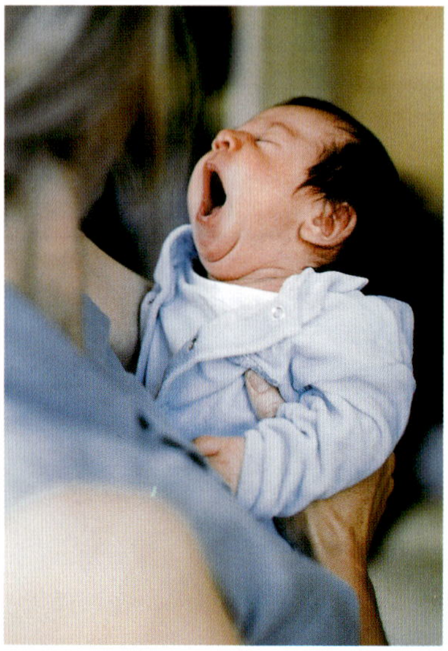

A yawn is a sign that this baby needs sleep.

Yawning is when you open your mouth wide *involuntarily* (without trying to) and inhale, then exhale. People and animals may yawn when they are sleepy, tired, or bored. Yawning is a sign that the body needs sleep.

Yawning is an involuntary *reflex*—something the body does by itself, without having to think about it. Once a yawn starts, it is almost impossible to stop. Even if you close your mouth, the muscles used to yawn continue to contract, or pull. One reason for yawning may be to wake you up by stretching your muscles and helping the blood move around inside your body. Yawning also increases the amount of air you breathe in.

Other articles to read include: **Reflex action; Respiration; Sleep.**

Yellow fever

Yellow fever is a disease caused by a kind of germ called a *virus.* The virus that causes yellow fever is carried by mosquitoes. It damages many parts of the body, but especially the liver. *Yellow bile* (a substance made by the liver) builds up in the skin. It makes the skin look yellow, giving the disease its name. Today, people get yellow fever only in parts of Africa and South America. But in the past, the disease was more widespread.

In the wild, mosquitoes often pick up the virus by biting infected monkeys. Mosquitoes then carry the virus from person to person through bites.

Signs of yellow fever include a sudden fever, headache, muscle pain, backache, weakness, and *vomiting* (throwing up). Most people get only a mild case of the disease and recover quickly. People who recover cannot get the disease again. But some people die from the disease.

People have gotten rid of yellow fever in many areas by keeping mosquitoes under control. It can also be prevented by a vaccine. The vaccine can protect a person from yellow fever for at least 10 years.

Other articles to read include: **Disease; Public health; Virus.**

Yogurt is a popular and healthful food enjoyed by people throughout the world.

Yogurt

Yogurt *(YOH guhrt),* also spelled *yoghurt*, is a smooth, sour food made from thickened milk. It is a healthful food. Yogurt provides the same vitamins and minerals as milk.

Yogurt is made from the milk from cows, goats, buffaloes, or other animals. People add harmless *bacteria* (tiny living things) to the milk. The bacteria change milk sugar into lactic acid. The acid thickens the milk, turning it into yogurt. Lactic acid gives yogurt a sour taste that many people enjoy. Other people like to make yogurt sweeter by adding fruit flavoring.

Yogurt is a popular food in many parts of the world. People in Iran, Turkey, and other countries have eaten yogurt for thousands of years.

Other articles to read include: **Bacteria; Food; Mineral; Vitamin.**

The index is an alphabetical list of important topics covered in this book. It will help you find information given in both words and pictures. The page number or numbers after a heading tell you where to look for information about a topic. For example, there is a reference to **Adam's apple** on page 359.

When there is an article on a topic in *The Discovery Science Encyclopedia,* the page number or numbers appear in **boldface.** For example, the boldface page for the article on **Adolescent** appears along with references to that topic in other encyclopedia articles. When there are many references to a topic, they are sometimes organized under subtopics, as they are under **Animal.**

Sometimes, an index heading refers you to information in other headings in the index. For example, **Agriculture** has a "See also" reference to additional information on this topic under **Farm and farming.** The "See" reference for **Backbone** tells you that all the information on this topic will be found under **Spine.**

When an entry can mean more than one thing, there are words in parentheses to help you distinguish between these different meanings—for example, **Depression** (illness) refers to the medical rather than the economic condition.

A page number in *italics* refers to an illustration only. For example, a picture for **Ascending colon** appears on 208, but there is no other reference to this topic in the text on this page or the facing page.

A

D

N

O

P

Q

R

S

T

The publisher gratefully acknowledges the following sources for photographs. All maps and illustrations unless otherwise noted are the exclusive property of World Book, Inc.

A - L

8-9 © John Watney, Photo Researchers
10-11 © Adrian Sherratt, Alamy; © Dreamstime
12-13 Carla Cioffi, NASA; © Shutterstock
14-15 © Shutterstock; Monsanto; © Photo Researchers
16-17 © Adrian Sherratt, Alamy
18-19 © SIU/Photo Researchers; © Thinkstock
20-21 © Extreme Sports Photo/Alamy; © Shutterstock
22-23 © Pictorial Press Ltd/Alamy; © Shutterstock
24-25 © Hulton Archive/Getty
26-27 © Photodisc/Thinkstock
28-29 © David Young-Wolff, PhotoEdit
30-31 © Fernando Morales, Agence-France Presse; © Dreamstime
32-33 © PhotoDisc
34-35 © iStockphoto/Thinkstock; © Shutterstock
36-37 © Giulio Andreini, Alamy
38-39 © J. Delafosse, Discovery Channel
40-41 © Shutterstock
42-43 © iStockphoto; © Shutterstock
44-45 © David Young-Wolff, PhotoEdit; © PhotoDisc; © Robin Nelson, PhotoEdit
46-47 © Corbis
48-49 © USDA/SS/Photo Researchers; © Hulton Archive/Getty; © Washington University School of Medicine Library
50-51 © Gunter Ziesler, Peter Arnold, Inc.; © Brian Bell, Photo Researchers
52-53 © Shutterstock
54-55 © D. Faulkner, Photo Researchers; © PhotoDisc/Getty; © David Parker, Photo Researchers
56-57 © Hank Morgan, Photo Researchers; © Science Source
58-59 © Bob Daemmrich, Image Works
60-61 © CNRI/Photo Researchers; © Shutterstock; © iStockphoto
62-63 © Will & Deni McIntyre, Photo Researchers
66-67 © Hank Grebe, SuperStock; © iStockphoto/Thinkstock
68-69 © Larry Mulvehill, Photo Researchers
70-71 © Julie Thompson, Alamy
72-73 © Shutterstock
74-75 © CRNI, Phototake
76-77 © Corbis
78-79 © Corbis; © Shutterstock; © PhotoDisc
80-81 © Shutterstock; © Biophoto Associates/SPL/Photo Researchers; Science Museum, London/Topham-HIP, Image Works
82-83 © Biophoto Associates/ Photo Researchers
84-85 © Hulton Archive/Getty
86-87 © Sam Ogden, Photo Researchers; Mark Clarke, SPL/Photo Researchers; © Shutterstock
88-89 © Shutterstock; © Corbis
90-91 © Nigel J. Dennis, Corbis
92-93 © Universal Images Group Limited/Alamy
94-95 © Exactstock/SuperStock
96-97 © ERRG Photography/Alamy; © Shutterstock;
98-99 © Thinkstock
100-101 © Shutterstock; © John Alves, Mystic Wanderer
102-103 © Shutterstock; © Michael Philip Manheim, Imagestate; WORLD BOOK Photo
104-105 © Shutterstock; © Art Resource
106-107 © Corbis/Bettmann; © Glow Wellness, Alamy
108-109 © Corbis/Bettmann; Granger Collection; © Janine Wiedel, Alamy
110-111 © David J. Slater, Alamy; © David Young-Wolff, PhotoEdit
112-113 © Shutterstock
114-115 © Art Archive; © Jim Reed, Corbis; © iStockphoto
116-117 © Ed Young, Photo Researchers
120-121 © Corbis/SuperStock; © AfriPics/Alamy
122-123 © Bill Aron, PhotoEdit
124-125 © Jonathan Nourok, PhotoEdit
126-127 © vario images/Alamy; WORLD BOOK Photo; © Shutterstock
128-129 © Jaime Souzza, Reuters/Landov; © Shutterstock
130-131 © Gary Gaugler, Photo Researchers; © Shutterstock
132-133 © doc-stock/Alamy
134-135 © doc-stock/Alamy; © iStockphoto; © Shutterstock; © Airell-Joubert, Photo Researchers
136-143 © Shutterstock
144-145 © Shutterstock; © Thinkstock
146-147 © Lennart Nilsson, Behold Man 1974 Little, Brown, and Company
148-149 © A&J Visage/Alamy
150-151 © J.C. Allen & Son; WORLD BOOK Photo; © Thinkstock; © Shutterstock
152-153 © Shutterstock
154-155 © Robin Nelson, PhotoEdit
156-157 © Shutterstock; © Daniel Cima, American Red Cross
158-159 © SuperStock; © Shutterstock; Granger Collection; © Joel Nito, AFP/Getty
160-161 WORLD BOOK Photo; © Thinkstock
162-163 © Michael Newman, PhotoEdit; © Shutterstock
164-165 © David Young-Wolff, PhotoEdit; © Everett Collection/Alamy; © Images & Stories/Alamy; © Shutterstock
166-167 © Shutterstock; © Corbis
168-169 © Thinkstock
170-171 © Thinkstock; © Shutterstock
172-173 CDC; WORLD BOOK Photo; © David Young-Wolff, PhotoEdit
174-175 © Shutterstock
178-179 Granger Collection; © Shutterstock; © Lawrence Migdale, Photo Researchers
180-181 © SuperStock
182-183 © Amoret Tanner, Alamy; © Thinkstock; © Thinkstock
188-189 © North Wind Pictures; © Stephen J. Krasemann, Photo Researchers; © Thinkstock
190-191 © Thinkstock; © Scott Camarzine, Photo Researchers
192-193 © Mauricio Anton, National Geographic; © Shutterstock
198-199 © Joseph Project-Malawi/Alamy; © PhotoDisc; © David Young-Wolff, PhotoEdit
202-203 © ImageState/Alamy
204-205 © Spencer Grant, Alamy; © Shutterstock
206-207 © Studio City/eStock Photo; James King Holmes, Photo Researchers
210-211 © Shutterstock
212-213 Granger Collection
214-215 © Getty
216-217 © Thinkstock; © Shutterstock; © Tony Freeman, PhotoEdit
218-219 © Corbis/Bettmann; © Bianca Lavies, National Geographic; © Thinkstock
220-221 © Thinkstock; © Will Hart, PhotoEdit; © Corbis/Bettmann
222-223 © Shutterstock; Red chalk (c. 1514), Biblioteca Reale, Turin, Italy, © SCALA/Art Resource; Pen and Ink drawing (c. 1510) by Leonardo da Vinci, Windsor Castle, England, Royal Library © Her Majesty Queen Elizabeth II
224-225 © Shutterstock

M - Z

230-231 © Ed Lallo, Corbis; © Scott Camazine, SPL/Photo Researchers

232-233 © Asia File/Alamy; © Peter Turnley, Corbis; © Shutterstock

234-235 © Hulton Archive/Getty; © James King-Holmes, FTSS/Photo Researchers; © Shutterstock

236-237 © Shutterstock; © Shutterstock; © Thinkstock

238-239 © S. Fraser, Photo Researchers

240-241 © Shutterstock; © Science Source

242-243 © Jame Cavallini, Photo Researchers; © Shutterstock

244-245 © Shutterstock; © Charles E. Mohr

246-247 © Deco Images II/Alamy; © Corbis

248-249 © Shutterstock; WORLD BOOK Photo

250-251 © Alexander Tsiaras, SPL/Photo Researchers; WORLD BOOK Photo; WORLD BOOK Photo; © Doug McFadd, Getty Images; © P. Marazzi, Photo Researchers

252-253 © Shutterstock

254-255 © PhotoDisc; WORLD BOOK Photo

256-257 © Blend Images/Alamy; ©AFP/Getty

258-259 © Scott Camazine, Alamy; © Corbis; © Angela Hampton Picture Library/Alamy

260-261 © Mauro Fermariello, Photo Researchers

262-263 © D. Hurst, Alamy; © Art Explosion; © PhotoDisc/Getty

264-265 © Shutterstock; © Hank Morgan, Photo Researchers

266-267 © Phanie, Photo Researchers

268-269 © Creatas/Alamy

270-271 © Dwight Kuhn

272-273 © SPL/Custom Medical; © E.R. Degginger

274-275 © PhotoDisc

276-277 © SuperStock

278-279 Austin Fire Department; Granger Collection; © Shutterstock

280-281 Louis Pasteur in His Laboratory (1889) oil on canvas by Albert Edelfelt (Granger Collection); CDC; © Roger Ressmeyer, Corbis

282-283 © Shutterstock; © Biophoto Associates/Photo Researchers

284-285 © Comstock/Thinkstock

286-287 © Michael Newman, PhotoEdit

288-289 © Shutterstock

290-291 © Comstock/Thinkstock; © Thinkstock; © Custom Medical

292-293 © Gary Gaugler, Photo Researchers; © Tom McHugh, Photo Researchers; © T. Brain, Photo Researchers; © Biophoto Assoc./Photo Researchers

294-295 © Oliver Meckes, Photo Researchers; © Cathy Melloan

296-297 © Rachel Epstein, PhotoEdit

298-299 © Cameramann International, Ltd.; © Cameramann International, Ltd.; © Shutterstock; © Shutterstock

300-301 © Charles Lenars, Corbis

304-305 © Comstock/Thinkstock; © St. Bartholomew's Hospital/Photo Researchers; Cognitive Evolution Group, University of Louisiana at Lafayette

306-307 © Sebastian Bolesch, Peter Arnold, Inc.; © Will & Deni McIntyre, Photo Researchers

308-309 CDC; © Custom Medical; © Neil Borden, Photo Researchers

310-311 © Alamy

314-315 © ISM/Phototake; CDC

316-317 CDC; March of Dimes Birth Defects Foundation; © Shutterstock

318-319 © Shutterstock; © Cultura/Alamy; © BSIP/Alamy

320-321 © C. Madsen, ESO; © Damita Delimont/Alamy; © Joe Songer, Birmingham News/Landov

322-323 © Dreamstime; © Susan Leavines, Photo Researchers; © Shutterstock

324-325 © Y. Ibata; © Arthur Hess; © Shutterstock; © Shutterstock

326-327 © Shutterstock

328-329 © Getty; © Des & Jen Bartlett, Bruce Coleman Inc.

332-333 © Shutterstock; © Shutterstock; © Bettmann/Corbis

334-335 © Shutterstock; © Thinkstock

336-337 © Grapes/Michaud/Science Source

338-339 WORLD BOOK Photo

340-341 © Shutterstock; © Peter Macdiarmid, Reuters/Corbis

342-343 © Dreamstime

344-345 © Phanie, Photo Researchers; © Getty; © Scott Camazine, Photo Reseachers

346-347 © iStockphoto/Thinkstock;

348-349 © Terry Wild; © Jacques Marescaux, reprinted by permission of Nature, © Macmillan Magazines Ltd.

356-357 © P. Marazzi, Photo Researchers

358-359 © Shutterstock

360-361 © BSIP SA/Alamy; © Andia/Alamy; NSF Oasis Program

362-363 © VEM/Photo Researchers; © Shutterstock; © LADA/Photo Researchers

366-367 © Cathy Melloan; Granger Collection

368-369 © Omikron/Photo Researchers; © SPL/Photo Researchers; © Brand X Pictures/Getty

372-373 © Tim Thompson, Corbis; WORLD BOOK Photo; © Shutterstock

374-375 NASA; © Cheryl Power, Science Source

376-377 © Sally & Richard Greenhill, Alamy; © Shutterstock; © Christie's Images/Corbis

378-379 © Corbis/Bettmann; © Photographer's Choice/Getty; © iStockphoto/Thinkstock